Victims of Development

V

Victims of Development

Resistance and Alternatives

JEREMY SEABROOK

VERSO
London · New York

This edition published by Verso 1993
© Jeremy Seabrook
All rights reserved

Verso
UK: 6 Meard Street, London W1V 3HR
USA: 29 West 35th Street, New York, NY 10001-2291

Verso is the imprint of New Left Books

ISBN 0–86091–385–6
ISBN 0–86091–611–1 (pbk)

British Library Cataloguing in Publication Data

A catalogue record for this book is available from the British Library

US Library of Congress Cataloging-in-Publication Data

A catalogue record for this book is available from the Library of Congress

Typeset by York House Typographic Ltd, London W13
Printed and bound in Great Britain by
Biddles Ltd, Guildford and King's Lynn

Contents

Foreword	vi
The Tehri Dam	1
Development and Economics	7
Manila	23
São Paulo	43
Rio de Janeiro	51
At the Frontier: Delhi	60
Replacing the Biosphere	79
The Unsustainable City: Bombay	89
The Place of Flowers: Survival in the City	92
Industry in the Third World: A Tale of Three Factories	98
Regenerating the Countryside	110
Death of a Socialist: The Chattisgarh Liberation Movement	125
Migrants and Refugees	147
Life of Migrants	152
Dispossessings: The 'First World'	159
Women Who Stay	167
Britain's Third World: Cornwall Undermined	174
Britain's Third World: The Land of Broken Toys	186
Scenes from a Developing World	193
Development and Human Needs	201
The Tourist Malignancy	207
Thailand	215
What is Development? Voices from the South	226
Conclusion	249

Foreword

The Western path of development, whatever its advantages, brings at least two intractable problems. The first of these is the worsening of social injustice, the growing gap between global rich and poor. The second is the damage, some of it already irreversible, to the resource-base of the earth, on which all economic systems depend.

With the eclipse of Communism, a critique based on the threat to social peace from widening inequalities, it seems that the dispossessed no longer pose any serious obstacle to 'development'. Relieved of this apprehension, the rich, who are only too aware of the environmental threat to their own well-being, may be tempted to see environmental issues resolved at the expense of the poorest.

Avoidance of this harsh possibility is the objective of those seeking another form of development: a decent sufficiency for all, in this and future generations, within the limits of what the earth can bear.

This book depends on the insights and work of many people to whom I am grateful; especially Winin and Nikhil Pereira, Sara d'Mello, Charu and Mukul, Bharat Dogra, Dhirendra Sharma, Susan Dhavle, Aleta Fernandez, Celeste and Jojo Sambales, Vandana Shiva, Urvashi Butalia, Cathie and Tony McCormack, Titos Quibuyen, Greg del Pilar, Vim-Vim Santos and Philippines Global Exchange, Sophie Dick, Chantawipa Apisuk, Natee, David Cavalier, Mohamed Idris, Martin Khor and the Consumers' Association of Penang, Mary Assunta, Ashok Row-Kavi, Randolph David, Sunderlal Bahaguna, Rameshwar Prasad, Rajendra Sail, Shashi Sail, Leonor Briones, and Derek Hooper. I am grateful to Satish Kumar of *Resurgence*, Ian Jack of the *Independent on Sunday*, and especially Steve Platt of *New Statesman & Society*.

The book is for Naoroli, Tulsi and Jagat Negi, with affection.

JEREMY SEABROOK
London, March 1993

The Tehri Dam

Tehri-Garhwal, in the Himalayan foothills, is one of the poorest districts in India. In the hills there is one hectare of land for 17.6 people, and there is very little flat land that can be irrigated. The inhabitants, however, have traditionally freely been able to take fodder, fuel and other produce from the forests; for every hectare of cultivated land, 11 hectares of forest and communal land have been available. The people have been self-reliant farmers for generations. Here, the Chipko movement was born, the successful efforts of the women to limit commercial felling and to replant the traditional, familiar species of trees. But the people are still being compelled into a market economy, which can only dispossess them of traditional life-ways, force them into the cities in the plains: Delhi and Lucknow.

The poverty is masked by the extreme beauty of the hills; the terraces of cultivation on the slopes create emerald staircases in the winter sunshine; the crests of bare blue hills, sharp as blades, cut deeply into the sky.

Tehri is the site of a proposed dam, which will displace 86,000 people. It is a posthumous monument to the former Soviet Union. Russian engineers and experts had spent twelve years in India; Rs600 crore (1 crore = 10 million) have already been spent. The ideology of the conquest of nature by industrial society (on this occasion, it its socialist guise) has been successfully exported to an area of the world where people had lived in balance with a fragile ecosystem, in a way of life now being swept away in the imperial interests of 'development'.

January 1992. The bus from Delhi is full of pilgrims from Rajasthan going to the holy city of Hardwar, where the Ganges comes down from the Himalayas and touches from the plains. They are going to celebrate the festival of Makhar Sankranti – the day when the sun returns over the Tropic of Cancer in its northward journey: rich farmers muffled in quilts against the cold. The women wear brilliant sarees of orange, vermilion and lime-green, and heavy silver anklets. There is a long delay at a police checkpoint on the outskirts of Delhi, when the officials demand money, which the bus driver refuses to pay. The journey to Hardwar takes about eight hours. From there, on to Rishikesh, where the Ganges flows fast in the dying light of the sun. People are lighting candles and setting them off in little boats of dried leaves piled with marigolds and rose petals. The lighted tapers are carried away by the fast-flowing water, pale in the fading light; they float for 20 or 30 metres before capsizing in the current. It has been estimated that in the event of the Tehri Dam bursting, floods would reach Rishikesh in one hour and Hardwar in 75 minutes; both would be washed away in a wall of water 250 metres high.

The 80 kilometre drive to Tehri takes three hours. Road construction has damaged the fragile foothills of the Himalayas, and everywhere there have been landslips. At one point, a bulldozer is clearing a recent fall of rocks; as it slides, the mountain crumbles to dust, rubble and earth, with scattered boulders and more substantial slabs of rock. The debris is swept back against the mountain side.

The hills have been intensively farmed, every cultivable square centimetre; terraces cut into the hills and strengthened with stones. Some of the higher terraces have been abandoned and reverted to thin grass, but the lower altitudes are fertile steps of spring wheat, and in the valleys, small patches of fields demarcated with a line of grey stones. The water falls in tiny rivulets and cascades, a clear cold splash of weeping hills. In the little towns, snack stalls, tea kettles black on the fires, sellers of dal and mungphal, little markets with creamy cauliflowers, purple *brinjal* and chillis. Women everywhere collecting fuelwood, some with headloads of twigs, leaves and branches making long journeys onto the denuded slopes. Patches of melting snow, with higher peaks streaked with white; and beyond these the Great Himalayas, blue hills covered with perpetual snows and framed against curdled clouds.

The descent into Tehri is through an altogether different landscape. The Bhagirathi river – one of the main tributaries of the Ganges – suddenly emerges into a great gulf of desolation and disturbance, where the excavations for the Tehri dam have been taking place. For the people of India, the Bhagirathi has a profound spiritual significance; it reminds them of the high ideals of penance and selfless service with which the story of its origins is connected. The sides of the hills have been cut away, and the river diverted through a stone tunnel, pouring its blue turbulence into the black mouth of the diversion channel. This leaves the former riverbed empty. At the bottom, there are some stretches of stagnant water, yellow with algae at the edges. But for the most part, it is dried out, sand and stone. The hills have been blasted to extend the water catchment area: boulders, pebbles, slate and dust have fallen into the valley bottom, tearing away the fragile green covering of succulents, thornbushes, karu and small shrubs, so that the hillsides show the flaking grain of the still-forming hills. The contractors have flattened approach roads across the debris for trucks and earthmovers.

Since 14 December 1991, the roads have been blocked by a group of protesters against the dam, led by ecologist and activist Sunderlal Bahaguna and some of the women of the small town of Tehri, which is to be completely submerged when the dam is completed. They have built their camp, a fragile provisional shelter in a scene of utmost dereliction, mountains reduced to their bare mineral content, just as the forests have become timber, the rivers water resources. The shelter is of corrugated metal with a polythene roof in the middle of the approach road, so that the bulldozers and earthmovers are immobilized. On a lower level, on the same zig-zag road, there is a kitchen and some small tents where Bahaguna and his wife live, and some cruder tents for the sympathizers who come to stay. Most nights between 20 and 30 people sleep here, and a constant vigil is kept to see that the camp is not disturbed. The contractors have spoken of evicting them by force, but this is not so easy in a small town, where sympathy lies with the protesters, even though there are few active in the dharna.

On the outskirts of the town many houses have been abandoned; there is an air of dejection; the *kachera* (rubbish) and dust from the blastings and excavations rise in the hazardous clouds, which hang over the single-lane metal bridge which spans the Bhagirathi.

In October 1991, an earthquake shook Tehri-Garhwal, the centre in Uttarkashi some 60 kilometres from the dam site. This killed 800 people and left more than 250,000 homeless. One of the principal objections to the Tehri dam had been that it is in a site of high seismic activity, and therefore a danger to the surrounding areas. Those who had protested imagined that the earthquake would put an end to this project of building what will be the highest dam in Asia, 260.5 metres. But instead of conceding what geologists, seismologists and the people's movement alike had been saying, the engineers pointed to the fact that no damage had occurred to the existing structures, and saw this as a sure sign that they were secure against earthquakes. They have agreed to strengthen the dam further, so that it will be proof against even greater tremors than the 6.5 registered on the

Richter scale in October. Even after the earthquake, the central government released a further Rs30 crore for continuing work.

During the day, the people in the camp work, collect fuel for cooking fires, sing and devise strategies to sustain their resistance. The labourers employed by the construction companies sit on the roof of their buses playing cards in the cool winter sunlight. The professionals cluster around their still earthmovers and wait, completely resourceless, in contrast to the camp people, who are always busy, cooking, winding wool, strengthening their shelters against the cold Himalayan winter. Surveyors move over the heaps of pulverized mountain; with every step they take, small landslips occur. Bahaguna greets them courteously; most can do nothing but reply similarly. There is still respect for the moral force of nonviolent protest. The camp though is at the base of a landfall: it could be wiped out at any moment by a spontaneous slip of boulders and rock.

Today is Makhar Sankranti. A group of women and children appear at the bottom of the valley coming from one of the villages further down the valley. They wear brilliant sarees, a line of vivid colour on the sad monochrome of the wasted mountain. Bahaguna takes his megaphone and calls out, 'Ganga bachao! Himalaya bachao!' ('Save the Ganges! Save the Himalayas!'). Their voices come back from below, echoing around the naked walls of the hill. All the people in over a hundred villages would be displaced by the dam.

So much money and prestige have now been invested in the project, it would involve an intolerable loss of face to the experts, engineers and professionals to admit that it has all been a costly mistake. Accordingly, the arguments they use have become more refined and seductive. It will ensure development for the impoverished region of the Uttarkhand. Those who are resisting are enemies of the poor. Those in the West who are saying it is dangerous and ill-conceived do not want to see India develop into a major industrial power.

However, the dam will not increase the area of irrigation in the hills: only 12 per cent of land is now irrigated, and this will not change. The dam is actually a filter, not so much for the conservation of water as for conveying wealth out of the region. 'The power station will be at Meerut', says Sunderlal Bahaguna, 'to give peak-time energy to the industrial belt of the Uttar Pradesh. The water will go to the rich farmers in the plains, to help them grow sugar-cane. Sugar-cane is the most voracious consumer of water. The sugar industry is to help India's exports; in other words, it is a means of exporting India's water, its most precious and scarce resource. The Worldwatch Institute has estimated that by the year 2000, India will have 24 per cent less water per capita than it has now; and here they are, busily diverting water for the most supremely redundant crop that could be imagined.'

Indeed, the whole journey from Delhi to Tehri provides a panorama of malign development. Everything is designed to enrich the already powerful – brickfields, which are a means of exporting the soil fertility of the region, fuelcakes of cow-dung, which is a way of consuming valuable manure, the growing area under sugar-cane. The cities, Muzzaffarnagar, Modinagar, appalling generators of pollution, which must be absorbed and paid for by the poor.

The dam has already become a lucrative source of corruption and waste. There has been a flourishing activity in the building of rough houses in the submergence area. Officials can then be bribed to declare that these are long-established family properties, worth Rs100,000, for which the owners then claim compensation. The officials expect to pocket about a quarter of the proceeds. It is estimated that some 5,000 such bogus houses have been built, and compensation claims lodged. Only the real oustees are unlikely to benefit from the scheme, in spite of the resettlement promises. There is a plan to construct New Tehri; but that will be at a higher altitude, where the land is poorer and the air colder, so that fresh costs will be incurred.

This is not to say that the protesters are against 'development'. But they conceive of this in quite different terms. The local people should be the beneficiaries of development, not the sugar lords and factory owners of the plains. Sunderlal Bahaguna says that run-of-the-river hydro schemes on a small scale would be sufficient for the sustenance and regeneration of the hills; because of the swift cascades of water, enough energy could be generated for local electricity needs; small dams and tanks could feed flourishing small-scale fruit- and nut-growers on the hillsides, for temperate fruits thrive here, cherries and pears and walnuts. Water can be pumped higher up the hills. But the Tehri dam is not intended to serve the local people; it is for the servicing of a distant economic necessity, which involves only loss, pain and disruption to the valley of the Bhagirathi.

Lunch is prepared on a fire in the improvised kitchen; rice, dal, vegetables in steaming vats, and served to visitors on metal plates. The camp is supplied with food – cauliflowers and aubergines, spinach, carrots and onions – by well-wishers in Tehri town. Quilts have been given for those who sleep out in the freezing January nights. We offered a donation, which was refused. Sunderlal Bahaguna said, 'Your visit is your donation; we should be offering you gifts for coming to see us.'

Dhoom Singh Negi, an activist and small farmer from Kumaon, says that he joined the dharna in mid-December. 'Within a few weeks of the earthquake, they began blasting again in the hills. The people were terrified. Instead of heeding nature's warnings, they increased their efforts. If the dam should burst, the water would wipe out the holy places at Rishikesh and Hardwar. We are urging them to rethink the whole Himalaya policy. The hills are very fragile. The idea of the steadfast, immovable Himalayas is an illusion, at best a poetic truth. There has already been one accident in the region. The whole village of Jamakh, beneath which a tunnel had been built, subsided suddenly, and seventy people were killed or injured. In any case, the life expectancy of the dam is limited – no more than 50 or 60 years, because of siltation. Since the earthquakes, many cracks have appeared in the hills. As these fill up with water, more landfalls will occur. The dam is a temporary solution to a permanent problem.'

Here, the war between the economy and the environment is at its fiercest. 'The battle was formerly between environment and development', says Sunderlal Bahaguna; 'now it is between survival and extinction.'

As we walk through the dried riverbed back towards Tehri town, the sound carries over the silent valley: 'Bacha Ganga, Bachao Himalaya'; the only other sound is the shifting minor cascades of rock and earth from the ravaged hillside.

Later, Bahaguna began a silent fast, which he ceased only when the government promised to look again at the Tehri project. The prime minister, P. V. Narasimha Rao, ordered blasting at the site to stop in a bid to persuade Sunderlal Bahaguna to end his hunger strike. By mid-1993, however, it seemed as though the project would indeed be resumed. The logic of the existing form of 'development' to which the present government of India is committed leaves them no option.

Development and Economics

All over the world, more and more people are being disadvantaged by a version of development which, even as it creates wealth, leaves them with a sense of loss and impoverishment. When they resist the violence done to them in the name of development, they are often branded by their own governments as 'extremists', 'criminals', 'wreckers'; at best, enemies of progress and modernization.

Among the people marginalized in this way are many indigenous communities; the inhabitants of forests and uplands, evicted by loggers and mining companies; those forced from ancestral lands, who have no choice but to live in squalid city slums. There, they die of grief for their defunct way of life, or they destroy themselves with the destructive consolations of alcohol and drugs, which industrial society offers them for their loss. Nomads, pastoralists, fishing communities, those ousted from subsistence or self-reliant farming, are seen as obstacles to development, as indeed are the urban poor themselves. The urban poor had fled to the harsh refuge of the cities precisely because they could no longer earn a living from devastated lands. Many had been compelled to give up farming by the rising costs of inputs or the pressure of agribusiness. Even when they arrive in the urban centres, they find no peace; their fragile shelters are routinely broken up by police and the military; the land they occupy is required by a different kind of 'developer'. There are, worldwide, more and more environmental refugees, developmental displaced persons, those caught up in wars, many of which are caused by a struggle for resources or ethnic differences between people who had lived without conflict for hundreds of years. Indeed, the victims of development are far more numerous than those removed from their habitat by mega-projects like dams, hydroelectric schemes, airports and military installations. Upheaval, displacement and endless moving on are part and parcel of processes which have at their heart the subversion of self-reliance, the undermining of sufficiency, the destruction of satisfactions, which are found outside an expanding global marketplace.

For what is this version of 'development' if not the export model of an economistic ideology, which has served the West so well for over two hundred years? Anisur Rahman says that 'development' was originally a Western promise to the South, designed to counter the danger of socialism. 'It was the threat of Bolshevik revolution inspiring social revolutions in the Third World that was countered by a promise of "development" and "development assistance" to help underdeveloped societies to catch up with the "developed". Development was exclusively defined as economic development, reducing the degree of progress and maturity in a society to be measured by the level of its production. The attraction of massive external finance and thrilling technology generated client states in the "underdeveloped" world, where oligarchies able to capture the organs of state could enrich and empower themselves as a class relative to the wider society, to whom "development plans" one after the other at the national level, and subsequently, at the global level, were offered as a perpetual hope for prosperity.

'The result: the economic benefits of such development have not even trickled down to the vast majority of the people in most countries honourably referred to as "developing". But the most fundamental loss has been the obstruction of the evolution of indigenous alternatives for societal self-expression and authentic progress.'

The Western – it should perhaps be called global, now that alternatives to it have been declared both inefficacious and unnecessary – economic system is an ideological construct. It is a mechanism for transforming all the varieties of wealth on earth into money; for concentrating it in the hands of those who already have; and finally, for legitimizing the process that provides so happy an outcome. It is a rationale for global social injustice and institutionalized exploitation. The union of the logic of capitalist expansion and the furtherance of a Western tradition of colonialism is consummated.

Economics is neither science nor art, but ideology. Its system of accounting is extremely selective about what it includes and what it omits, in terms of both costs and benefits, profits and forfeits, advantages and penalties. This partial and fragmented view of human affairs is now the focus of an evangelizing fervour by Western governments and financial institutions.

Indeed, the ideological underpinning of its economic system is now the bearer of a far older universalizing mission of the West. Formerly, this mission was carried in a less sophisticated, and now officially discredited, belief; namely, that it was the destiny of the West to civilize and convert the backward peoples of the earth to the truths vouchsafed to the West alone. The certitudes that animated earlier generations of missionaries, colonists and bringers of enlightenment now work through far more effective vehicles of domination. The IMF, the World Bank, the GATT negotiators, the transnational corporations and those Western governments that insist that the recipients of their aid must provide evidence of 'good governance' and 'sound economic policies' are now the eager transmitters of messages of economic salvation. Within the Western countries themselves, the ideology of economics is so deeply rooted that even radicals and dissidents rarely call into question those revelations that have deserted Bibles and scriptures, and have taken up their abode in the prescriptions and edicts of economists, those masters of what they call 'the real world'.

The sanctification of the 'science' of economics serves to conceal the narrow, partial and, above all, fiduciary nature of its accounting system. The exclusions, the violence and dispossessings which the Western system now inflicts on the South are seen by its votaries as nothing more than the unfortunate byproducts of processes that are as necessary as they are ultimately benign. Yet it simply eliminates everything that is inconvenient to its version of profit and loss – the ruin of the resource-base of the earth, the reduction of biodiversity, the injury to a large proportion of the world's people, the multiple forms of impoverishment which accompany its limited vision of riches. These consequences of its workings are referred to as 'externalities', that is, as having nothing to do with economics; and yet economics continues to colonize and expand over more and more areas of our experience.

The quasi-religious element in the economic dogmas of the IMF and World Bank is scarcely new. The 'hidden hand', whereby the pursuit of private gain is transmuted into public virtue, was always, presumably, the hand of God.

The laws of political economy were seen as a regulatory mechanism, whereby a fallen human nature could none the less redeem itself through the creation of wealth. These convictions, hardened, concealed beneath the self-justifying, opaque and impenetrable calculations of economics, underlie the sweeping, universalizing doctrines now being imposed on the whole world, notwithstanding the human and environmental desolation they cause. Thus, the IMF looks approvingly on 'the timely and decisive policy reforms of India'. The British prime minister, John Major, agrees to limited forgiveness of Third World debt, on condition that the countries thus favoured submit to the advice of the IMF. His foreign secretary, Douglas Hurd, insists that the conditions for disbursement of the EC aid budget should be 'the pursuit of sound social and economic policies'. Indeed, during the negotiations between the government of India and the IMF in the summer of 1991, one of the 'conditionalities' of the loan, which the government resisted, was a cut in food subsidies. (The word 'conditionalities' is an interesting euphemism; it sounds less harsh than 'laying down conditions', which is what victors usually do to the vanquished.) That the representatives of the Western financial institutions should even consider the option of reducing food subsidies in a country where as many as 40 per cent of the people do not have sufficient purchasing power to provide themselves with an adequate diet indicates something of the priorities of the IMF. It is clear that hunger, if not starvation, has become an instrument of economic adjustment.

Earlier justifications of Western dominance obviously had to change. Assumptions of a civilizing mission based on racial superiority suffered a severe setback in the middle years of the twentieth century, as a result of the devastation wreaked by Nazism and Fascism in the heartland of Western civilization itself. That these excesses were no temporary aberration in the ideology of the West may be understood by anyone familiar with the apologies offered for Western violence against those people whom centuries of colonists and empire builders had sought to subdue militarily. 'The coolie, though fond of money, prefers perfect idleness, and it is frequently necessary to drive him out of his village to force him to earn a good day's wages on the neighbouring railway works,' they said with a candour which their descendants have learned to avoid. After the Second World War, however, the open expression of that form of arrogance ceased to be a respectable vehicle for the continuing mission of bringing the backward and recalcitrant peoples of the world to an acknowledgement of their own inferiority, dependence and subordination.

A more subtle and efficient form of domination was required. And what could have been more acceptable and benign than a promise to share with the whole world the secret of the West's spectacular capacity for self-enrichment? That this secret involved centuries of subjugation and plunder of the South has not deterred many Third World governments from eager acceptance of the advice, instructions and, indeed, orders now issuing from the IMF, World Bank and Western governments. As decayed Communist regimes and disillusioned, sometime independent former colonial territories alike hasten to implement these prescriptions, we are clearly in the presence of mass conversions of an order and scope to which those other bearers of revelation, the Marxists, could never, in their wildest, most scientifically socialist dreams, aspire. Their transforming visions were, by comparison, the most idle of utopias. Anisur Rahman describes how, under the promise of 'development', 'the vast majority of the people were classified as "poor", and therefore as objects of sympathy, paternalistic intervention and assistance. May of these people, under the blinding light of compassionate observation which was flashed upon them, have internalized this negative self-image. Perceiving themselves as "inferior", they have sought to be "developed" by the "superiors", surrendering their own values, cultures, their own accumulated knowledge and wisdom. Others have been forced to do so by the sheer power of "development" effort, which itself has concentrated power and privilege and wealth in a few hands with the ability to subjugate and exploit the broader masses; and which has uprooted vast masses of people from their traditional life and life-styles *to become inferior citizens in alien environments*. Thus they have suffered not only economic impoverishment, but also a loss of identity and ability to develop endogenously, authentically, within their own culture and capabilities; *a deeper human misery* which as economists we were not trained to recognize.'

The exuberant and self-confident advice now being tendered to the countries of the South by the IMF and World Bank should be seen as part of Western rejoicing over the death of all rivals to its definition of development. It is certainly no celebration of the end of misery and injustice. Far from it. It is simply that misery and injustice no longer appear to have the power to pose a threat to Western interests; which suggests that new, unimagined poverties may still be in store for those who already see themselves with nothing. Indeed, so powerful has the West become, that seductive voices are raised once more, declaring not only that inequality and social injustice are irremediable, but that they are necessary, even an essential prerequisite, for the creation of that form of wealth whose showy iconography has seized hold of the imagination of the people of the world.

That we are confronted by blind faith in the 'miracles' of Western economics is clear from the fact that it is not disconfirmed by mere evidence. Those countries that have faithfully followed IMF structural adjustment plans and corrective macroeconomic policies (and how mechanistically Marxist some of these sound, as though the ideological winners had learned a thing or two from those they have vanquished) – Brazil, Peru, The Philippines, for example – have seen their landscapes ravaged, their resources gutted, in their effort to service fathomless debts; they have seen their forests felled, their cities teeming with refugees, the indices of ill-health, malnutrition and mortality worsening. This has not prevented other, desperate Third World governments from following the same path, hoping perhaps that they will somehow be delivered from the inescapable consequences of their imposed policy 'choices'.

There is another aspect of the ideology of economics which betrays its continuity with earlier, supposedly archaic, assumptions of racial superiority. For the world's rich are still mainly white and Western (or Japanese); while the overwhelming majority of the poor remain non-white and non-Western. The closely kept secret of the economic evangelists is that there is a virtual replication of the effects of overtly racist doctrines in the outcome of the workings of impersonal economic necessity. In fact, the economic ideology is more effective, for it provides a minority of non-whites among the rich, thereby permitting the West to distance itself from accusations of racism, by declaring that economics – unlike colonial administrators – is colour-blind; while the structures of domination nevertheless remain intact.

Perhaps this is why the issue of apartheid has been so fundamental in recent years. For there, frozen in time, a spectral graveyard relic of dogmas of racial superiority, it remained to haunt and remind the world of those former high principles which once stood at the heart of the West's civilizing mission. It was not by chance that among those most anxious to abolish apartheid in South Africa have been some of the most prominent capitalists: their prescience, and their understanding of the functioning of the global economy, permitted them to foresee that the workings of the economistic creed would preserve familiar forms of domination and ensure the survival of Western supremacy in the world.

This mutation of ideology serves to buttress and justify global patterns of power. Those who speak of pluralism, of open societies, of freedom and the clash of ideas in Western society, exaggerate. All societies need a cohesive and coherent world-view which holds them together; and Western economic ideology serves this purpose. The fact that it is not seen as ideology at all only strengthens its hold on us; and when it is spread with such zeal to the rest of the world, those at the heart of the imperial project are even more secure against seeing what they take for granted relativized, undermined, challenged by other beliefs.

Ruth Benedict in the 1930s recognized the psychological effects of the Western universalizing impulse on the West itself. In *Patterns of Culture*, she wrote,

Western civilization, because of fortuitous historical circumstances, has spread itself more widely than any other local group that has so far been known. . . . The psychological consequences of this spread of white culture have been out of all proportion to the materialistic. This world-wide culture diffusion has protected us as man had never been protected before from having to take seriously the civilizations of other peoples; it has given to our culture a massive universality that we have long ceased to account for historically, and which we read off rather as necessary and inevitable. We interpret our dependence, in our civilization, upon econo-mic competition, as proof that this is the prime motivation that human nature can rely upon, or we read off the behaviour of small children as it is moulded in our civilization and recorded in child clinics, as child psycho-logy or the way in which the young human animal is bound to behave. It is the same whether it is the question of our ethics or of our family organization. It is the inevitability of each familiar motivation that we defend, attempting always to identify our own local ways with Behaviour, or our own socialized habits with Human Nature.

The means of Western dominance are flexible and protean; they have migrated from one set of beliefs into another; but they have not changed their most fundamental characteristics. This is perhaps why, in the last decade of the twentieth century, we can now see coming together diverse social forces in the West, dedicated to the preserva-tion of existing patterns of privilege in the world. On the one hand, Western governments have become obsessed with the exclusion of those they refer to as 'economic migrants', as distinct from 'political refugees'. Economic migrants are themselves a creation both of Western policy (the flow of wealth from poor to rich, the uprooting and impoverishment of peoples in the Third World), and of a Western iconography of affluence, which is projected with seductive and growing intensity all over the world. The raising of barriers against those seeking to enter Europe or the United States serves as a powerful declaration of the intention to conserve wealth where it is now concentrated. At the level of popular reaction, we have seen the firebombings of migrant hostels in Germany, the rise of neo-Nazism; in France, the National Front now claims to represent the sentiments of one third of the people. In certain housing estates in Britain, there exists a de facto apartheid, under which no black families are permit-ted to live on all-white estates, not as a consequence of government policy, but because of the refusal of the inhabitants to allow it. In this way, the emergence of increasingly articulate racist forces in Western society and the reactions of their governments only make easier the promotion of values and policies by the Western financial institu-tions, which will ensure the continuing dominance of the West.

13

Nothing now apparently stands in the way of Western expansionism in the world. Nothing can prevent its violent incursions into lives and livelihoods, its evictions and uprootings of people, its forcible refashioning of custom and tradition, in order to maintain the flow of wealth from global poor to rich. For the promise of the West that it will show the rest of the world how to attain its levels of affluence is simply an illusion. That experience of the West, which has crucially depended on centuries of exploitation and plunder, and the sustained transfer of riches from South to North, is not replicable in those countries now following Western prescriptions. There, we can expect to see only intensified social dislocation, further excesses of violence, secessionism and terrorism, casteism and class conflict, kidnappings, bombings and repression. This will be viewed in the North as evidence only of corrupt rulers, instability and the inferiority of those people afflicted by it. Its model of development will remain untainted; its faith in its ideology will not be impaired by the rumblings of distant atrocities and televized brutality; its unquiet enjoyment of poisoned privilege will be untouched.

It is a strange paradox that at the very moment when the West no longer sees any obstacles to its unlimited expansion in the world, it is also becoming clear that such visions are not so easily realizable; not because of moral or political impediments, but because of constraints imposed by the finite carrying capacity of the earth.

Recently, the term 'externalities' has entered the vocabulary of economics. This idea has come to indicate certain environmental costs, until now rigorously excluded from the economic calculus. This is important, because it marks the first recognition that the increasingly totalizing claims of economics may have been exaggerated. For it is now admitted that nature cannot be relied on, either as an inexhaustible supplier of resources – what has always been called 'raw materials' in the reductionist lexicon of industrial society – or as an external, silent and unresponsive absorber of wastes. Acknowledgement of this has come as a great shock to the economic system, and the agitation caused has given rise to much uneasy discussion about 'sustainable economics', environmental audits, green consumerism. Efforts have been made to incorporate the costs to the environment within the economic paradigm, to price the priceless, to give a monetary value to those excluded aspects, indeed, to force into the economic straitjacket much of that which its totalizing impulse had overlooked, discounted or suppressed. In other words, the West has, perhaps predictably, looked to economics to remedy the damage that economics has caused.

In fact, what we are now seeing is the conjuring trick of the millennium; namely, the attempt to subordinate environmental 'externalities' to the existing accounting system. If this is can be done, it will overshadow all the preceding economic miracles that have come out of the West. If it cannot be done, the economic system may require such drastic modification that it will no longer be recognizable; indeed, may be transformed. The unalterable laws of economics are pitted against the all too mutable fabric of the planet. One of them will have to give.

A profound intellectual dishonesty underpins the effort of the West to salvage what is a mere ideological construct. (This is, perhaps, the one example of recycling that we could dispense with.) For this enterprise is potentially even more disastrous than discredited 'socialist' attempts to absorb all human existence within the single economic and social paradigm of Marxism. The dissolution of that unhappy experiment has served to conceal the fact that the West is engaged in a similar undertaking. The West has used the disintegration of Communism as an argument for proclaiming the unique and universal validity of its own economic system, which it is proceeding to impose on the whole world.

For even as the West greedily extends its influence over the blighted lands of formerly existing socialism and the Third World alike, it also declares its conversion to 'green values', and expresses its eagerness to incorporate 'sustainability' and resource conservation into its plans for the world. Now those who have pointed out that sustainability is at odds with the industrial system miss the point. First of all, when the West speaks of sustainability, it means sustaining its own patterns of living and privilege. And second, such an unjust system is indeed sustainable, and for the foreseeable future. As the Indian environmentalist Anil Agarwal says, 'Those who say the present system is unsustainable are talking nonsense. It is sustainable. The only question is, who will pay the price for the powerful to sustain their riches and their privilege? This is why questions of environment are also questions of social and distributive justice. But there is no objective reason why the present system cannot go on dispossessing the poor, with more and more casualties of environment, more and more urbanization, social dislocation and degradation in every sense.'

There is another way in which economics is the agent of colonization, not only in the poor countries, but also within the West itself. For 'development' in the rich countries means more and more areas of human experience being brought under control of economic relationships. At an earlier stage of growth, this had involved the privatizing

15

of the commons – just as is occurring now in many countries of the South. Later, we see the enclosure of the human commons, the ability to care for and support each other, and its reappearance in our lives as commodity or service.

In the rich world, we see ourselves increasingly impotent without the empowering possibilities of money; our human powers decay and fall into disuse, our creativity and ability to do things freely for ourselves and for each other become redundant. Where the spread of industrialization promises liberation from repetitive, destructive or backbreaking labour, it is welcome; but there comes a point where human autonomy, our capacity to act and do things for ourselves, becomes impaired, precisely by this division of labour; and then we find further industrialization invasive, disempowering and inhibiting. Strange new industries arise in this scheme of things – a sex industry, a health-care industry, an information industry, an entertainment industry, all of them, little by little, usurping our own capacities and vesting them in services, institutions and enterprises, which means that we have to buy them back. Those without sufficient money to participate in this game are the poor. It is this dynamic process that gives a sense of movement and change in Western society; it requires accelerating use of material resources, and a growing neglect of human resources. To the poor of the earth, those whose energies are confiscated totally in a desperate search for survival and food, this must appear as a liberation; but it becomes, in the rich world, a compulsion, an obligation, a mechanistic process from which disengagement becomes unthinkable. It becomes dependency and unfreedom.

For one thing, there are enormous costs involved when human beings are dispossessed of those activities which it is quite proper for them to carry out for themselves and for each other, freely, outside the money economy. Skills are struck from the hands and imagination of women and men; people are robbed of function and purpose. One of the problems of the growing arena of economic activity means that these costs must be borne by a shrinking number of the non-economic. This in turn places more and more pressure on women, and on those people who must bear the brunt of the often violent and disturbing changes that occur as we pass more deeply into the money economy. To take a specific example from the South: a young woman, the daughter of a rice farmer, migrates from the impoverished region of north Thailand to Bangkok, where she enters the sex industry. The cost of the change in sensibility from countrywoman to sex worker involves a great violence to her. She bears that cost. For a few years, perhaps, she will earn money in the bars of Patpong and remit something to her parents each month. She will not tell them that she is working as a prostitute, but that she is a receptionist in a hotel. The cost of this lie will be borne by her. The only appearance of her activity in the formal economy will be the few thousand baht she remits each year; also no doubt in the income generated by foreign tourists, and the profits that have gone to bar-owners and brothel-keepers. After three or four years, she becomes ill. She seeks remedies in private medicines and treatments. Later, her illness is diagnosed as AIDS. She then returns home; used up, full of shame, terminally ill. She must confess to her parents and siblings the truth of her life in the city. Again, they will collectively bear that cost. They will not turn her away, but will welcome her back into the family. Unable to earn anything, they will somehow manage to feed her and cherish her and ease her dying. Who will carry the unbearable burden of doing so? It will certainly not show up in economic benefits to anyone; indeed, the pitiful cash that she earned during her brief career marks her only passage into the GNP of Thailand; and the shrinking area of the non-economic – the caring family, the fractured rural structures, the dispersed loved ones – will have to bear an even greater share than if traditional society had remained intact. The mother and the sisters in particular will be there in her last illness.

Vandana Shiva describes this process:

> The market has depended upon women and their efforts to keep going. Women have continued to live a life where their contributions are not bought and sold. Their invisible work has helped the system to perpetuate itself. Women know that no market can be all-embracing. Women's role is to act in the areas of the exclusions created by the market. They must bear ever greater burdens of degradation inflicted upon both the resource-base and humanity. The same role devolves upon the Third World in the global economy. It is for us to make visible the parallels between the world of nature, the role of women and the Third World in this scheme of things; the degradation of all three are symptoms of the uncounted costs which the world must bear as the price of the success of the market economy. Until the South articulates itself along lines that parallel and mimic the feminist critique, we will be trapped into new subjugations.

At the same time, the West expresses its dedication to cleaning up an environment which it has recklessly polluted for two centuries. This can be understood only in terms of its intentions towards the South. What is not spoken in this project is that it can be accomplished only at great cost. And while the West restores and landscapes and ritually cleanses its own damaged and degraded industrial sites, it is at the same time passing on the costs of sustaining business as usual to other, less defended parts of the world, precisely in the name of 'development'. This is the meaning, not only of the dumping of toxic wastes in the Two-Thirds World, but also of the export of dangerous technology prohibited in the United States or Japan, of the more intensive resource-culling of the seas, the forests and fertile lands of the South, of the accelerated ransacking of the earth. The deepest dishonesty lies in persuading the people of the South – or at least its leaders – that by following the path pioneered by the West, their people, too, can freely partake of the fruits of industrial growth, which the people of the West so conspicuously enjoy.

The poor cannot have what the rich have without irreparable damage to the resource-base. The promise that they can is an illusion; and while the credulous leaders of the Two-Thirds World seek to accommodate themselves to the exhortations and advice coming from the West, their people, especially the poorest, are paying the costs of this lie. The spread of the West's dogmas cannot liberate these countries. For under the influence of these, the people of the South will have to reduce their claims on their own resources in order that the West may continue in the way of life to which it has become accustomed; indeed, upon which its people have developed a terrifying dependency. The conspicuous environmental improvements in the West, like its conspicuous and continuing extravagant life-style, are paid for by the ousting of the peoples of the South from the sites where valuable minerals lie, by the evictions from the forests of Sarawak, Indonesia or the Philippines; by the impoverishment of Lima, the violence of São Paulo, the slums of Calcutta; by the chaotic growth of Lagos, Cairo or Nouakchott; by the poisoning of the peoples of South-East Asia by Japanese technology, the appropriation of the natural beauty of Penang or Goa for tourists.

The role of the South in the new world order proves to be a very old one: to be suppliers of labour, cash-crops, amenities, playgrounds for the rich. It used to be called colonialism, but continues under the – until now – less controversial designation of 'development'. The servicing of debt, the flow of wealth from poor to rich, the terms of trade, the brain drain, transfer pricing and the multiple manipulations of the transnationals are a few of the mechanisms whereby older patterns of conquest and domination have mutated into more efficient and more opaque forms, now ennobled by being allied to economic necessity.

More and more people are caught up in this monstrosity as it rolls over the earth, laying waste, not merely the face of the planet, but all human societies and relationships that stand in its way, all other ways of answering need, all customs and traditions that are an obstacle to its further expansion. What we see is a confrontation between an aberrant version of riches and a grotesque form of poverty in a world which could – which still could – furnish all humanity with a decent, and even noble, sufficiency.

But even the hesitant and ambiguous recognition by the West of inadequacies in its economic laws has some unforeseeable consequences. Once one cluster of 'externalities' (the environmental impact) of the ecnomic system has been acknowledged, it soon becomes clear that there are many others. It is obvious that those who have accepted economistic measures of the 'costs' of labour have also radically falsified and underestimated the true costs *to* labour, before it can even make an appearance in the industrial marketplace. That the cost of labour is simply the least amount of money that a worker will accept bears no relationship to the experience of the people who find themselves standing outside the factory gate. Who has ever calculated the true price of that violence done to peasants and countrypeople as they are transformed into industrial workers? (If they are lucky, that is; many more become urban without even the disputable benefits of industrial employment.) For the passage of people into an urban setting involves radical disruptions and discontinuities with traditional cultures. It means a breaking of the sensibility of human beings and its reassembly in the image of industrial society, a coercive readjustment from the rhythms of the natural world to those of manufacture. The migrations from the home-place to the city, the eviction from settled ways of life, and forced resettlement into the security and pain of life in city slums, have never been costed, because they are incalculable. Indeed, they do not occur in the realm of what can be counted in money, and cannot be expressed in economic terms at all. Therefore, they simply disappear from the economic calculus. The burden is borne by 'society', which is a kind of dumping ground for problems and costs unrecognized by the economy; and indeed, is a diminishing area, as the colonizing thrust of the economy invades the last refuges of the non-monetary economy, the few demonetized zones in which human beings give and take, exchange and provide freely for one another.

Much was written at the time of the industrial revolution in Britain, and afterwards, about whether the people experienced that trauma as a rise or fall in their standard of living. Much of this debate has missed the point: whatever monetary increments there may have been, the experience of a majority of the people was of an overwhelming, disorienting and violent disturbance in their lives. To argue that a higher monetary income could compensate for that is absurd. In any case, their deeper dependency on the cash economy and the forfeit of much they had gathered and taken freely from the countryside, and what they had grown and cultivated for their own consumption, meant that more money was indispensable if they were not to undergo a serious depletion of an existence already on the edge of survival. They were well aware, as peasants in the South are today, that they were losing control over many aspects of their life in which they had until then been self-reliant; and because that also defies the familiar 'costings', it too failed to be recorded by a system which was responsible for such elisions and suppressions.

There are similar considerations in the examples of violent trans-formation now being undergone by people all over the South. They, too, are subject to upheavel, trauma and loss of control over their lives. One of the most significant of these losses is the fateful passage of the frontier, where direct dependency on the biosphere is exchanged for dependency on the industrial technosphere; for once that change has occurred, the technosphere becomes, apparently, the primary source of human survival, and the deeper dependency of the technosphere on the natural resource-base disappears from view. No means exist to count the cost of these forfeits and exactions; and even if they did, they would not be calculable in pecuniary terms. How much easier to ignore them!

Because the industrialization of the world has gone so much further than anything known to the early nineteenth century, the scale and intensity of it have increased in the contemporary world. The movement of handloom weavers from the hills of Lancashire to the slums of Manchester seems a relatively minor upheaval com-pared to the migration of the children of rice farmers entering the sex industry in Phuket. What profound changes occur in their concept of themselves and their purposes in their shift of livelihood. (Perhaps, with the prevalence of AIDS, it should be called deadli-hood?) Perhaps some of the enthusiastic advocates of the universal extension of the Western model should talk to the children of peasants in the bars of Bangkok, where, barely out of their teens, they become merchandise to be consumed by rich and greedy Western or Japanese tourists, who regard them as a legitimate 'reward', to be purchased like any other self-administered treat, as a consolation for their own heroic labours of wealth-creation. Indeed, the very exis-tence of a 'sex industry' suggests that the laws of supply and demand are infinitely extensible and liable to invade all kinds of areas of our experience, unsuspected in the early industrial era.

Nowhere are the continuities of colonialism, and its mutation from the military into the economic arena, more plain than in the fate of those in India, compelled by Great Britain to grow opium in the nineteenth century. The British wanted to create a commodity that would break down the self-reliance of China. In the process, tens of thousands of subsistence farmers, especially in Bihar, were forcibly dispossessed of their livelihood and made to cultivate the opium poppy. Many of them starved. In the 1980s, Britain ceased taking its legal supply of morphine from India, which had remained its chief supplier until then. Britain is now supplied from Australia, which in recent years has perfected a high-technology process of extracting the drug from opium poppies. As a result, the poppy farmers of Bihar have once more been robbed of a livelihood which they had never sought in the first place. In theory, the land on which they cultivated the poppies has been taken out of production. In fact, since they were so inadequately compensated, much of the surplus has found its way onto the domestic market of India. In consequence, there are 100,000 heroin addicts on the streets of Bombay alone.

And what of the people of Goa, Langkawi or Penang, or of any of the other places that have become the sites of intensive Western tourist penetration, where local people can no longer afford to buy the food they produce because it is monopolized by the big hotels? What of those countries, recently self-reliant in food, that have been compelled to turn over land to cash-crops in order to increase foreign exchange, to pay off debts of which they were never beneficiaries? What of the people compelled by unfair trading practices to renounce their traditional foods in favour of foreign eating patterns? The Philippines, with its variety of indigenous fruits, its mangosteens and lanzones and abundance of sweet bananas, its custard apples and rambutans, now sees its fruit-stalls laden with Washington Red apples, Californian oranges and grapes, grown for their appearance, genetically engineered for cosmetic and not nutritional purposes.

There are many other 'externalities' of the economic system, notably those of time. A long-term perspective in economics means five or ten years at most; the immediate concern is for the current balance-sheet. It has no care for the burdens it may pass on to generations to come, just as it makes no acknowledgement of anterior wrongs, which have impoverished and destroyed ancient and digni-fied life-ways which had persisted for millennia and were disturbed only by the violent irruptions of the West. Instead of Britain congratulating itself on the generosity of its aid to India, we ought to be talking about the incalculable reparations we owe that country. How could we compensate for the ruin of sustainable agricultural and industrial practices which we destroyed, in order to dump inferior British manufactured goods on India? How would we recompense those weavers, long dead, whose thumbs were cut off, so that they should be deprived of their skill to make cloth far more delicate and durable than anything known to Lancashire? Or would this, in the treacherous lexicon of free trade, merely be considered a non-tariff barrier?

One thing is becoming clear in the last years of the twentieth century: among the multiple 'externalities' of the system and its version of 'economic development' are increasing numbers of human beings, by no means all of them in the countries of the South. This can mean only one thing – that their lives and deaths do not register on the crude and simplistic measuring devices whereby wealth is judged. This book is concerned with those people who are, and are becoming, 'external' to that system, their lives, their resistance and their efforts to build alternatives to it.

Manila

Holy Week in the Philippines. There are few Christian countries where religious fervour reaches such heights – the candlelit processions at dusk, the carrying of crucifixes in the oppressive heat, the re-enactment of the Passion by countrypeople dressed as disciples and Roman soldiers. Each year there are reports of real crucifixions; in some places, these have become a tourist attraction. In 1991 it was reported:

> A 24-year-old fish vendor wept and stared at the sky as he and other devotees were nailed to wooden crosses on Friday, in a ritual marking the Crucifixion of Jesus. Six men, including the fish-seller Chito Sanggalang, were nailed to the crosses in the middle of a rice field in Pampanga. Hundreds of flagellants beat their backs with bamboo whips as they led the procession to the field where the nailings took place.

To be in the Philippines at Easter is to experience what popular fervours might have been in medieval Europe. At the same time, you gain a sense of the force of the colonial power which originally christianized the country with such ineffaceable violence.

In recent years, the urban poor of Manila, taking advantage of the intensities of Holy Week, have organized an alternative Kalbaryo (Calvary), identifying the sufferings of the present-day poor with those of Christ.

Outside Malate church, devoted to Our Lady of Remedies, almost five thousand people gather under the hot sun. A truck carries a choir whose voices will accompany the procession, with the cast of the Calvary on foot, a crowd of vendors, jeepney drivers, labourers, the unemployed, dressed as Roman centurions, Christ and his disciples, including Judas. There are seven figures in black masks with blood-stained T-shirts, carrying heavy wooden crosses on which are inscribed the sources of the pain borne by the poor: Debt, Unemployment

Corruption, Militarization, Cronyism, the Transnationals, IMF and the World Bank. In this Calvary, Christ is taken prisoner outside the American Embassy, is crucified outside the Assembly building and resurrected at the Mendiola Bridge, which is as close as the demonstrators are allowed to the Malacanang Palace. Behind the actors come radical priests and nuns – not very numerous – then representatives of the urban poor communities, then foreign visitors. There are five of us.

The American Embassy is guarded by the military; all corpulent, with sharp metal buckles over well-filled bellies. By contrast, those they are controlling look thin and defenceless. There is negotiation over whether the procession will be allowed to halt and perform outside the Embassy. This year, for the first time, permission is granted.

As the cortège winds through the concrete canyon of Taft Avenue, the heat of the sun is trapped in the stone and strikes the procession both from above and below. Motorists sound their horns impatiently, and some drive dangerously close to the people on the road. Some passers-by stop and applaud and others join the procession, with the result that, as it nears its destination, there are twice as many as at the beginning. The crowd advances slowly through the ruinous cityscapes, scarred by recession, poverty and neglect. The pollution from buses and jeepneys creates a permanent metallic fog. In the shadow of luxury hotels, squatter settlements have grown. Some people carry a banner protesting at the shooting of residents in a slum during demolition in February. At the bridge over the Pasig, where huddled shanties overhang the glassy, stagnant water, the dome of the mosque, gilded by Marcos as a concession to the Muslims in the dying days of his power, hangs like a mock sun over the fetid slum beneath.

The crowd is silent; young women and men, their beauty made more poignant by crowns of thorns, garlands of evergreen and flowers. Some wear straw hats, a cloth over their mouths to protect them from pollution. The emotion is heightened by the uncertainty as to whether the military might turn their guns on them. They calculate that in Holy Week they are safe, and they can turn the religion of the powerful against them, under protection of the most solemn week in the Christian year.

At Mendiola Bridge the procession halts and forms a semi-circle in the space created by the road intersection. The resurrection is acted out. Prayers are asked for a government of the poor. The soldiers watch the kalbaryo impassively. They know that if they should waver in their support for those in power, they too will find themselves in the same precarious position of the urban poor, from whom, in any case, so many of them come.

Dolores is one of the organizers of today's march. A frail, dark-haired woman in her thirties, she says that even if the leaders of the urban poor are under surveillance – which they surely are – they have no option but to continue to work for social justice. She says, 'The urban poor in Manila are always threatened, by demolitions, by evictions, by prison. We are one of the most vulnerable groups. Others are part of an international network – trade unionists, women, environmentalists, all have their counterparts in the West. But the urban poor have no support groups abroad. We are isolated. If there is one thing the urban poor need, it is friends.'

Dolores came to Manila from Bicol in 1964. 'Our land was seized by land-grabbers while my father was working in Manila. Then we came to join him. We lived in a house owned by his employers. He worked in a factory making heavy machinery. He died two years later, at work, of a heart attack. My mother received 4,000 pesos [about $80] in compensation. I was twelve years old, the first of six children. My mother was a dressmaker and I helped her. I made buttonholes and sewed beads onto dresses.

'We had to leave the house and went to live in Tondo down by the docks, one of the biggest slum areas in Manila. I used to work in the morning and study in the evenings. Even at that time, the urban poor were regarded as an obstacle to development. Houses were always being demolished. The poor were not seen as a resource to the city, but as an encumbrance. When we protest, we attract the attention of the military, who send their goons to wage psychological war, to scare us off. Sometimes, they burn down poor communities: fires are started which rage through the poor areas in no time.'

Dolores now lives in Dakota, a huddled cluster of shacks and poor huts behind Mabini Street, a district of downmarket entertainment, a place of karaoke bars, VD clinics, money-changers, strip shows and seedy bars. Dolores's house is on the main road, a tiny strip of garden in front; a structure of wood and concrete, an upper storey and corrugated metal roof. The land has recently been claimed by the Landcom Realty Corporation, owned by Lucio Tan, a Marcos crony, and one of the richest men in Manila. The company presented bogus documents to the court to establish its claim. They plan to demolish the long-established community and replace it with a commercial development. This is a strategic tourist area, and land is worth 15,000 ($300) pesos a square metre. 'If big business gets hold of it, the people will be relocated miles away, beyond Metro-Manila, with no job, no transport, no schools. People want to stay here. It has taken them so much effort and pain to create work for themselves here.'

The people of Dakota provide vital services to the city – vendors of vegetables, newspapers, fish, bread. The women work in hotels, laundries, and as domestics. Many work in the sex industry, as pick-up girls on the streets, or go-go dancers in the bars and clubs. Most of these are owned by American, Japanese or German interests. 'The women work from 8, through the night. The customer pays half to the bar and half to the woman, who then has to share this with her pimp, or in some cases hand over the whole lot. Sometimes, I say to the women "When you sit at a bar and drink with a customer, who gets the profit?" There is the bar owner, of course, the pimp, the liquor companies, the bartenders, the government, the tourists – everybody except the women. By the age of twenty-five, their career can be finished. They start very young, and many dream of marrying a foreigner. Some do get out that way; but even when they go to other countries, they find it a great cultural shock. Filipinos are very friendly and sensitive. They often find life in the West harsh in a different way. In the Philippines, social relationships are frozen, colonial, archaic. Women feel they must be submissive and docile, and men are their masters. This is what attracts some Westerners to come and find Filipino brides, because Western women have become more assertive.'

Dolores has three children. Her husband, Aquilino, grew up in Malate, and his mother lives with them. Aquilino's father was a carpenter, but died when Aquilino was six. His mother worked as a laundress and cook for an American family. Aquilino started work at ten, first watching parked cars and then selling newspapers.

Dakota consists of 700 households, 900 families; 4,500 people on 1¼ hectares. In one house, there may be three or four families, occupying one room each. People who don't have water connections must pay 50 centavos a can to vendors. One family will take a legal supply of electricity, and then illegally serve five or six others.

Ten years ago, Dolores had typhoid and TB. TB is common in the slum areas. She had to stop organizing for a year and went to Saudi Arabia as a domestic. She stayed twenty months. 'People dream of earning dollars. They think that will change their life. I came back home because my husband lost his job as the result of a strike. I knew dressmaking, so I worked in a shop here, but I couldn't bear to see the shopowner shouting at the women sewers as though they were not human beings. Then I had a job working for the Basic Christian Community programme in Malate church.'

The urban poor first began to organize in Tondo in the early

1980s, when Marcos's grandiose City of Man project was conceived. This was to drive a main road through the Tondo area, to facilitate an enhanced import–export drive by means of containers at the docks. A plan to develop the domestic port would have evicted some 27,000 families. The poor organized the first demonstration to take place in Manila under martial law. Marcos promised not to demolish, and said he would provide on-site development to upgrade the slum area. The government would buy the land and sell it at 5 pesos per square metre. All the people had to do was pay for the infrastructure. The project was financed by the IMF and World Bank. But because of corruption, the drainage system was inadequately constructed. The pipes were too narrow and the system collapsed. One result of this is that the streets are constantly flooded. Sheets of stagnant water covered with a carpet of green algae spread over the area, and in the monsoon, the houses are contaminated by sewage.

The problems of Dakota are compounded by its proximity to the entertainment district. There, drugs are readily available – shabu (a heroin derivative), marijuana, glue, amphetamines, cough syrups. Many people live by hustling. Romero makes a living by offering high rates of exchange for foreign money – 40 pesos to the dollar. He operates from a snack stall, inviting foreigners to change their cash for the highest rate in Manila. He then employs boys to follow the customers and pick their pockets. They don't always succeed, but overall, he makes a good profit.

Carisima Balatrayo came to Manila from Visayas twenty-one years ago. Under Aquino, she says, things became worse, and under Ramos there is no change. 'In Marcos's time, there were "salvagings" of people, there was unemployment and drugs. But now, our land has been claimed by Lucio Tan. We are a small community, what can we do against their wealth? There was a court hearing on the ownership of this land. Our attorney was ambushed and killed.

'There is no work for the young people. Aquino promised homes for the homeless, land for the landless, jobs for the jobless. None of these happened. There is insecurity, no livelihood, price increases. My son works in a ceramics factory in the United Arab Emirates. My husband has liver amoeba and cannot work.

'Even basic necessities are beyond the reach of the people. A gas cylinder costs 132 pesos and it lasts barely two weeks. I have five children and one grandchild. We need 14 kilos of rice a week, but the cheapest rice is 7.50 pesos a kilo, and it smells bad. Beans cost 5 pesos a small bundle, kamote leaves 2 pesos for a handful, kangkong the same. Galungong is the fish everybody in Manila eats. It is 8.50 pesos a kilo, dried; fresh it is four times the amount. Oil is 20 pesos a litre. We pay 139 pesos for electricity each month, 33 pesos for water, and the pressure is always low. Some children here are malnourished. We had to form our own fire brigade, because we were afraid they might try to demolish us by setting fire to the houses. People say this land was a cemetery in Spanish times. It is unlucky to live here. When we first came, it was marshland, tall grasses. We have built up the land, improved it. Now it is valuable and they want to take it away from us.'

Gregorio Gimpayan is from Cebu, the youngest of seven children. He runs a small cooked-food store on the main road. His mother and father began their working life in Manila by selling water. His father died in 1978. His mother gets up at 4 in the morning, to buy the food; and the store is open until 8 at night. Gregorio was working as a technician, but with his salary of 80 pesos a day and the price of transport, it was not worth it. He says his life's dream is to have a stable job so he can marry and bring up a family. Not exactly extravagant, he says bitterly, but impossible in today's circumstances.

Gregorio had been underground during the Marcos era. He returned when Aquino came to power. He was driven underground because his family's land was confiscated. Only now, many of his friends are wondering whether they should have stayed under-ground: now there are more human rights violations, more killings, constant police extortion from the poor.

Camilla is over sixty, but she still sells newspapers in the morning, and washes clothes in the afternoon, working twelve hours a day. Her son has bought a pedicar, a cycle rickshaw, a form of transport devised by the poor themselves as a means of taking passengers short distances within the neighbourhood. His wife is from Iloilo. She came when she was seventeen to work in the bars; but now they have a baby she has stopped work and wonders how she will survive. 'By the grace of God.' Dolores says you can't eat the grace of God.

Four women working in the bars share a single room, reached by an almost vertical ladder. It is early afternoon and they have just got up. They yawn, push the hair out of their eyes and sit hugging a teddy bear or a pillow, rocking to and fro. The only furniture in the bare wooden room is a plastic table and a scattering of cushions. A rack of clothes – sequined blouses, lurex miniskirts, ra-ra skirts, incongruous in the bleak setting. There is a Holy Family calendar on the corrugated metal wall. There are no cooking facilities, no run-ning water. A red plastic bowl holds some plates. There is a row of San Miguel beer bottles and Coke tins. Merle, a thin, youthful-looking woman, is forty-one and embittered by her experience. She has ten children, who are with the violent husband she left. She has been in dispute with the management of the bar where she works, because they want to dismiss the older women and replace them with younger ones who are arriving in Manila all the time. Merle earns 700 pesos a month from the bar for waiting. The rest she must make up from clients. There are no amenities for the workers, not even a comfort room for the women.

Colette is twenty-two. She is a dancer, 'not go-go, but a floor-show model'. There is a strict hierarchy of respectability. She is, she says, 'tired of bedspacer living'. She is pregnant, but thinks she will not have an abortion as she did last time. The father of the child has promised to look after her, although he is married and has three children. Colette would love to give up this life, but she doesn't know whether she can trust him. Merle scoffs at what she calls 'a two-bit romance'. 'Men make you promises in bed, then afterwards, nothing. Once a man is in a woman, he'll say anything. Do I believe in love? When I'm in love, yes I believe. But that never lasts long, so no, most of the time I don't believe. Life has made me selfish', says Merle, 'because the world is so stupid.'

Cora works as a waitress through the night. 'Most of the girls take drugs, shabu, syrup, even cocaine, because if you take drugs, you can forget the shame, you don't mind what you do.' She leans against the wall, and her hair falls over her shoulder. Her eyes close, puffy with lack of sleep. She cuddles an electric-blue teddy-bear, still wrapped in protective polythene; a present from an admirer, she says. A toy. Because they think of us as playthings too.

Dingdong sits in the wire-mesh cage of the window of his house, curled up in the narrow space provided by the ledge. He wears a red football shirt, red silk shorts; a beautiful boy of fourteen, who is autistic and has no speech. His real name is Marcos. He was, says Fely, his mother, a martial law baby. At the time, it seemed both prudent and hopeful to call him Marcos. Her other children are called Mona Lisa and Ronald, after Reagan. She is, she says, ambitious for her children. Fely's husband works as a cook and houseboy for a family who own a wine factory. Fely came from Leyte ('like Imelda') in 1964, and worked as a housegirl for 60 pesos a month. Her family had no land, but were tenants who tilled the earth as sharecroppers, growing rice, grains, corns and *kamote* (sweet potato). Fely came to Manila to better herself. On the wall there is a glossy picture with the caption: 'Look upon the Rainbow and Praise Him That Made It.' There is also a McDonald's growth chart for measuring the height of children who have been nourished by McDonald's food. On the window ledge, a canister of TNT roach and flea killer. Fely is tied to Dingdong, who cannot feed himself or go the toilet on his own. Although he cannot speak, he communicates by touch with those he knows and trusts. She says, 'He lives in a different world. Let's hope it is better than this one.'

Ricky is eight and has developed a precocious puberty. He is a strange, small adult, whose voice has broken and with hair on his lip. His father works in Saipan as a waiter. His mother cannot work because she cannot leave him, but his grandmother sells cigarettes on Roxas Boulevard, outside the American Embassy. The family pays 700 pesos monthly to the owner of the hut, although it is constructed on public land. Ricky cannot be allowed out on his own, because his sexuality is a danger to other children. There is something oddly symbolic here: so many families have fathers who are forced to go abroad to work, who have to leave home, to abandon their children; it seems as though Ricky, the child, has sought to replace the absent males of the neighbourhood.

Like all poor communities, Dakota has many sick and handicapped people, and the burden of their care falls overwhelmingly on women. Many of the sick are overprotected and do not go out. Eduardo lives in a dark, windowless room on the ground floor of a hut in a maze of little paths behind the main thoroughfare of the slum. He has cancer, a growth on the spine, and never goes out. He sits on a wooden platform where he sleeps, a towel covering his withered legs. He is ashamed to be seen in public, because one of the consequences of his illness has been loss of bladder control. He is an intelligent young man of nineteen, and keenly interested in politics. He needs an operation that would cost $450, but it might just as well be $45 million. His mother has TB and his brother, who has just finished an engineering course, is jobless.

Tessie is a manicurist. 'Call me Tessie Crazy,' she says. 'I was born in purgatory and I've lived in hell, so whatever comes next doesn't scare me.' Tessie is a cosmetologist. She does hair care and make-up. When people go out of their houses, they always want to look their best. In any case, with all the women in the sex industry, there is no shortage of work for Tessie. She says, 'Nobody employs us. We have to make our own livelihood.'

At one o'clock in the morning, the foyers of the hotels in Malate are full. Women parade in sequined blouses and short skirts across the illuminated flooring of the discos, while the foreign tourists appraise them critically, and wonder which one to buy. It would not occur to the clients that they might live in impoverished hutments, only 200 or

300 metres from the synthetic luxury, the sanitized refrigeration of the hotels where they labour.

SURVIVING

Jun is one of the hundreds of thousands of young people whose dream is to leave the Philippines. He says, so many do, 'There is no future here. There is no money. I want to get out while I'm young.' Jun is nineteen, a bright and able young man, who is studying for his Commerce degree. He spends much of his time at a dance and modelling studio in Mandaluyong, a place where young people are trained to become entertainers for Japan. The building is a boarded-up shop window, with a stifling basement, where the young people practise, an office and a kitchen. Jun sometimes prepares meals for the dancers. His friend, who runs the studio, sometimes lends him money. Jun is fascinated by the glamour of this seedy place. He is himself not agile or talented enough to be a dancer. The eagerness, beauty and hope of the young people, their unself-consciousness, are being marketed by those who know how to sell these qualities. If they succeed, it will be a question of short contracts (six months at a time) for a few seasons, and then the return, used up, disappointed, without skills. The culture of 'disco-dancing', of being an 'enter-tainer', is an ambiguous and precarious occupation, without duration or substance. But it represents the chance of meeting a rich for-eigner, of marrying a Japanese, a fantasy of escape into the blinding light of the agent of their dispossession. Jun is eager to please his friends at the studio; whenever he has any money he treats them all to ice-cream and beer.

Jun's mother was one of fourteen children who came from Iloilo to work as a domestic when she was fourteen. Later, she worked in a garment factory and somehow met and married the son of a lawyer. The marriage was vehemently opposed by her parents-in-law, who would not let them live with them in their substantial stone villa in Mandaluyong. Accordingly, Jun's mother built an annexe alongside the house; a long railway-carriage of a lean-to, with a perspex roof. It is impossible to stand up in this shelter, and it is built over a drain which carries the waste-water from the adjacent houses. In the rains, the living-room is flooded, and mildew and damp stain the lower part of the walls. Jun's mother has raised the concrete floor, and painted it red. There is a peeling plastic sofa and plastic chairs. The kitchen is raised by a step, and because of the slope of the ground, the water doesn't reach the kitchen. The single bedroom is on a level with the kitchen, but the roof leaks, and tins stand to catch water from the most violent downpours.

Jun is the youngest of three. He has two older sisters. One of these has now left home and gone to live in the cosmetics factory where she works. Their father has run away with his girlfriend. The children grew up knowing that there was something wrong – their father used to take rice and vegetables to feed his girlfriend and her family, often leaving them hungry. He now works in a factory in Taiwan, and there is no communication with him. Jun's grandfather is dead, and the relationship with the grandmother has become worse. She wants them out, barely tolerates their presence, and is constantly threatening to evict them. Also in the house is another cousin, a boy of twenty, who has no work but helps around the home. Jun's mother has taken in the twin children of her sister's daughter, Charmaine and Charlene, who are just twelve months old. Their mother has gone to Japan as an entertainer, and the father has deserted them. The twins are pale, wide-eyed children, and Charlene, who has just had pneumonia, is thin and listless. Their grandmother works in a biscuit factory and cannot look after them; so Jun's mother, who at the moment has no permanent job, is looking after them. She works as a hairdresser at home, but the work is irregular. Cathie, Jun's other sister, is just finishing her degree. She has been doing accounting – like many young people who study commerce, business, accounts, they hope that their familiarity with money will magically produce some.

The place where they all sleep, with mattresses on the floor, is a windowless 2x3 metre space. Jun goes to college in the evenings, because it is less crowded then and he can concentrate better. He is very proud of his English, which is very fluent. He has great charm and warmth, and thinks he will find work in public relations. He saw an advertisement for a waiter at 4,000 pesos a month. When he applied, he was told the only jobs were for 'receptionists', which meant receiving the clients of the gay club. He worked there for a few days, but is not gay, and detested having to service the clients. He gave it up.

His family knew nothing of what he was doing. They are devoutly Catholic and would have been deeply distressed by it. His mother had done everything to enable her children to finish their studies. He feels it is his duty to provide for her. His dream is to leave the Philippines. He says, 'I'll do anything. I'll do anything. I'll give up my studies. I'll be a janitor, work in a factory. Anything.' He says, 'If I have to be unhappy, I'd rather go away where they will not see it. And at least, I'll be able to send them money.'

Manila

SMOKY MOUNTAIN

In June 1991, the people of Manila had to live with the fallout from the eruption of the Pinatubo volcano in Pampanga. The air was thick with ash and dust. Life in the chaotic city became almost unbearable, as people tried to protect their houses and their bodies from the pollution and clouds of choking dust. Although few people drew the conclusion, what was happening to them was very much like the daily experience of the 3,500 families – almost 20,000 people – who live permanently on Manila's human-made Smoky Mountain, perhaps one of the most infernal living-places on earth.

Smoky Mountain is a vast garbage dump; something of a human dump too, where humanity – refugees from damaged farmlands and degraded ecosystems, from militarization and social injustice – is also being recycled, like the objects among which they must scavenge for daily survival. They labour on the sulphurous smoking slopes of an area which for a quarter of a century has been receiving the 2,500 tons of garbage produced by Manila each day.

Smoky Mountain is reached by the Marcos Highway, which cuts through Tondo. The road is covered with a thick layer of dust, so that as the silver-painted jeepneys pass, they set in movement whirlwinds of sand that reduce visibility almost to zero. Indeed, the desolate highway, with its loops of power-lines, its metal shacks and stalls, its heaps of wayside rubbish, has the air of an abandoned frontier town. The covering of dust fades all objects to the pale monochrome of an ancient film.

At the foot of the mountain some huts of recycled metal are anchored in an expanse of viscous seawater, so still that the reflections look more substantial than the structures themselves, which can be reached only by walkways of rotting planks. The lower slopes of the hill have been completely occupied. About forty concrete steps constructed in the now solid flank of the mountain lead to a road that encircles the higher levels, where the trucks come to unload their wastes. There is an embankment alongside this road, where layers of compressed rubbish still reveal shreads of undegraded plastic, pieces of rusty metal and the imperishable logos of transnationals – Sanyo, Pepsi, Toshiba.

A rough plateau covers the top, with its shifting ridges and valleys, as the randomly dumped garbage finds its own level. Silver seabirds swoop and wheel. The smell is overwhelmingly of methane, sulphur dioxide and especially smoke, which unfurls in endless coils of acrid fumes, intensified by the heat of the sun.

Everything in the people's homes is made of salvaged objects; a curious junkyard culture, which is a vast exercise in recycling. The huts themselves look like an emanation of the artificial mountain, jagged tin, rust, decaying wood and plastic. Many are surrounded by rectangles of rusty bedsprings, from which the mattresses have rotted away. The metal whorls provide an open-work fencing around which creepers and morning glory flower, the bright blue trumpets and veined hearts of flowers and leaves in defiance of the polluting smoke. Herbs grow in Maggi soup cans or tins of Infant Formula. Some men are playing pool on a ragged baize table, propped up by stones; others play tinny cassettes. A boy sits in the shade of his hut and sings 'Unchained Melody' to his own accompaniment on a battered guitar.

Here, nothing is wasted except the people, their bodies eroded by overwork and malnourishment, their lungs corroded by heat and fumes, the children weakened by respiratory diseases, diarrhoea and worms.

As the trucks – painted with the message Environmental and Hygiene Improvement (Japanese Grant in Aid) – deposit the new day's rubbish, a crowd of people surges after it, foraging with hooked metal poles, turning over the stinking material and picking out anything that is saleable. Virgilio from Pampanga is filling a hessian sack with dingy underwear, soiled by the trash, knickers and padded bras, vests and pants. He takes them home to his wife, who washes and cleans them and sells them to the tribal people of Pampanga. He makes a profit of about 20 pesos a day, and this, together with the produce from his small piece of land, will just sustain his family of six.

Some people look only for particular objects of value – glass, unbroken bottles, ferrous metal or brass. Others fill sacks or baskets with anything that will earn a few centavos – printed circuits, plastic radio cases, cans of del Monte pineapple, San Miguel beerbottles. A thick swarm of flies hovers over the scene, barely distinguishable from the scintillas of dust in the fierce sunlight; their aggregated hum the only sound, apart from the chink of glass and metal as the rubbish is turned over. Children, too, are working; many have red eyes and are covered by a film of dust. One ten-year-old has a huge carbuncle, which has distorted one side of his face. He is the only earner in his family. He has no father and his mother has TB.

Robert from Zambales is twenty-three. He wears a US flag as bandanna round his head to protect him from the sun. His hut has a small yard filled with garbage. Inside the hut, there is green lino on the floor, a 1988 Pepsi calendar. The walls are beaten panels of old oil-containers rivetted together, the roof uneven strips of wood. There is a cracked plastic sofa, its foam gaping. The interior of the house is well maintained; the discarded consumer items are a gesture of deference by the excluded to those who can afford to throw out such things. A useless refrigerator is used as a food cupboard. Robert's parents have been in Manila for thirty years. His father worked on Smoky Mountain until he had a stroke, two years ago. His mother is blind; a thin woman in a red floral dress, with wasted arms and blank yellow eyes. She was knocked down by a government truck during the demolition of the barangay (slum) where they were living, and this was a result of her injuries. On the door of the cabin in black crayon Robert has written, 'God Bless Our Home'. It isn't an ironic comment; he means it.

Alvin Lopez sits in the compound of his more substantial house. He buys bottles, which children collect and sell to him. He pays them 25 centavos per item, and sells them to a glass factory in Manila for 35 centavos. In order to set up even this rudimentary business, capital of about 5,000 pesos is needed (about $200) for storage space and transport. Gina Reni is from Negros Oriental, where her family works and lives on a sugar plantation. Now twenty-five, she earns about 35 pesos a day, just enough to feed her three children, the youngest of whom is one month old. All were born here on Smoky Mountain. Her husband makes 50 pesos a day; together, they make less than the official minimum wage for one person.

Rebecca Sibilia is twenty-nine. She collects wood, which she sells as cooking fuel. Consuela burns wood on the foreshore and turns it into charcoal. She lights a fire and covers it with sand, so that it smoulders. She can make two sacks of charcoal a day, and sells them for 40 pesos each. She is from Bicol, where her family are share-croppers, giving 70 per cent of their harvest of rice and coconuts to the landlord. There, she earned 10 pesos a day and was permanently in debt. She says that life on Smoky Mountain is better than in the province. Her husband is down by the stagnant pool where the waste-water outlet reaches the sea. He is fishing for frogs for them to eat.

In a little wayside chapel, with a brass cross and a glossy photograph of a painting of the Virgin, a varnished coffin is laid out on a trestle. In front of it, two candles are burning. The dead woman is twenty-six. She died of a pulmonary infection on Monday. Today is Friday. They are waiting for her mother to arrive from Samar. The husband sits, dazed and numb, and her three children, all under six, cling to him. His brother is there, but he himself has six children. How can his wife take three more?

Smoky Mountain has expanded. At the edge of Tondo, Aroma Beach is being reclaimed from the sea: rubbish and paper, decaying vegetable matter, create a swampy landfill. This has blocked the waste-water outlets of Tondo to the sea, with the result that its streets are permanently flooded, canals of black water, 'little Venice', they call it.

One of the biggest employers in Tondo is Procter and Gamble. Jobs here are well paid and much sought after. The company employs about one thousand people. However, it sends its soapy pollutants into the air, a thin greasy drizzle, which irritates the throat and chest. It is the supreme mockery of the people of Tondo – a polluting factory in one of the most polluted settlements in Manila, which is in the business of manufacturing cleansing items for private use.

In May 1993, President Ramos announced the closure of Smoky Mountain as a dumping site. This may deter foreign TV crews from taking pictures of one of the most shameful human habitations on earth, but will do nothing for those evicted once more from their fragile livelihood.

FREEDOM ISLAND

In Manila Bay, there is a small island of 65 hectares which remained unoccupied until the late 1970s. It is a marshy strip of land, covered with coarse grass, creepers and shrubs. It has been named Freedom Island by the 12,000 people who now occupy it, because for many of them it appeared to offer a solution to the long forced march which had driven them from their homeplace fifteen or twenty years ago. They have been on a continuous, insecure pilgrimage ever since, which took them from the islands of Leyte and Samar into the capital, where they have been endlessly harassed and their houses repeatedly demolished. Eventually, they were 'relocated' to Bulacan, in a rocky region with neither work nor land for their sustenance. When they discovered Freedom Island, it seems they had, at last, found a place where they could live in peace.

Freedom Island is only 10 minutes from the mainland by canoes that are stabilized by bamboo frames. The island is clearly visible from Aguinaldo Highway, the coastal road, and it is not far from the concrete bulk of Imelda Marcos's Cultural Center. There is a narrow causeway of sandbags and boulders, where the *bancas* (canoes) pick up and set down their passengers; and the shore is a soggy area of coconut shells, pineapple tops, plastic bags, cans, old sandals. It looks like a garbage dump, but is, in fact, the beginnings of further reclamation of land from the sea. This gives way to the spiky olive-green of salty mangroves around the margin of the shore. The stagnant water trapped by the garbage is emerald green with algae.

The soil of the island itself is sandy, with fragments of uncrushed shells gleaming with pearly fire under the sun.

During the 1980s, more and more developmental refugees have come here. For the first few years they were relatively undisturbed. They bored wells, which provide water for washing and bathing, although it is too salty for drinking. Drinking water has to be brought from the mainland. It is stored in metal tanks and sold at 2 pesos a can, in plastic petrol containers.

There are now 1,756 families on the island, living in four barangays, or villages. Each one has a dusty central plaza, with a chapel, a few *sari-sari* (general goods) stores, and houses of varying solidity. Some are basic, cool traditional barong houses of bamboo, on stilts, with nipa roofs; others of corrugated metal, which intensifies the heat of the sun; some are of concrete.

Within the past few years, the people of Freedom Island have had their fragile liberties curtailed. The Aquino government's Total War policy against the insurgency in the Philippines led to the erection of twenty-four watchtowers on the island, set on concrete blocks, with soaring wooden frames and surmounted by metal observation platforms. Ostensibly, these towers were to prevent further 'squatting' on the island, but the people know they are intended to suppress any activity that might be contrary to the perceived interest of the government. And with so many migrants, it is felt that Freedom Island might be a hiding place for fugitive members of the New People's Army. The residents suspect that there is another purpose to the intensive monitoring of their lives. Freedom Island has become a desirable piece of real estate, which may already have been promised, if not actually sold, to 'developers', as the future site of yet more five-star hotels, condominiums for the Japanese, for whom the amenity of weekend golfing excursions or sex tours must be provided in order to help them sustain their economic miracle.

There is a striking similarity in the testimony of the people. Most left their land when deforestation of the hilly regions where they lived eroded, washed away or silted the fields which their families had cultivated for generations. A group of families from Bicol had originally settled at Makati in Manila, the district that subsequently became the business and finance centre of the city. They originally took over unused private land, and earned a living as vendors, construction workers and domestics. Their shelters were demolished to make way for the curious high-rise enclave of Makati, an area like an unfinished part of downtown Atlanta, a transplant into the middle of the city, which peters out in scrubland and urban dereliction. Later, the people went to Paranaque, on the foreshore of Manila Bay, where they learned to make a living from the sea, from fishing or shellcraft. When the highway was built and more of the coastline reclaimed, they were forcibly relocated in Bulacan, far north of Manila, where there was no means of earning a living. It was in the late 1970s that a group of some eighty families came to the island, and were given permission to remain there.

They have planted trees, and many have little thornbush enclosures where they grow fruit and vegetables and medicinal herbs. There are mangoes, plantains, ipil-ipil, acacia trees. There are no roads on the island. The air is relatively pure, with a constant sea breeze. Some of the people work on the mainland, as vendors, carpenters or drivers; but the fare across the water is 10 pesos each day, and since many are paid so far below the minimum wage, this is a severe strain on the monthly income. Some make a living from the sea, fishing in the polluted and depleted waters of Manila Bay.

The first time I saw Freedom Island it was a public holiday, 9 April, Bataan Day, the day which commemorates the Death March from Bataan to Tarlac following the Japanese invasion of the island. They, too, have been on a kind of death march, uprooted, evicted, moved on, and many of their children have died during their reluctant and functionless wanderings. Indeed, on Freedom Island itself there are many malnourished children, many of whom fall sick and die. The only question now, said one woman, is whether the forced march of the people has been instigated by Filipinos themselves or by foreigners; indeed, in part by the Japanese themselves, who play such a significant role in dictating present patterns of development in the Philippines, and who are called by some the latest colonial invaders.

'When we first came to the island, it was empty,' says Peter Pianeta. 'It was unpoliced then. We were free to create our own homestead, to grow cassava, kamote (sweet potato), peanuts, tomatoes. We lived peacefully. It was only after 1987 that the authorities came, the baranagay police and security guards hired by the military.' Peter was a restaurant supervisor in Malate, but had to give it up when he developed a tumour behind the eyes, which impaired his vision. From Bicol, his home, he remembers how the transnational companies clear-felled the slope of trees. 'They took all the narra, the mahogany, dau, apitong, which is a beautiful, hard, yellow-wood tree. We used to grow rice in the hollows that we made on the low slopes of the hills; but once the trees were gone, the rainwater simply swept our rice-fields away. By that time, the logging companies had gone as well, so there was no one to turn to for compensation.

'In Spanish times, all the people in one community were given surnames beginning with the same letter, A or B or whatever. In my village, everyone's name began with a P. That helped the colonial authorities control people – they could tell where anybody came from by the initial letter of their name. At least then they made no pretence that we were free. That's the difference from today.'

Peter Pianeta says he is lucky, even though he never achieved his life's ambition, which was to become a doctor. He has educated all his children, and he is proud that they are all committed to changing Filipino society. He says, 'The government wants people to go abroad, to earn foreign exchange. What a policy, to export your own people like any other crop. I want my children to stay here and work for reform and improvements in society here, so that millions of future Filipino families won't have to suffer the wrench and the partings of mass migration.'

There is no school on the island. This year, there were only six high school graduates and three college students. 'What a waste of future human resources,' says Peter Pianeta. Eighty per cent of children stop schooling here after grade three, because their parents cannot afford the fares to send them to the mainland.

Daisy Alvares runs a small sari-sari store, selling oil, fish, kerosene, soap, sugar, salt, coffee. She is also an accomplished dressmaker. She identifies the major problems of the islanders as stability and security of their homesteads, human rights violations by the guards, liveli-hood ('With Japanese trawlers coming right into Manila Bay at will, how can the small fishing communities make a living?'), health ('We counted sixty-nine children malnourished to the third degree'). She says, 'We are called squatters. How can we be squatters in our own country? If we are squatters, what are all the foreigners who come and buy up prime land? What are those coming with all their money from Hong Kong, Japan and the USA? We are told that we are an eyesore. The truth is, we are refugees in our own land. In Bicol, we were happy to grow rice, bananas, coconuts, but we cannot plant now. Everything that is planted is just blown away by the wind.'

The government has been offering people 10,000 pesos to leave Freedom Island, but the community leaders are sceptical about whether anyone who was tempted to go would ever see the money. A survey of opinion was organized by the residents themselves. 'We suggested three choices: to go back to the province, with or without 10,000 pesos; to go into tenement housing, where the rent would be 500 pesos a month, with the costs of water and electricity added to that; or to stay on Freedom Island with on-site development. Over 90 per cent of the people would prefer the last choice; but even then, they would never be able to afford the cost of the infrastructure, which they would be expected to pay for.'

Daisy came to the island from Las Marinas in Cavite, where she and her family were relocated after many years in Manila. 'When they moved us, they promised complete facilities. When we arrived, there was nothing. They throw you into a resettlement area with no light, no water, no job. People had to come back to Manila. We have no option. But still they are relocating people, throwing them back onto the hillsides where they have two choices – to starve or to come back to the city again.'

In the dusty square, the fish vendors sit before upturned wooden crates with small heaps of galungong and milkfish. The fish costs up to 60 pesos a kilo, and 40 pesos for poor quality. The cheapest rice is now 8 pesos a kilo, and almost inedible. Good rice is 12–14 pesos a kilo.

In the shadowless noon heat, some of the unemployed young men play billiards or table-tennis on improvised tables. Bonny Aniano is twenty-four, from Samar, one of the most impoverished islands in the archipelago. He says it was a long journey to exchange one kind of poverty for another. He works as a delivery boy for factories on the mainland; he and his wife have two children. His hut is on stilts, so that it doesn't get flooded in the monsoon. He fetches his guitar and plays, first of all, a fierce and beautiful anti-colonial song from the Spanish era, which tells of the unfreedom of the people; it has a sad contemporary resonance. People gather in the shadow of the ugly watchtower, and join in the singing. Then he plays 'Unchained Melody'. All around, on the sandy soil, cerise and pink Vietnam roses open to the sun. A woman comes to the threshold of her house, drawn by the singing. In the bare interior, oscillating in a muslin sling, is a two-month-old baby. The woman's stomach is still distended; she has cancer of the ovaries, a grotesque mockery of pregnancy, but there is no money for treatment. She is about thirty-five; dark rings under her eyes. 'Who will look after my child when I am gone?' she asks.

Many people rely on traditional herbs and plants for medicines: upo grows in some gardens, a squash-type vegetable, the leaves of which are good for hypertension. Talisay trees have broad leaves which are used for diarrhoea; aratelis is a purgative, while ipil-ipil is used for fever.

Concepcion Negrita has a cool, traditional house of rattan and bamboo close to the shore. She was offered 250,000 pesos to give up her work on behalf of the people of the island. Later, she was threatened with abduction. The guards said to her, 'Aren't you afraid of what might happen to you?' She said, 'My fate is in God's hands, how can I be afraid?' Her husband works on the mainland in a shellcraft factory, where he earns 3,000 pesos a month. She has four daughters. She says, 'All we want is to stay here and improve our lives. Here, there is no crime, no drugs, no robbery, no sex industry. If we are allowed to build up by our own efforts, it will be a good place for our children. There is no electricity for us, but there are direct lines to the watchtowers. What use of resources is that, providing facilities to control and spy on the people, and denying them the chance to achieve a dignified life?'

Many people point out that because Aquino was credited internationally with having 'restored democracy', the policy of her government, and that of Ramos, her successor, has no longer been subjected to the same scrutiny which Marcos's was in its dying years. This means that the killings, disappearances and salvagings have been given a kind of tacit legitimacy. It is agreed that certain democratic spaces were opened up by the coming of Aquino, but the war against dissent has intensified at the same time. The people of Freedom Island do not even figure among the million or so internal refugees created by the Total War policy. Many feel that the administration has been able to pursue the most malign policies, subjecting a majority of the people to even greater poverty and degradation than they knew under Marcos; and this has been done under a cloak of international respectability, and sanctified in the name of economic necessity.

The intensely religious atmosphere of Manila does not come so much from the ubiquitous churches, the monstrous bulk of the Iglesia ni Christi, the more homely arcades of Quiapo, where country people sell medicinal herbs and barks, not the stiff formality of Manila Cathedral in Intramuros. It comes, rather, from the fact that this city is the site of countless human sacrifices to the articles of faith of an apparently invincible economic system. The lives it claims, in one guise or another, are the subject of the most casual conversations – too commonplace an occurrence for any great ceremony. Gerardo shrugs when he tells how his brother flew back to Manila after two years in Saudi Arabia, bringing his gifts to the airport, while his wife, mother and three children travelled from the province to meet his flight in the early morning, and were all killed in a head-on collision with a truck. He shows no anger at the drivers' licences that can be bought for 2,000 pesos from corrupt officials; he accepts that the Philippines cannot afford adequate roads for the cars that flood the country, that the motor manufacturers make the profits and leave the wreckage of lives and vehicles to the people. In the same way, the voice of Jimmy remains cool when he tells how his wife died three years ago of an illegal abortion. He bears a terrible guilt, because they had wanted to give their five children a good education by limiting the family. He feels it was a punishment. The oldest child is now fifteen, and all are in school. In order to earn enough money, Jimmy drives a cab 24 hours a day, from 7 in the morning to 7 the next morning. He works every other day, and pays 700 pesos rental and 250 pesos for fuel. His earnings start only after he has made 1,000 pesos; the pressure is to work the whole 24 hours without a break.

With around ten million people, Metro-Manila now holds almost one sixth of the population of the Philippines. Every year, many more thousands arrive here, forced from their land by usurious debts, land-grabbing by the big haciendas, militarization, environmental ruin. 'You think you'll make enough money to go back home,' said a prostitute from Malate. 'At least in the city, you think, you'll eat; but after a few years, you find it is you the city has eaten.'

São Paulo

Crossing the industrial frontier is a common experience all over the world. The arrival in the city is itself often not the beginning of the process at all, but only the definitive move that comes itself as a consequence of the industrial invasion of fields and forests, the incursion of forces that have uprooted those who would otherwise never have had any reason to abandon their dependency on the biosphere.

At ten o'clock in the morning, the dim Gothic interior of São Paulo's Catedral de Sé is full. The people are not praying, but sleeping, a ragged humanity slumped in the hard pews, their heads covered by coarse blankets. Here, at least, they are safe from the predators who roam the Praça de Sé outside. A cathedral of impoverished dreamers, cold and silent, a *Totenschiff* with its drifting cargo of refugees from economic and developmental violence.

In the faces of the migrants to São Paulo can be read an epic story of rural dislocation, environmental breakdown and monstrous social injustice: Indians from the degraded habitat of the Amazon, subsistence peasants dispossessed by the encroachments of cattle ranchers, unsuccessful *grimpeiros* (prospectors), people fleeing debt and hunger on plantations of coffee, oranges and pineapples; as well as the heirs to the legacy of slavery, which has left Brazil with the second largest black population in the world after Nigeria.

Industrialization – and two-thirds of the people of Brazil are now urban dwellers – is quite unlike the experience of the early industrial period in Britain. Then, a severe discipline required by the factory system was imposed on the rural sensibility; now, the process is accompanied by an orgiastic consumerism, which is, perhaps, more seductive to those whose lives are being so radically reshaped, but which also unleashes great violence, particularly when the advertised better life remains beyond the grasp of the great majority of the people.

The life of the migrants to the city is pervaded by an iconography of privatized dreams, which call into existence strange new divisions of labour. Economic development to a poor woman from Mato Grosso means paid employment to clean the floor of a porno movie-house, where the men masturbate in mechanistic accompaniment to the images of brutal sex. The vendors on the viaduct of St Ifigenia stand guard over the detritus of capitalism, as though they had been entrusted with its greatest treasures – T-shirts emblazoned with obscenities, value-added, nutrition-subtracted foodstuffs, magazines with titles like *Girls Who Dig Girls, Anal Sex*, manuals that promise *prazer sim limite* (limitless pleasure), horoscopes, Tarot readings, Barbie dolls and war toys.

The square outside the cathedral is part marketplace, part fairground. It has the aspect of a rural meeting-place. Gipsy women in lime-green and scarlet flounces read the hands of credulous passers-by; sellers of traditional medicines, barks, herbs and roots (many of which are now attracting the attention of ethnobotanists in the pay of transnational corporations) offer relief from syphilis, ulcers, cancer, worms, depression and madness. A man attracts a crowd by breaking glass bottles with his bare feet. Another escapes from iron chains, simply by flexing his overdeveloped muscles. The ornamental fountain serves as bathing-place to the homeless, and the faded washing of the poor is laid out on the green-painted benches. Young boys, gnawed by unappeasable hungers, haunt the public spaces, robbing with balletic co-ordination and speed, offering sex or stolen goods with the same huckster's indifference; picking pockets with a dexterity that deceives the eye. The sad, creased faces of Indians appear above publicity sandwich-boards, like living playing-cards, advertising good money rates for gold, fortune telling, xeroxing, or sex therapy from certified practitioners.

São Paulo with its fourteen million people is the biggest city in South America. The state of São Paulo produces over a quarter of the national product of Brazil. Its function as banking and commercial centre places pressure on the poor, more and more of whom are crowded into illegal subdivisions in *corticos*, or tenements, where four families of seven or eight people may occupy a single apartment. As many as three million people live in such conditions.

One *cortico* in the central *bairro*, or neighbourhood, of Liberdade, a place where faint traces of an older European colonial city remain; houses of a single storey, with shingled roof and peeling ochre-washed walls. Number 99 rua Tomaz de Lima is deceptive. It looks like a rundown villa, with broken windows and a ruinous staircase leading to a solid front door. In fact, it is a tenement sculpted out of the side of the hill, four storeys deep, almost underground. There is a central shaft in the middle of the building, which is the only source of daylight to the dwellings beneath. A metal roof at the base of the shaft sags with garbage thrown from the floors above; the narrow court-yard at the bottom is dank and muddy from recent storms.

In the corridor, a man is skewering pieces of greasy beef onto kebab sticks. In the early evening he will barbecue these in the open air, and sell to the homegoing crowds; a cheaper fast-food for those who can't afford McDonald's.

Luisa and Edson live, with her three children and his brother, in one room with a small kitchen. Edson's brother is a drummer and works in the clubs. Edson used to make Persian carpets, a craft he learned from his first wife, intricate, delicate patterns in muted blue, gold and fawn. He can no longer buy the camel wool he requires, because of the government's financial plan, which froze and deval-ued his savings. He and Luisa are now selling lottery tickets in a street-booth. Edson says that the poor are prevented from exercising their skills and crafts. All they can do is go onto the streets to rob, and then they are thrown into prison. 'Nobody knows the owners of this building,' says Edson. The rent is collected by agents. The rent is about $40 a month, while the minimum wage is $50 a month. Landlords all over São Paulo are selling property, so that the land can be resold for commercial development. Edson points to an apart-ment block about thirty storeys high, which shadows his building. There are twenty-five flats on each floor, every one occupied by four or five families. He calculates that this single block shelters around seven thousand people.

At the side of the tenement, a flight of stone steps leads to the bottom of the sunless pit; apartments consisting of single rooms without air or natural light; damp, concrete floors, mattresses, the trunks and suitcases of those who plan to stay only a few weeks or months, but who never go home again. Angelica, from Bahia, lives at the end of a corridor, bare, plasterless walls, festoons of flex which take an illegal electricity supply to each room. Angelica's room is at an even lower level, across a stagnant pool, with only a plank giving access to her room. This contains two beds and a big cupboard. Her husband and children lie on the bed, watching football on TV. In Bahia, says Angelica, the only work was on the big plantations, moving from place to place seasonally, lodging in wretched shacks. Her family were not allowed to grow anything for their own con-sumption, and had no guarantee of regular labour. Is life better here? She says, 'It is bad in a different way. There, we knew hunger

and insecurity; here, there is violence and drugs. They call it Liberdade – liberdade is a rotting building in a heartless city.'

Many people in the West are now familiar with the destruction of
Amazonia and the disastrous consequences for the indigenous
peoples, such as the Yanomami, whose way of life has been contaminated and destroyed by invasions of *grimpeiros*, gold-prospectors,
loggers and ranchers. But this is far from the only human sacrifice
exacted by development. In the *favelas* (shanty-towns) on the periphery of the greedy megalopolis of São Paulo, as in Rio de Janeiro,
death-squads operate, whose victims are mostly young men, small-
time criminals and petty crooks, and whose elimination is paid for by
those keen to 'clean up the city', with the connivance, if not participation, of the police. The Pé de Pato squads, as they call themselves, are
vigilantes, *justiceiros*. While the poor destroy one another, the rich
remain inviolable, protected by the very wealth that is the object of
veneration to the dispossessed.

Padre Jaime, of Mboia Mirim, in the south of the city, says this is the
result of the 'third world war' which is being waged globally against
the poor. There are a million unemployed in São Paulo, many as a
result of government 'rectification' programmes. Not all of these can
possibly create work for themselves. Last weekend, within a radius of
500 metres from Padre Jaime's church, there were twelve murders,
many of the killings of the *ladroes de pe de chinelo*, as they call the street-
boys who terrorize the neighbourhood. 'Others are murders that are
caused by anger. Two men were arguing in a bar; a third intervenes,
and he is killed. The two men flee, and take the murdered man's car
to make a getaway. They run down and kill a child on the way. Some
of the killings are a consequence of gang warfare; if the houses in one
street are robbed, the young men of the area will get together and
take revenge on those they believe have robbed their neighbourhood. The problem, of course, goes much deeper. The trouble is that
the destiny of our country is not decided here, but it is here that
people must live with the consequences. Even government policy is
not determined here.'

Padre Jaime called a meeting to discuss the terror on the streets.
Two days later, a leaflet was being distributed in the area, threatening
that anyone who is out after ten o'clock will be shot.

The testimony of Padre Jaime is echoed by Padre Paul at Campo
Limpo, also on the south side of the city. He says that one recent
Monday was marked by forty funerals in the local cemetery. More
than half were murders that had occurred over the weekend – the
rest mostly the deaths of young children, the other victims of economic violence, through avoidable diseases and malnutrition. Activists

in the city are increasingly making the links between human rights and economics. 'The rich have hardened their hearts,' says Pedro Jacobi, a researcher at the Centro de Estudios de Cultura Contemporanea. 'They see the poor as deceivers and swindlers. But people who get up at 5 a.m. in the slums to look for work are not idlers or vagabonds.'

During the long period of military rule that ended in 1985, it was openly said by economics ministers that the workpower of the factories was located in the interior. These migrations fed the long-faded economic miracle of Brazil. But the people still come, although perhaps in smaller numbers now, at least to São Paulo, deterred by media images of violence, kidnappings and social dislocation.

At Nossa Senhora de Paz, a church in the shadow of an elevated concrete motorway, there is a refuge for newcomers to the city, with bed-space for two hundred people. Lone individuals may stay three days, families up to ten days, the sick somewhat longer. In the inner cloister, beneath ragged palms, migrants sit; faces of uprooted peasants, weatherbeaten and sunstained, faces of people not yet adapted to the necessities of urban life: they still smile at strangers. Some have already had their first bitter encounter with the city at the bus-station, where they have arrived after a journey of two or three days. There, they attract the attention of people on the make – many of them also recent arrivals – whom they recognize as their own countrymen, and who offer to find them a home or a job and then disappear with their money or belongings.

Olesia da Silva, who is twenty-six, arrived yesterday. Her husband died of drink six weeks ago, leaving her pregnant and with three small children, Angelica six, Angelo four and Lidiano two. Her husband had a newspaper stall in a small town in the north-east, and she worked as a domestic to provide for the children. She has no living relative – her own mother died at the age of twenty-four – and the only other work is on coffee or orange plantations. Her most precious document is the reference from the woman who employed her as a servant, a hand-written note on a piece of embossed paper, which, Olesia is sure, will guarantee her a job. She says she will never abandon her children, as so many poor women do in the city. Recently, six brothers between the ages of two and ten were abandoned by their father under the motorway when their mother died of TB.

José Carlos Ferreira comes, like so many of the migrants, from the north-east. He had been working in São Paulo for a week, when he was knocked down by a car and badly injured. He will stay in the hostel until the metal pins in his arms and legs are removed. José do

Batista from Bahia is twenty-three; he used to drive truck-loads of sugar-cane from the fields to the factory, but the work was available only twice a year, at the time of the sugar-harvests. He came with his wife and four-month-old child, and is proud to have found himself work on his first day here, as a construction worker at 70 cruzerios (about 60 cents) an hour. José do Nascimento worked on the latifundia, travelling from estate to estate, living in workers' barracks. Forbidden to grow his own food, he had to buy from the employer's shop. He has been to São Paulo before. He hates the city. He says in the city people lose their humanity; but in the province you lose your life and your children.

The women of Mboia Mirim – Anna-Maria, Annalise, Ifigenia – run a feeding centre for malnourished children. They are well aware that there were over 2,500 reported murders in São Paulo last year; they have seen the gang-fights and the young people corroded by drugs. Yet they say that life is better here than in the countryside. There, their families were *meieros*, share-croppers, but were indebted to the big landowners, or had been disemployed by the transformation of plantations into cattle ranches, which require less labour. Their optimism about life in the city is tangible; visible in the improvements they have made to their houses, in the hope that their husbands or children may secure a safe job in a factory belonging to a transnational company. Pedro Jacobi says that with the rising price of land, there is no longer as much mobility in the *favelas*. People are compelled to stay where they are. This means that they are far more likely to invest in and improve their property.

In other areas, there have been organized occupations of unused government and private land. One such is the *mutirão* (self-build) community near Campo Limpo. Eight hundred families – about five thousand people – forced out of the slums by rising rents and unemployment, occupied the land. ('We don't say invaded, because that makes it sound as though we are aliens and have no right to live anywhere.') They were supported by John Drexel, a Catholic priest and author of *Childhood and Poverty*. Both civil and military police tried to dislodge the people. They went to the mayor, who promised to send bulldozers to level the land so that they would be able to build. When nothing happened, two hundred residents slept in the square outside City Hall. Early in 1990, they gained the right to stay.

The people have built their own homes in groups of twenty-five – *mutirão* – and then drew lots to see who will occupy each house. No one moves in until all are completed, thus ensuring that each one receives the same care and skill during construction. On this site, the houses are 100 square metres, far more generous than the space provided by the city's limited housing programme, which are barrack-like structures and cost five times as much. Self-build houses cost only a fraction of those erected by commercial builders.

Nowhere is the creative ability of the poor more clearly visible; of people like Maria Lausinha, who walked out on her husband, because she is of a generation that will no longer tolerate a selfish and violent machismo. She lives with her daughter, and has worked on the construction with great enthusiasm. She says, 'Half the families here are women, deserted wives or widows. When we have finished, this will be the best-organized community in São Paulo.'

Some of the sites cleared of their tenements in the centre of the city have been occupied by people who have built makeshift shacks of wood and tin. Maria came from Minas Gerais seven years ago. She has seven children, and they led a nomadic existence around the edge of the city, until she settled on the debris of a derelict building in Liberdade. In the downtown area, there is always work of some kind, especially for children. Maria's oldest child, a girl of thirteen, works in a dress factory from 1.00 to 6.30, after she has finished school. The oldest boy is eleven, and has been working for two years. He carries money and documents from factories to the bank in an innocent-looking old pouch. Nobody expects a poor eleven-year-old to be carrying money, and he is considered the safest courier, secure against robbery.

Pedro Jacobi points out that the history of São Paulo has been obliterated by the rapidity of its growth. Brazilian cities were built in the image of those of the colonial power, unlike the cities of the United States, which were crude, functional places; this is because the life of the US colonizers was essentially small-scale farming, oriented towards the open countryside, whereas in Brazil, the colonialists were owners of plantations, city people who dreamed of returning to Portugal, and in the meantime sought to reproduce the grace and amenity of Portuguese urban life. However, nearly all traces of São Paulo's past have been overwhelmed by the glass, marble and concrete of commercial construction, and the poverty of the streets. Jacobi says, 'There is nothing romantic or desirable about the life of the streets. It is too harsh and indeed, too faithful a reflection of the dominant values of rapacity and accumulation of the rich. This is why the middle class hate the poor so: if they call them cheats and swindlers, this is because they see in them a distortion of their own values. No wonder they seek to distance themselves from those upon whose services they depend.'

The Partido dos Trabalhadores, or Workers' Party, governs São Paulo, but it can do little to mitigate the ugly inequalities. On the night sky, triumphal emblems of the transnationals burn, blood-red: Sony, Toyota, McDonald's, Sharp, Coca Cola. Beneath them the poor live out a degraded form of consumerism, their homage to wealth. A girl emerges from the cathedral wearing aT-shirt that says 'Fuck You'. A man in a suit seduces boys in the amusement arcade with promises of food. On a traffic island, a couple from the countryside sit on an abandoned plastic sofa: she wears a ragged skirt and lilac turban, he a straw hat and trousers tied up with string; they have the numb look of mental disorientation of the uprooted. In a rubbish-cart, resting on discarded wrappings and vegetable refuse, a man sleeps, arms and legs hanging limp over the edges.

Perhaps we may understand here why the leaders of the rich industrial countries were so eager to cry victory over socialism. For they know better than most that the issue of social justice has not disappeared, simply because there no longer appears to be any significant opposition to the Western system. The sonorous funeral orations of Western leaders over the end of socialism are also a blessing on the injuries to those who wander through the desolation of São Paulo, one of the most savage shrines to capitalism on earth.

Rio de Janeiro

The sharp crack of gunfire disturbs the night in the northern suburbs of Rio; the guns echo from the *favelas* of Casa Branca and Borel across the Tijuca Forest, part of UN designated human heritage, and the most spectacular urban forest in the world. After several nights, there is silence again. Control over the distribution of cocaine has finally been settled in the hillside slum communities.

Rio, city of permanent pleasure and carnival, now rivals Johannesburg and Lagos in the number of murders per 100,000 people. More bodies of street children – over two hundred killed in the first three months of 1992 – are found in a stagnant ditch in a place called Nova Gerusaleme, done to death by extermination squads in the pay of city businessmen who believe they are bad for business and frighten the tourists away. Cocaine is traded openly in the *favelas*, which are controlled by quasi-fascist parallel authorities of the druglords. The tourist hotels of Copacabana are half empty. People are afraid to use the buses because of armed hold-ups. And it is only a question of time before cholera, raging in the north of Brazil, reaches Rio.

Even the middle class are troubled in their gilded enclaves in the south of the city. Spiked cages surround baroque colonial villas; apartment doors are reinforced and guarded at gunpoint. In antique Portuguese interiors, dark, silent maids serve nervous guests under the shadow of grilles, whose ornate design scarcely conceals their function. The rich strip themselves bare of watches, jewellery and chains before they venture onto the menacing streets.

Sixty per cent of the people of Brazil now live below an ungenerous poverty line. The top 10 per cent receive half the annual revenue. One per cent of Brazilians hold 53 per cent of the wealth; distribution is more unequal than in India.

Rio is a city of refugees; people displaced by epic dislocations from subsistence farming by the growth of *latifundia*, agribusiness and ranching, by deforestation, drought, the laying waste of the Amazon

51

and worsening social injustice. These upheavals have now created a society in which more than three-quarters of the people are urban.

Even in the richest quarters, poverty is visible on the streets. A woman from Minas Gerais living close to the beach at Botafogo offered her child to strangers for $500: she wanted a job as live-in maid, but with a baby it is out of the question. A mentally disabled woman, enormously fat, is paid by men in a bar to insert an empty Coca Cola bottle in her vagina: the owner of the bar breaks up the party, and she waddles out of the bar, clutching the bottle in one hand and a bundle of 100 cruzeiro notes in the other. In the bus station, women sit writing on pieces of cardboard for children to distribute in the buses: 'I am an orphan and am hungry, please buy a packet of sweets for 300 crusados'; these are the 'good' mothers, who do not abandon their children. In the *favela* of Santa Marta, 360 steps cut into one of the hills overlooked by the monumental Cristo Redentor, the community has been well organized, but cannot escape the culture of unemployment, recession and drugs. The hillside is covered here and there by concrete: the result of landslides, the most recent of which killed twenty-nine people when uncollected rubbish and debris rolled down the hill, sweeping away the precarious shelters on stilts.

But for the most part, Rio has been cleaned up; not only the grisly environmental 'improvements' of the murder of its street-children, but by constant clearances of the poor, exiled to vast settlements on the periphery, down the long, dangerous, ten-lane concrete canyon on the Avenida do Brasil. This violent thoroughfare, with its fumes and speeding trucks, its bandits at the traffic lights, is like a medieval representation of the road to hell. It leads to Nova Iguaçu, a satellite of Rio, and now itself the eighth largest city in Brazil, with over a million people. A bleak dormitory city, a barracks for the poor, many of whom work in Rio; arcades of desolate shops, loops of power cables and dim lighting, hectares of *favelas* and tenements, devoid of basic facilities and without amenity or grace. Its streets are haunted by the wraiths of former country people, the uprooted and displaced, desperate to sell – cigarette lighters, biscuits, pornography, novelties, second-hand junk, old shoes, themselves, even their children.

The bus from the centre bears the stark message INDUSTRIAL; it goes to the edge of Nova Iguaçu, the periphery of the periphery; through a landscape of deforested hills and wide, shallow valleys, industrial buildings with the logos of transnationals, Coca Cola/ Kaiser Beer, Volkswagen, Fiat, Bayer, Bosch, Inega.

Santo Expedito is a township of about four thousand people, off the main road, down a rough track where the bus sets up a cloud of hot red dust. Small plantations of beans, avocados, aipim (a kind of potato) and the pale yellow flowers of kiapo (okra). The houses are single-storey, of hollow red bricks which the people make for themselves, and roofs of corrugated, impacted cardboard. The people have nothing: the only water is from artesian wells, now contaminated by the industrial effluents from the factories, and from the huge rubbish dump where all the garbage from Nova Iguaçu has been partly ploughed back into the despoiled hillside; a gaseous stench of decaying refuse hangs over the countryside. There are no medical facilities, no public drainage. The only public services are electricity – not for street-lighting, but as a conduit for television, the most important bearer of promises to those whose lives are lived at the limit of endurance; and, of course, buses, to get people to and from work.

Many of the houses have handwritten notices offering some service: manicure, pedicure, literacy teaching, hairdressing; one or two have turned their front windows into small shops for sweets, Coca Cola, combs and trinkets. Those men who are working are principally in construction or security; there are few women to be seen in the daytime, for most of them work as maids in Rio, a journey of two hours each way. Maria says they are taken away from their own homes, where they are needed, to work in the homes of people who have everything; the small wages can never compensate for the confiscation of their labour by others. Ismael sits in the street outside his house. He is working in a sweet factory, at the minimum wage (around $50 a month). He has come from Rio, he says, because here it is less dangerous. The streets of Ipanema and Copacabana, that is where the danger and the violence are. We are quiet here, we know each other. More and more people are leaving Rio because they are afraid of violence from paramilitary groups, or simply because there is nowhere to live. Robinson is from Pernambuco in the north. He says proudly, *Tenho professon, ma não tenho trabajo* ('I have a trade, but I don't have a job'). He is a driver; but where are the roads in Santo Expedito to drive on?

Santo Expedito has an active residents' group. Its leader is Israel Vincente da Silva, who came to Rio from Recife to join his uncle who was in the navy here. Through *mutirão* (collective self-help) they have constructed a health centre: a whitewashed building with cool rooms, but no equipment or drugs or employees. He says it is easy to get people to protest here, but much more difficult to sustain solidarity for a long time: the daily attrition of labour, exhaustion and hunger uses up people's energy. The land here belonged to the Caixa Economica, and was occupied illegally by the families. The police did nothing to remove them. On the edge of the settlement, there are a number of smallholders, growing vegetables and fruit for their own consumption.

The people's associations of Nova Iguaçu are affiliated to the Federaçao das Associões de Baisso de Nova Iguaçu (MAB), the city-wide residents' organization. The people have no illusions that anything will be given to them without a struggle; and even then, they are as likely to be jailed for their efforts as to achieve their ends. 'We need basic *assaneamento*, health, work, security. The rich talk about population, not people. We know that population only stabilizes when people have security. But security would mean redistribution from rich to poor. That is the last thing on their agenda – quite the opposite, they believe in more for the rich and less for the poor. So when they talk of cleaning up the environment, what they have done in Rio they will do for the whole world – sweep the poor away.'

If Novo Iguaçu is a melancholy place, Duque de Caxias is infernal. In the centre of this smaller satellite city, the cathedral is locked, a cage-like barrier preventing access to the baroque interior. Under the portico and in the cathedral grounds bodies are sprawled, a tangle of limbs of malnourished young men, utterly exhausted. The site is like a battleground, or a visitation of the plague. Nearby is the triumphal double yellow arch of a McDonald's. A rootless, needy humanity wanders through the desolate streets of Caxias, under the municipal notices that say 'Era Lixão-Lembra-Sé', remember this was a rubbish dump; small vendors of the most worthless things, trinkets, snacks, sweets, combs, brushes; the addicted, whose hunger is now for money to nourish their craving for cocaine. A little girl of about eight works, threading minute beads onto a string, and then spreading them for sale on a coarse blanket on the sidewalk. Her father, a man in his thirties, rocks to and fro in despair. She pauses in her work from time to time to comfort him, passing her tiny hand across his hair and neck in a gesture of compassion.

Josenaldo's family comes from Paraíba, in the north-east of Brazil. There, as landless plantation workers, the children grew up under-nourished; many lost their teeth, and still suffer from digestive and growth disorders. José and his wife, Iara, live in the *favela* of Jacare-zinha, which has the reputation of being one of the most dangerous in Rio. In the spate of recent kidnappings, many were traced to the tangle of shanties and huts of Jacarezinha. Under the elevated metro line, between a fetid canal and the railway track, a dozen or so young men stand in line waiting to buy cocaine from one of the salespoints in the slum. The dealers wear extravagant silver and gold medallions, rings and earrings, fashionable shorts and trainers. The small packets of cocaine are wrapped in white paper and tied with cotton – preparing them is a cottage industry in itself – and they are exchanged for $5 and $10 dollar notes. In these slums, there is a parallel economy, which generates more energy than anywhere else in the *favela*. An earlier alternative economy was through the *jogo de bixio* – an illegal form of lottery, controlled by big business and which financed many of the *scolas de samba*, the organizations which spend six months of the year preparing for carnival; and this now coexists with the more vibrant drug economy. Once the dominant drug gang is established, its members become the effective authority in the slum, and indeed, are often seen as benefactors of the people: 'When a child is sick, the people will go to the druglord for money, and they will give.' José says the people have become tied to the drug culture, not only through addiction and fear, but also through gratitude. 'This makes the work of the people's movement the more difficult.'

And the workers in the popular struggle labour under constant threat, even of their life. Josenaldo is under unofficial sentence of death. They have no choice but to pursue the work with courage and tenacity. 'Marx spoke of socialism or barbarism. It isn't a prophecy for the future. The choice has already been made. It is here and now in Brazil. It is not a dignified life for a human being. One of the richest countries in the world, how can such misery have been conjured out of the natural riches of our country? What is worse, we are governed by a perverse world order that sees no advantage in changing anything.'

Out of Caxias the road leads to the plain of the Baixada Fluminense. The hills have been scarred by deforestation and the excavations for construction work. Close to the Petrobras, the largest refinery in South America, there is a small community along a road which peters out in marshland and coarse grass. Here lives Iara's mother, who sits with the women of the community in the Sunday afternoon heat, in the shade of the amandouera trees. It is a brief time of peace and relaxation from work. Yvonete, who works in the nearby cigarette factory, takes us to her husband's workshop, where he makes wooden effigies of the Christ of Rio, for sale to tourists. He works under contract to a factory in Caxias. He has a vice and a machine for cutting the figures, and he receives 150 cruzeiros for each Christ, which will then be sold for 10,000. Marisa is a domestic worker, earning the minimum wage, and she travels daily into Rio; her husband works in an aluminium factory. Most of the people here are working, and this is reflected in the improvements they have made to their houses: more space, more comfortable furniture, television, fridge and music-centres. Irinede is divorced; she travels into Rio and works as a saleswoman in a dress shop. Patricia is seventeen; she works in a Rio sweatshop, making dresses for less than the minimum wage; Vanya travels to Uzina for work in a supermarket; it takes 2½ hours to get there and 2½ back. She gets up at 4.30 in the morning, takes the bus to Caxias, then another to Uzina, and returns by 7.30 at night. Yvonete says that many men have two jobs, one by day and another by night, as watchmen and security guards, one of the few growth industries in Caxias. The women here are organized; they make clothes as a co-operative to sell in the neighbourhood.

Emilio is fifty-seven. He came to Rio in 1957 from the north-east, and is a baker. His family had land, but as the forests were cleared, the rain ran off and no longer watered the earth. Walter is seventeen. He arrived from Paraíba just a few months ago when his mother died, and he lives with relatives. He left school when he was ten, and has no skills. He works as a general labourer in construction work, casual and intermittent. He hates the city. He would rather be back home. In his sad eyes you can see the violent reshaping of the country sensibility in the image of urban life; only there is no going back. All that remains in the end is regret, a persistent idea that people might have been happy in the home-place, if only they had been able to survive there if it had not been degraded.

The hot wind blows up a storm of dust, leaves and wastepaper. Some of the women take the chairs back into the houses. The road simply disappears in a mass of capim (marshy grass) and stagnant water, in which broad-leaved aguape grows, a plant that purifies water. The silver chimney of Petrobras refinery sends its perpetual flame into the afternoon sky. Towering clouds of creamy cumulus build up over the silver peaks of the distant mountain range that borders the plain. People have to dig wells for water here: there is danger of contamination, not only from raw sewage which seeps into the earth, but also from the dump of toxic chemicals, hexachlorine. There is one close to a cowshed, which provides the people with milk, and the fowls and pigs rummage among the poisoned wastes. The pipeline from Petrobras passes beneath this community; an explosion could occur at any time. Yet by comparison with the fate of most people in Caxias, this is a haven of relative security and well-being.

About 2 kilometres from Caxias is the railway station of Gramacho. A suburban railway station, where the poorest people sell pitiful things – a few cloves of garlic, a meat stall of foul-smelling offal, tripe and cattle-hooves, a woman with six tins of Coca Cola, little piles of sweets and biscuits on an upturned box, secondhand magazines. On the other side of the bridge a raw new settlement, plots of land demarcated by barbed wire. On a piece of white painted wood are the words, 'Benvindo a Vila Chico Mendes'. This is land only recently occupied. Occupations always take place on a Friday night, so that by the time any legal action can be taken, the people have already constructed their shelters. Vila Chico Mendes was originally settled by twenty-six families; now there are over a hundred. It is low-lying ground, with a stagnant pool the only supply of water. Some of the houses are only of cardboard and plywood, but most are the site of energetic activity: people building, mixing cement, fetching loads of red bricks, sand, stone chips for flooring. Aurelio pauses in his work: already his is the biggest house in the new community, four rooms, with barbed wire marking the boundary; two rooms already inhabited, with a battered fridge, a plastic sofa and bedding, a small gas stove. The *tejole* – red building tiles – cost 1,000 cruzeiros each (about 66 cents), and 500 are needed for a reasonable single-room dwelling. Some people are building in groups, *mutirão* – mutual help; others build alone. The roofs are of corrugated iron, and inside, the burning afternoon heat of the plain is suffocating. Illegal light connections have already been taken, loops of wire with bare bulbs. Some people are digging a trench to carry water pipes which will take water, again illegally, from the pipes on the main road. Aurelio comes from the north-east. He knew Chico Mendes, the rubber-tappers' leader and social activist, whose murderers were released from jail. Aurelio is working as a cook in the local prison. His wife is a maid. Wages in the north-east were only $26 a month – half the present legal minimum. He worked on plantations of sugar and tobacco. Life here is better, in spite of the hardship, the social violence. Here at least, they eat. There is no going back to a life of itinerant intermittent agricultural labour; he doesn't want to see the children's bellies swollen with hunger, their skin covered with sores and their hair falling out.

After the occupation of the land, the police came next morning to confront the twenty-six families who had constructed their shelters overnight. The police had no official warrant to destroy the houses, because it was a Saturday. They were told that if they demolished the shelters, they would come under attack by the people with bottles and stones. The police said, 'We have guns.' The people said, 'Go ahead and shoot – you will kill women and children with no warrant.' The police destroyed the houses whose occupants were not present and then went away. Within 24 hours the lots had been demarcated, people had finished the first rudimentary structure: the hundred families now here are from Belém or Paraíba; others have already lived in Rio, but were displaced by demolitions and the fear of violence. Beyond Vila Chico Mendes is Vila Esperanza (Hope), newer shelters, a foundation of brick, with temporary cardboard structures.

Most women are domestic workers, while the men are in construction or factories; some are electricians, plumbers. Vando is a baker by trade, but is working on construction sites. He is from Paraíba , and one of the new leaders of the community. They are planning a new occupation, about 2 kilometres away, for next weekend. They discuss buying the wood, with delivery to a safe, remote place, where it can remain undisturbed overnight, so that people can build after dark on Friday. They have researched the ownership of the land: it belongs to the government, and is therefore easier to occupy than private land. Vando has a list of fifty or more families who are eager to take part, but when the *favela* is established, many others will find the courage to join them.

Selma sits outside a house that has been turned into a rudimentary shop. She has a son who went to Germany, and has not heard from him for many years. She is a domestic worker in Copacabana; her employer pays her fare to and from work; without this, it would not be worth her while to travel. She says women have a harder time than men. They are up before dawn to prepare food, and then when they come home from work, they have to look after the children, clean and cook. She is from the neighbouring state of Minas Gerais. Why did she come to Rio? To see what it was like. And how is it? As it looks. She gestures to the uneven parched ground, the dust and flies.

There has been something of a battle for the image of Rio in the past few years. This is the reflection of the conflict between the forces of the social democratic populist Brizola, the ruling party, and those forces embodied by the media conglomerate of Roberto Marinhoso, whose fortune was made under the military dictatorship: his television station, newspapers and radio stations constitute one of the largest media conglomerates in the world. This conglomerate has an interest in promoting the culture of fear that dominates Rio, for this helps to undermine Brizola. In turn, this leads to calls for 'a strong man', for 'a return to law and order', which can mean only one thing – the army. Inside the fortified salons, places of archaic colonial grace in south Rio, the talk is already apocalyptic: beneath the real violence there is an ideological struggle which actively seeks to promote the image of lawless, ungovernable city. In this struggle, the poverty and despair of the poorest are just one more exploitable commodity.

It is a tense, fearful place. I was robbed only once, and that by the police. Coming away from one of the *favelas*, a federal policeman wanted to see my papers. 'They are at the house of my friends.' 'What are you doing here?' 'I have been visiting some people.' 'You came for

drugs.' 'Why don't you search me?' He took me to a café and
intimated that if I didn't pay him, he would take me to be searched at
the police station. I gave him the $12 I was carrying. The police are so
ill-paid that they have to undertake a little private enterprise to make
a living salary.

Candido Grzybowski is a human rights worker with the Brazilian
Institute for Social and Economic Analysis, IBASE, in Rio. He says
that the realities of the conditionalities of the IMF and World Bank,
and the GATT negotiations, signify that we have entered the most
destructive phase of colonial occupation in the history of his country.
'The mechanisms are more clearly in place than ever before for the
transfer of resources from poor to rich. Because no local models of
development exist, there is little resistance to what is imposed upon
us, with its resulting social disintegration and violence: the killing of
street-children is just part of this dispossession. There has been a vast
impoverishment of people over the past decades. If we take 100 as
the base of the purchasing power of the minimum salary in 1956, the
equivalent today is around 30. This is after the so-called economic
miracle, a drastic and brutal military government, and the piling up
of unserviceable debt.

'At the same time, we are also seeing a new internationalism, a
solidarity which is not yet systematized. But we can see the shape of a
new global struggle: a struggle of humanism against the free market.
This is what we have to build on. There are many small initiatives in
Brazil and elsewhere, but as yet, no mass movement. There are a
number of issues around which such movement could crystallize. For
instance, one of the struggles is over food. All over the world, people
are being compelled to give up local and traditional foods, in order
that they might be fed by transnational companies on value-added
staples determined by the West. When you give up traditional food,
you give up everything, for these are the roots of identity. Brazil is
exporting its nourishment while the people are malnourished.'

At the Frontier: Delhi

After a night of torrential rain, the poor who sleep on the streets are drying out: clothes and bedrolls on railings and improvised washing lines between the trees. The purple fruits of the jamun trees which line the streets of New Delhi have fallen, and children collect them for sale: rich in vitamin C, they provide a brief livelihood for those with the patience to pick and sort through them.

Many people sleep through the day, since their night was disturbed by the downpour: a woman sleeps with a child inside her saree, a handkerchief over her face for privacy. The tricycle rickshaws are stationary, drivers sleeping on the plastic seat, their bodies balanced on the crossbar, feet on the handlebars. Everywhere the rain has left spreading puddles, and the long summer's dust has been churned to paste.

In Wazirpur to the east of the city, the rain has mixed with the effluent from the factories to flood the streets with indigo mud. In this area, there are about 45,000 people working in the steel industry, mills, forges and factories making steel vessels, tumblers, beakers, knives. There are more than 1,500 factories, 200 of them making utensils. Most of the workers are men, but women and children are employed to clean the steel in acid vats. The work is dangerous, and the number of accidents is suppressed. Between August 1988 and February 1989, there were 83: 8 workers died and 75 were disabled. Official statistics show only five accidents during the same period.

The steel is made into strips 30–32 inches long, cut and pressed in a hydraulic machine, then elongated in acid tanks. After this it is fired, then with a cold 'fortis' machine pressed to 90 inches. The acid vats give off poisonous fumes, and the acid eats into the hands and legs of the workers. The workers who mould the steel wrap sacks round their feet and towels round their heads and wear cloth gloves as protection against fire, smoke and dust. The steel is moulded into the shape of the utensil, pressed, then beaded and polished. Many

60

accidents occur with the cold 'fortis' machine. While pressing steel pieces on this machine, particles escape like bullets and pierce the workers' bodies. The machines are not covered. The power press leaves so little space for workers that their hands, palms and fingers are always a mass of cuts. Beading requires physical effort to complete the shape of the vessel; the machinery is old and dangerous. Many of the workers are unskilled or semi-skilled and working on machines that require training and skill. Because labour is cheap and replaceable no effort is given to this; the skills are acquired from observation, experience and practice. There is no record of the lives of the workers, and their deaths therefore go equally unrecorded.

The roads between the small factories and the *jhuggis* (huts) are almost impassable after the August rains. Rickety planks cross expanses of mud; some stepping-stones are the only way to reach the factory entrances. Singalpur is a well-established settlement. The houses are mostly of brick, and in the evening, the doors stand open to the humid heat; small rooms of a few square metres contain six or eight rough beds, where migrant workers live. The houses are close together, with only narrow passageways between them, and ragged metal roofs almost meet across the paths. In the main thoroughfare – itself little more than a lane – there is a cattlestall, with cows and buffaloes eating from broken bathtubs. Dung, which would be a valuable resource in the countryside, here mingles with waste-water, creating crooked rivulets across the uneven ground. The small shops are stocked with the comforts of the poor – *paan* (betel-nut), *bidis* (cigarettes), sweets, biscuits, toiletries bearing the name of transnational companies. In one of the alleys, a man is milking a buffalo; jets of white milk splash into a dusty steel bowl. Some string beds have been brought outside the huts, and men are sleeping in the early evening, before their 12-hour night shift – 8 hours with 4 hours compulsory 'single' overtime. Kerosene lamps hang from the ceilings of some rooms, shedding a greenish light into the indigo dusk. There is no privacy: people bathe, cook their evening meal, sleep, in full view of one another.

It is a predominantly male community; migrants to Delhi from other parts of Uttar Pradesh, from Madhya Pradesh, Bihar and Orissa. The women are left to manage as best they can. The places where the men live have the air of temporary arrangements, but they become permanent; battered suitcases and trunks contain their clothes and belongings. Some come seasonally and return for two or three months at harvest time. They do not necessarily regard themselves as city dwellers: all they know of Delhi is this small area, and the bus route back to Bareilly, Lucknow or Bhopal. They all work in a dangerous environment, sometimes in semi-darkness by the light of the forge. In the evenings, in the red glow, they can be seen, almost naked, the flames of the fires reflected on their sweating torsos. Their bodies are frail and vulnerable to the pieces of metal, which fly from cylinders of incandescent steel.

Most of the men are landless, or with so little land that it will not support their families. They send money home, but their wages are far below the 'legal' minimum. In some cases, all the men have migrated – a father, his brother, a son of eighteen and one of twelve. In the village, the wife and daughters on half an acre of land wait for the men to come home for one month in the year. Nearly all the workers are scarred by traces of metal which have flown from the press or the rollers and struck them in the chest, stomach or arm. Some are covered with the epithelial shine of multiple scarrings; others have cavities in the stomach, chest or face.

The conditions in the factories are reminiscent of Engels's descriptions of England in 1844. The units are dirty and cramped. Often there is no drinking water, and the temperature inside the factories is far higher than the 40°C heat outside. Ten or twelve men work in a confined dark space, feeding the metal into rollers or presses, banging and hammering hot steel sheets in smoky metal sheds, with barely enough room to stand back from the constant showers of sparks and flame. The industrial effluent and *kachera* (rubbish) from the cooling processes flow into the streets. There is a cat's cradle of wires, cables and power-lines above the buildings. Tea-stalls, snack stalls, small houses are crammed into the gaps between the factories. A low monsoon sky is reflected in the pools of stagnant water and effluent; malaria, dysentery and cholera weaken people already enfeebled by overwork and the pollution of their living-place. Inside, the little houses are overcrowded and stifling; the fan only moves the hot air faster. A child of about nine is recovering from malaria; his eyes huge in a wasted face, his arms and legs those of a four year old.

Perhaps the most shocking thing is the proximity of the owners' houses to the shameful living-places of the workers; new buildings with wrought-iron balconies and ornamental brickwork, ceramic tiles and glass. Couples sit reading or drinking in comfortable chairs on terraces overlooking the *jhuggis*. The lives of the rich are clearly visible from the narrow alleys where people sit selling a few miserable vegetables, bananas, onions or aubergines on a piece of sacking, where the cycle-rickshaw drivers encumber the narrow thoroughfares in a tangle of metal and thin limbs, where the workers linger for a moment of sociability before going home to sleep. Here, in the ostentation of the rich, is a strange phenomenon, a kind of urban feudalism, whereby the people from Bihar, accustomed to the arrogance of landlords and the power of caste and wealth, submit to the flagrant injustice of the factory owners with their lavish villas, built with black money and exploited labour. In many ways, the life of the city only replicates that of the countryside, although in a less oppressive form.

In one small house five brothers live together. There are three rooms and they are paying Rs500 rent. Four of them are working, two in steel factories, two in construction. They are proud that they can pay for the youngest to finish his studies so that he will be able to make a better life. Their generosity, and pride in his achievements, is very touching; a protective tenderness in a harsh place. The landlord wanted to raise the rent of the hut; he sent in *goondas* (hired thugs) to attack it. The same thing had happened to them in Bihar. The house is close to the concrete hangars and galas of the steelworks. On the floor, there is sacking for a bedroll, with a folded sack as a pillow; a candle burns in a bottle, and a book which the boy was reading has fallen onto the floor. In spite of the heat it is impossible to take a *charpoy* (string bed) outside; the black water laps at the little mound on which the hut is built; at one spot a *charpoy* stands in the water, with five small children asleep on it, marooned on their little island in a dark sea.

Where the ground is dry, bodies lie in rows in the open air, like the victims of a natural disaster awaiting identification. And this is what they are, victims, environmental and economic refugees.

Those who believe that all India needs is more liberalization could not be more wrong. An extreme of laissez-faire operates when it is a question of using and abusing human beings and their labour. Official regulations and labour laws give the impression of a country immobilized by an officialdom, which some call socialism. But that is illusion; these are simply a dead letter. This is what D. L. Sheth, of the Centre for the Study of Developing Societies, means when he says that India has had 'socialism by decree and capitalism by default' for the past forty years. The idea that less protection, lower wages for those exposed to the humiliations and dangers of Wazirpur could be advantageous in some way to the country only demonstrates how expendable people are, how 'external' they have become to development.

This city of men nevertheless also contains a sizeable minority of women. Many of those who are landless and have no hope of returning to the village, bring the whole family to the slum. The children paddle in the *kachera*, and play with jagged pieces of metal; coils, springs and sheets of metal piled up outside the industrial units.

The blank concrete fortresses of the factories, the red-white glow of furnaces, the churning of industrial effluent mark the limits of their horizon; everything is hard and unyielding, except the limitless sweetness and softness of the people with each other; the silent absorbers of such unspeakable costs and impositions, their endurance and dignity, which none the less temper this human-made desolation.

Shivsagal is fifteen. He has been working for a year in a steel mill as a machine helper. This means he carries the steel sheets for the machine operators. The sheets are 2 metres long, deadly, blade-sharp pieces of metal, which he bears in bundles of twenty. He earns Rs600 a month (about $20). His twelve-year-old brother earns Rs 500 doing the same work. Their mother has a couple of hectares of land near Bareilly in Uttar Pradesh. They came to Delhi when their father died. Shivsagal sends home Rs200 a month, his brother Rs150. They pay Rs250 for a single room, a small mockery of a lodging, where the rain comes in. The boys prepare the food, rice, vegetable and dal; food costs them about Rs400 a month. Together, this accounts for all their income. The two boys live in a real-world parody of children mimicking an adult household.

Munna is eighteen. He came with his father and brother from Bihar. He started work when he was nine, and now earns Rs1,200 a month as a skilled worker. The three men pay Rs300 for a room, and get one month's holiday a year. Two sisters are at home with his mother. His body is scarred with injuries from the hot metal. He smiles. The factories are dangerous, the employers cruel; but not as bad as in Bihar, where moneylenders steal from the poor and landlords rape their daughters. Arun is thirty-five. He is pulling a rickshaw and earning around Rs40 a day. His landless family is in Western Bihar. Sanjeev is earning Rs900 in a steel factory, and is paying Rs300 to learn TV maintenance and repair. He pays Rs200 for a room, sends Rs200 home. When he finishes the 12-hour shift in the morning, he goes to work in the TV repair shop for about 6 or 7 hours, and sleeps the rest of the time. The acts of self-denial and sacrifice, and the damage they do to the people, scarcely figure in the costs of production of the steel factories. Overwork, premature ageing, exhaustion, a struggle to replace the calories used up each day in the search for livelihood: the human resources, like the material ones, are depleted, but with this difference: there are plenty more people where these came from. In the concern for resources, the perishability of individuals is disregarded. The pool of labour may be infinite, but the lives of the people here are eroded, their strength undermined, their energies used up in ways that monetary rewards could never make good, no matter how lavish these were.

Rajkumar worked in Jindal factory in Wazirpur; he was disabled by an injury and laid off without compensation. It is a small unit, employing eighteen or twenty workers. He has no work now. At home, the family has a miserable two bighas (¼ acre) of land. His two children are there with his wife, to whom he has stopped sending money. He is ashamed to face his family. He sleeps with five other men in a single room. Formerly, he was a machine man, who could earn up to Rs1,600. He demanded compensation from his employer; the result was that he was told he would never work in this area again.

P. K. Shahi is the secretary of the Delhi General Mazdoor Front, which is affiliated to the Indian Federation of Trade Unions. He works from a small unofficial office in Wazirpur, at the top of a flight of stone steps, an austere room with bedroll, desk and files in a metal cabinet. Here, the union keeps an account of the injuries and injustices to the workers in the steel industry, which would otherwise go unrecorded.

'There is a complete factory life set up in this area; people are regularly employed. But there are no records, there is no muster roll, so the workers have no official existence. The pay is monthly, but liable to arbitrary cuts. They work twelve hours a day. The minimum wage is not applicable here; the pay is Rs450, 500, 550, (a six-day working week), no sickness benefit, no compensation for accidents.

'This area is officially sanctioned for industrial development, for hosiery and garment manufacture, non-hazardous, non-polluting industry. The owners are violating official policy. When a worker dies from an industrial accident, the owner, with the connivance of local doctors, police and Industry Department officials, persuade the workers to accept Rs10,000 – Rs15,000 compensation. Yet the Compensation Act provides one lakh (Rs100,000) for a factory death.

'Last week, some steel went into a worker's chest. He died. A private doctor was brought in by management. The doctor declared him dead. The management took him back to the factory. This occurred in the morning. No one informed the union, which found out only in the evening, when some workers came to inform us. The dead worker is a member of the *bustee* (hut) committee. When the news came out, 300 – 400 workers surrounded the premises. There was one constable there. The leader asked the police, "What are you doing?" They said, "This worker is not dead. They are taking him to the government hospital, why are you here creating hue and cry?" Various anti-social elements hired by management and the owners came to try to remove the dead body, saying, "There is no problem, we are taking him to hospital." But because there were hundreds of workers there, they insisted on photographs and police supervision.

'The local police station was alerted. A police inspector came with a photographer, and he photographed the body. It was clear that the worker was dead. At the post-mortem, no case was brought against management. We demanded that a formal case be made. He was a Bihari migrant worker, and his elderly father, wife and two small children cannot survive without him. The management and the police went to the family, asked them, "Why are you involved in this union thing? The case will be long. Accept the market value of compensation. We'll pay Rs10,000 over the amount, we'll give you Rs45,000." Because they were in desperate poverty, they accepted.

'Every other day in the utensils factory, there are injuries to chest, stomach, some fatal. The problem is old technology, faulty machinery, lack of safety. They use patched up machinery, and most of the workers are migrants. In the village, they have little or no land. In Bihar, ten years ago, they were small farmers; economic hardship converts them into landless labourers, landless labourers become factory workers, factory workers become rickshaw pullers. The small farmers in Bihar cannot afford the inputs required by new seeds, so the people go to Delhi, Bombay, Madras, and the rich gobble up their land.

'The price of basic goods rises, the official minimum wage is not increased, and it is not even implemented anyway. The devaluation of the rupee will lead to our wage being able to buy less and less. Not all workers have ration cards – to get one you have to know the *jhuggi dada* (slum boss). The *jhuggis* are controlled by Congress(I) and BJP *goondas*. Rice costs Rs6 in the open market, but this is very poor quality. A kilo of flour is Rs4½. Five kilos of potatoes are now Rs26; three months ago they cost Rs10. The Pepsi factory in Punjab is now taking the best potatoes, mangoes and tomatoes. Potatoes that were once cheap food are now being diverted to potato chips.

'The owners have tried to break the union. The factory *malik* (boss) threatens people to leave the union or they'll be laid off or hurt. Earlier this year, local Congress(I) *goondas* surrounded this office; they attacked the building with police connivance. They beat me and took all the files away, with the evidence of the infringements of labour laws. Then they try to infiltrate the union and take it over, either management-inspired plots, or they do it on their own initiative. People who float a new union in the name of the workers, to get money out of them. We are the only union fighting for workers' rights. Management bribe and threaten by turn. We have 1,200 members here, but active participation is much greater. Many people will not join openly, because they are afraid.

'There is another dimension to our activities. It is difficult to organize within small factory premises. Therefore, we also work in the *bustees*, because there the pressure is not so intense, there is more space, more freedom than in the workplaces. We are working on anti-liquor campaigns, for basic amenities, water, security of tenure, cultural expression, songs and plays. That is not to say that life in the *bustees* is safe. There is no security because they can be demolished at any time; but organization in the *bustees* makes the authorities hesitate before they destroy our homes.'

Shahi himself comes from Bihar. He was the son of a small farmer who had been falsely implicated in criminal activity because of his political activity. He came to Delhi to escape economic and political oppression. He worked in a factory making motorparts, and started a union in Singalpur. Later, he worked in a factory making aluminium vessels. One day, he was assaulted by the son of the factory owner; and that was what made him realize that the workers had to protect themselves against attack, exploitation and impoverishment.

'It hurts us to see the rejoicing of the West over the fall of the Soviet Union. They are happy because the struggle has been damaged, not because social injustice has been alleviated. Quite the opposite. To us, it sounds as though they are celebrating our worsening situation. There has been an adverse impact upon the working-class movement in India, but that isn't the whole picture. Everybody is now saying that the US path of capitalism is the best way of living. This is not the path for India. India is supposed to be a democracy, but after forty years of independence, democracy has nothing to do with the workers. There is too much legislation designed to suppress them – ESMA (Essential Services Maintenance Act), NSA (National Security Act), TADA (Anti-terrorist Act), all are used against workers.'

Tilku has just been dismissed from the chemical factory where he worked. Now, he says, the owners are starting new tactics. For some time they will use one name, then close the factory, and open up another with a different name. That way they get out of paying dues to the workers, including wages. When the factory closed, he demanded his legal dues. He was refused, and that was when he approached the union. Since then, the owner has victimized him, threatened that he will never get another job in the chemicals industry. Tilku comes from Uttar Pradesh, near Lucknow. He has no savings. His only child died recently. He has been four months without work.

Rambabu was dismissed for demanding the minimum wage in his

engineering factory. He says that you work in one place for a long time, you become a skilled worker, but you are still being paid at the rate for unskilled labour. He was a machine man, and was entitled to Rs1,140, but was getting only Rs700. He had worked eight years in the same place.

In September 1991, about ten thousand workers from the IFTU trades unions came together to march through New Delhi. Among them are some of the most abused and exploited people on earth. There were landless labourers from Andhra Pradesh, earning Rs15–20 a day for only six months of the year. There were survivors of caste atrocities from Bihar, workers from small repair shops in Bangalore and Trivandrum, displaced farmers from Punjab now working in steel mills, bitter about the Green Revolution, which they see as having robbed them of their land, workers from the sweat-shops of Uttar Pradesh, in textiles, pharmaceuticals and electronics, steel-workers from Delhi, rickshaw-drivers, recyclers of glass, their hands and arms covered with cuts that fester in the damp monsoon heat, students from Nagpur, the children of the landless from Hyderabad. A group of women from Kerala, coir workers and cashew workers, head the procession, with its red flags flying in defiance of all the obituaries that have been written over the death of socialism.

It is an immensely dignified and moving procession. Many of the participants are very young, like Raju and Kumar, both fifteen and Rajnesh, eighteen, from Harpur in Uttar Pradesh, working in leather goods, clothing and chemicals factories. They have come because they have seen their parents prematurely aged by poverty and exploitation, unable to sustain the little land, falling deeper into debt. Their instructor has not been Marx, but the injury to loved flesh and blood, the injustice that drives their youth and energy into dirty and dangerous factories. It is the opposite of fatalism that has led the fifty-year-old woman vegetable-seller from Ahmedabad to travel the 1,000 kilometres for the sake of a march the few kilometres from Tilak Marg to the Gateway of India. A frieze of insulted humanity, thin and undersized from generations of malnourishment and poverty. The well-filled bellies of the police hem them in on each side, although these are given no excuse to use their *lathis* (bamboo canes) against the solemn and silent crowd, which winds its way slowly through the chaos and disorder of this violent city. Rajdev is seventeen. Both his parents died before they were fifty in their village in eastern Uttar Pradesh. Oppressed by village life, overwhelmed by the predatoriness of Delhi, Rajdev lives on a footpath. With his bitten nails, threadbare trousers, imitation trainers with false Reebok labels, scars on hands where he has worked in the Delhi sewers, he has seen many other country boys destroyed by alcohol and drugs. His only protection against dereliction is his faith in socialism. Their slogans – Down with the IMF. Down with Congress(I). Long live the people's struggle – the battered lorry with the distorted sound-system broadcasting revolutionary songs, seems ineffective against a city irritated by this obstruction to the traffic, this hindrance to its daily business.

There is another level of sadness here. The colonizing of the people by the alien faith of Marxism-Leninism is as complete as the total surrender of their opponents to the sacred principles of the IMF and World Bank. Theirs is a double alienation, bearers of a foreign creed that has now lost its power in the place where it grew. That India might have found another way, with its Gandhian tradition of modest consumption, voluntary austerity and a decent sufficiency for all, has been lost between the warring foreign faiths, of which only one remains, to dance on the graves, not only of socialism, but also of the teachings of Gandhi, crushed by treacherous and unrealizable promises that the Western way is replicable here.

In the centre of Delhi is Connaught Place, a vast open circle, showpiece of the imperial Lutyens capital, bounded on its outer edge by white-painted arcades of restaurants, shops and airline offices. At the heart is a grassy rotunda, colonized now by those attracted by the growing tourist presence in Delhi, and who inhabit a very different world from the migrant workers of Wazirpur. Connaught Place is only a few hundred metres from some of the big hotels, and it has conjured forth a population of hustlers, survivors, conmen and salespeople, beggars and hucksters, as well as waiters, washermen and domestics taking a rest for their work in the servicing of the rich.

Hope is inscribed in the busy iconography of the city, the images of glamour, ministerial limousines, lurid film-posters, markets, even the exotic livery of servants. This is the place where the country sensibility of migrants is broken and reshaped in the images of the dreams, excitements and illusions of metropolitan life. There are always clusters of people standing outside the luxury hotels, simply watching the rich transients, and wondering, perhaps, what mysterious qualities differentiate these strangers from those whose labour they command so effortlessly.

In Connaught Place, you can find anything you want: fortune tellers, palm-readers (I. C. Clear), astrologers, masseurs (including those who offer head-massage, a violent friction that leaves you disoriented and light-headed), ear-cleaners – young men in smart red turbans, with bunches of cotton buds on sticks. There are people collecting for orphans, the blind, the Missionaries of Charity or themselves; vendors of fruit and vegetables, cloth and sandalwood, jewels and carpets, bangles and snacks, bhel-puri and bhajis, channa and agarbatti, sex, drugs and money at unofficial rates of Rs60 to the pound; those who ask if you want to do business, any other business, like the end of a committee meeting agenda; they will find you a taxi, a rickshaw, take you to brothels where there are girls to be had for Rs10 or Rs1,000; they will guide you round Delhi, show you where you can get gold, buy coloured birds from south India, find precious stones, valuable works of art that have come to market from the ruins of Fatehpur Sikri or prised out of the stones of the Taj Mahal itself.

Many of those working in the hotels are from Uttarkhand, the northern part of Uttar Pradesh, the foothills of the Himalayas. Everything and everyone coming from the hills is transformed. The forests become timber, the men become boys. Only the women, who stay, remain women.

From Garhwal and Kumaon, regions with their own separate languages and identity, they come to the plains. Servants, houseboys, waiters, cooks, they enter the service industry precisely because of the qualities they bring from their damaged hill-culture, their openness and honesty. It is an irony that just a few characteristics salvaged from the old culture are exploited, while all the rest falls into decay. Perhaps this is why there is such a strong undertow of melancholy in their exile, the hankering after a return, yet the sense of something having been changed irreversibly in the move to the plains: a flattening of the psyche also. It is significant that it is the women who remain, who cope and resist. The men escape. They are defeated. They run away. It is the women who must stay and create a decent life out of the degraded landscapes and the damaged forests.

Nainital in Kumaon was the old summer capital of the United Provinces of Agra and Oudh. Founded in the 1840s, many of the British churches, schools and hotels remain, some of them sadly in ruins. Elphinstone Hotel, overlooking Lake Nainital, is a cavernous building, with musty, lofty suites where once the wives and children of British officials stayed. It smells of damp in the monsoon rains, with flyblown mirrors, ornate colonial furniture, carved almirahs and dressers, and an efflorescence of mildew spreading on the peeling walls. British officials came up here in summer to avoid the oppressive heat of the plains; the settlement was originally all white, only the bearers and coolies were Indian, toiling up the tracks on the steep hillside, carrying the memsahibs in their chairs and palanquins and depositing them beside the cool, clear lake. The railway came to the bottom of the hill in the 1890s, but the first motorized traffic did not appear until the 1920s. It was only twenty years ago that Nainital became a resort of mass tourism. Foreigners still come in April–June, but when the rains set in, it is mainly Indians; everything in August is damp and the great pink and blue Himalayan galciers are obscured by perpetual mists, which settle over the marble terraces and crumbling ornate stonework.

The lake is now a polluted and glassy olive-green. It is surrounded by a cluster of stalls selling fast foods, mementoes, clothes, crafts and artefacts. At the bus-stop, the Nepali workers besiege every bus and taxi-van that comes up from Haldwani, looking for customers for the empty hotels, or carrying luggage of those men home for their annual holiday from the plains.

Jagat is a hill-boy who has never lived in the hills. His father was a farmer near Nainital, but died when Jagat was one year old. The father's brother would not let the wife and her two children stay, so she came with Jagat and her five-year-old daughter, Tulsi, to the plains, to Haldwani, which is the frontier town before the road climbs to Nainital. She found shelter in a shed on the land of a rich Gujerati family, who owned 100 acres of fertile farming land, as well as factories in Bombay and Delhi. She worked for them as a cook, and also on the land, especially at harvest time. Naroli Devi is now fifty-two, a small, thin woman, with hands disproportionately robust from the years of manual labour. By working sometimes 16 or 18 hours a day, she was able to save some money over the years. Her employers were good to her, she says, and with their help she was able to buy five bighas of land (a little less than one acre). Her daughter also worked in the fields with her mother, but Jagat was allowed to study. He went to university, got a degree in Economics and Commerce, took a physical education diploma and joined the Border Security Force. After basic training, he spent his time practising for inter-army athletics meetings. He is a good short-distance runner, and at twenty-five, has reached the peak of his form, and has been rarely absent from the winners in the 100 metres, 200 and 400 metre races. His ambition is to be a teacher of physical education in Kumaon, so that he can return to his region.

The bus takes eight hours from Delhi. At Haldwani, a cycle rickshaw takes a side road bordered by small workshops, which soon declines into a rough dirt track, with potholes full of rainwater. This leads up to Rani farm, which has to be crossed before we come to the small piece of land where Jagat's family live. He points out the now derelict shed where he grew up. In the fields, the women and children are cutting fodder for the cattle. Rani farm is set with soya beans and maize. Red, white and black butterflies hover over the fragrant grasses and wild flowers on the margin of the fields, clover and sweet orange karu. A row of eucalyptus trees divides Naroli Devi's small piece of land from the main farm. At the edge, there is a cattleshed, with three buffaloes and a cow. Over the shed a *lokhi* creeper, a kind of pumpkin with creamy yellow flowers. Two goats are tied to the bushes beneath the trees.

Naroli Devi has begun to build the house where Jagat will live when he marries. It is a single-storey building, with concrete floor, brick walls and pakka roof, on which the firewood for the rainy season has been stored. As yet, there is no bathroom, and no electricity. The five bighas are immaculately kept by her and her daughter: maize, soya and rice for their own consumption. The small plot of land was bought seven years ago for Rs25,000. Now the price has quadrupled. Every centimetre is used: there are papaya and mango trees beside the house, aru and sitaphul. There are medicinal herbs and the white starry flowers of red peppers. The mother appears, a frail figure, with a headload of fodder. She sees her son, but does not quicken her pace until she has placed the headload beside the byre. He touches her head in homage, and she smiles. He greets his sister in the same way, and then she goes off to cut vegetables from Rani farm, from where they are allowed to take what they need for their own use.

The house is raised on a red and black painted platform, so that the floodwaters do not enter. There are three rooms, one of which belongs to Jagat: a wooden bed, a small table, with two aluminium and plastic chairs. There is a small bookcase, and shelves with his running trophies, small tarnished cups and shields in inferior metal. The field is vivid green with the young rice, and the intermittent sunshine sparkles on the raindrops caught in the tender leaves like crystals. A tiny bird settles on a blade of maize; the plant scarcely bends beneath its weight.

The family are Rajputs, and pride in their caste remained even through the years of poverty; Jagat feels that it is his duty to redeem their fortunes. He does not believe in caste, but says his mother would not allow an Untouchable into her kitchen. There is a gobargas plant for cooking, which cost Rs10,000, half of which came from the state government. Naroli Devi points out the khimu and amruth trees, the karela creeper, the lemon trees and the mint which she grows to make chutney. Overhead the shintola and bulbuls fly; pale grey and saffron butterflies against a silver-grey sky. Beyond are the blue, tree-fringed hills, their sharp outlines blurred by mist which comes with the incessant monsoon rain. Alongside the plot of land is an irrigation canal which provides water throughout the year.

Mother and daughter get up at five to milk the buffaloes. They eat rice and dal at midday and chapati and vegetables in the evening. The mother wears a pink and green saree with a pink top. Her hair is greying. Tulsi Devi is sick. She has severe pains in her side, and must go for an operation next week. She shows the medicine she has been given: antibiotics in lurid orange capsules and a big bottle of tonic. Jagat will stay with her in hospital, take food and keep his mother company at night.

The two women sit and look at him all the time. Their expectation and their love are painfully tangible in the afternoon stillness. They show him the medicines. Will everything be all right? He feels their eyes on him, and is constrained by the weight of their feeling which fills the room with its intensity, and its anxious need for reassurance. He gets up and walks around the house. Their eyes follow him. Jagat knows that he must come back here and look after his mother and sister. Tulsi Devi was married, but her husband was a drinker, and he left her. There is no one else to care for them. He too feels the power of his own attachment to them: he is like his mother – the same hill people's eyes, the same hands, although his are not scarred, the same gap between the two front teeth. If he could choose, he would perhaps stay in Delhi; but choice is not an option when flesh and blood are tied together by such bonds of necessity. He will feel his life constrained and diminished after the excitement of being a champion runner, the trips to Calcutta and Madras for inter-army competitions. He walks up to the concrete roof; the heavy spots of rain splash the concrete and dry immediately in the subdued heat from a hazy sun. He points out the hut on the adjacent piece of land. There, the man is a sharecropper and the land belongs to an absentee landlord who receives half the produce. He recognizes his own good fortune because of his mother's industry and devotion. He cannot express the mixture of pain and love: the desire to leave, to migrate to the Gulf, the need to stay.

They speak Kumaoni. For Naroli Devi, Hindi is a foreign language; they lapse easily into the dialect. They ask him if he will marry next year. He says he is ready. He has saved Rs5,000 from his monthly salary of Rs3,000, a third of which he sends home. In spite of her illness, Tulsi prepares food. She wears a white saree with yellow and pink circles. Her face is thin and hollow. She washes the aluminium plates in a zinc bucket, and sorts through the grains of cream-coloured rice. The house is plain; tools for working the land – hoe, mattock and scythe – stand by the door. Jagat is intelligent, not intellectual, very physical, proud of his skill, which he takes very seriously. He has a hill-face which people often take for Nepalese, gold skin and amber eyes. He has been privileged by the women who love him; but the other side of this advantage is that he reciprocates their feeling, and will do what is expected of him, whatever violence this may do to his own inclinations. The modern world has under-mined his consciousness of himself, but not destroyed his sense of duty. The house waiting to be improved, the tired body of his mother, the small parcel of well-tended land on the one hand, the excitements of city life, the competitive exaltation of athletics meet-ings, the wider social contacts on the other. You can feel the lure of escape, individualism, on the one hand, and at the same time the tug of the rooted and the traditional; that tension that is repeated not only in the people from the foothills of the Himalayas, but with countrypeople all over the world.

Shekhar Pathak lives in Nainital and edits *Pahad*, a magazine about the life and culture of the hills. He lives on one of the hillsides overlooking the lake; steep steps and shallow zig-zag paths wind up the hills, overgrown with grasses and ferns, white daisies and blue gentian. In places the slopes are built up to a height of 200–300 metres, but in others they are too fragile. Shekhar Pathak chooses to live and work here at the University of Kumaon. Of 'development' in Kumaon, he says, 'Development is a necessity here. But Kumaon has special features that mean we must not just follow the Western path. Six lakh (600,000) people come here each year, especially from the north of India. This is one of the safe areas, because there is no trouble as in Kashmir or Punjab. But the numbers of people are more than the fragile ecology can bear. The British transformed a non-monetary economy into a cash economy; forests and minerals were to them only a source of revenue; and they turned so many of our young men into soldiers, who fought in the Afghan war and in the two world wars. Wool, skins, furs, herbs, stones, minerals, plants – the hill culture was in every way self-reliant; indigenous technology spun wool and made copper and iron utensils, arts, crafts and woodwork. The drain of men to the plains is an old story. Few want to come back; and indeed, rural society doesn't want them back. If as a migrant you return, that means you have failed, the land you will get is of poor quality. Our young go, and if they get good jobs they send money back, and this helps keep the population of Uttarkhand – 60 lakh here, but half as many again working outside. That is the contribu-tion to the sustainability of these fragile hills – they couldn't possibly all live here. They do dream of coming back, but they have been changed by the plains, and it remains a dream.'

'The environment is something to be lived in. Livelihood and environment interact. If you conserve an environment without change, that implies the people must be removed. Chipko started off originally as an economic movement. They wanted sustainable wood from the forest to start small-scale industry. If you talk of environment as pure ecology, there is less possibility of people's participation. Chipko is both a philosophical movement and an exercise in sustainable economics. A conserving economics and, at the same time, a vision of society. If we conserve and protect the trees, this is in order to be able to use them in modest and non-damaging ways; a practical use of resources. Deep ecology is attractive philosophically, but economically and socially impossible.

'It is the women who stay, although some girls who have been educated are now going outside. Men feel that with a degree they have a claim upon a job. Women have had no alternative. Women have been custodians of the forest. They are also fighting on behalf of the men, who also help sustain the women from outside the region. The economy and culture of the hills are maintained and transmitted by women.

'The region has been badly eroded. Only 10 per cent of forests are now virgin, with more than 60 per cent canopy cover. Twenty-nine per cent is forest cover, but that includes open forest, land without any forest. Forest with more than 60 per cent canopy is down to 10–12 per cent. Eighty per cent has been completely damaged. There are parts of Delhi where the tree canopy is thicker in places than in our forests.'

Shekhar Pathak is well aware of social and economic issues and their relationship to the environment. For the people of Kumaon, the process of 'development' itself is not in question; but the systematic abuse of the resource-base in its name is. Chipko is not a model so much as an idea, a philosophy; but unless the environmental struggle can be identified with its economic base, it will never gain popular acceptance. The problem now is that only a few marginal communities now *obviously* depend upon the resource-base: the 'development' of the West has actually sought to conceal that relationship – which is the same for all human communities. As a result, conservationist concerns come to appear the efforts for the 'environment' of those without material worries, those who would deny development to the poor, who in turn perceive access to the material production of industrial society as the most urgent and compelling hope for their future.

When people, driven by ecological breakdown or economic necessity, are compelled to leave the village or farm, they often assume that they will be free of the harassment and evictions of the rural areas.

But too often the urban experience continues the rural story of displacement and upheaval; and not only for the poorest.

Ashok Nagar, in the south-west of Delhi, was settled between 1972 and 1980: 450 families bought plots of land which had been sold by landlords to developers at what they considered a reasonable profit. The community was legally constituted, and the people living there expected to construct a modest dwelling on their land. In 1980, the residents formed the Ashok Nagar Welfare Association.

Throughout the early 1980s Delhi expanded, and land values rose rapidly. More than 160,000 people now come to Delhi each year. Some of these come for seasonal or temporary work, but most do not return to the villages. This places enormous pressure on housing, and because of the vast spread of the city, increasingly on land values. If people live in *jhuggis* (huts), they must pay money to the headman or slumlord, who will have links with the police or politicians. There are so many routine demolitions of unauthorized settlements that this no longer makes news for any but those affected. There is always a massive amount of construction going on in Delhi, yet the beneficiaries are always the rich. Even so-called low-cost housing goes to those who can afford the rent, who are not the poor.

The landlords who had originally sold the land realized that if they had held on to it, they would have made an even greater profit. Accordingly, they planned to repossess it by force, evicting those legally settled there. Some highly placed employees of Delhi Development Authority and the administration became involved in this scheme, in spite of the fact that these agencies had originally sanctioned the construction of the community. The landlords hired *goondas* to frighten and threaten people. Houses were attacked and robbed. Some were burned out. People were beaten and injured. After a time, some of the residents began to leave. Those who protested were beaten up. Mohan Singh, president of the association, was hit and badly injured. Mohan Singh had come to Ashok Nagar in 1978 from Hardoi in Uttar Pradish, and had a government job. With the other residents, he had helped clear the trees and scrub from the land. Most had secure though modest jobs – a peon at WHO, bank workers, owners of small businesses. Many took loans which they could no longer afford to pay after they were evicted. They complained to the police, the state and then the central government; they wrote to the prime minister and the president. Nothing happened.

The Delhi Development Authority, in alliance with the landlords, helped set up a Residential Co-operative Society, to the members of which the plots of land belonging to the oustees were sold. In 1980, under the Public Interest, in the name of the planned development of Delhi, under the Land Acquiring Act of 1984, the DDA announced its intention of acquiring the land. The correct procedures were not followed, and the residents knew nothing of it. In September 1982, DDA announced that it would develop the land itself. A falsified list of people who received compensation was prepared. All the legal proceedings were completed in one day in September 1982, by which time much of the land had already been disposed of.

The original residents petitioned the Delhi High Court in 1984. The court ordered that the sale be stopped. Nothing happened. The Court's orders were violated. According to DDA, Ashok Nagar was an unauthorized colony, like so many others in the city, and hence the residents had no right to land or compensation. It was assumed that Ashok Nagar was just another case of eviction of an illegal settlement.

The original settlement is now a desolate place, ruinous houses and wrecked plots. The Housing Co-operative is putting up multi-storey blocks. The land that was sold in 1971–2 for Rs25 per square metre, was resold in the 1980s at Rs400–500. The newly settled families are related to the landlords, and they formed a new Ashok Nagar Welfare Association in 1987. The land and houses of the displaced people are still being sold and resold, in defiance of the court order. No action has ever been taken to protect their rights. All authorities, including the highest, surrendered to the economic pressures of landlords and politicians.

Delhi must be one of the few places on earth where people advertise their services as 'Property Dealers and Colonizers' on boards outside their businesses. The demands of the Ashok Nagar residents, that their houses should be returned to them, that the illegal activities of landlords should be stopped, that there should be a high-level inquiry into the events at Ashok Nagar, have all been ignored.

Replacing the Biosphere

Within the next decade or so, it is expected that a majority of the worlds's 5.5 billion people will become urban. As a result, a minority, and a declining one, will be responsible for feeding the rest. This scarcely perturbs the people in the rich world, for they have become accustomed to a tiny proportion of people in their society engaged in agriculture. Nor are they unhappy that far more people are involved in 'the food industry' than in the growing of food.

This process, of rural–urban migration, has been in train since the beginning of the industrial era. It has required an ever more intensive cultivation of the land. Indeed, the industrial revolution in Britain and its colonial enterprise were both, in part, a response to an early ecological crisis, as the development of the country struck against the limits of its resource-base. The limited land-mass of Britain could not support its growing population; severe deforestation had already depleted the wood available for construction, fuel and shipbuilding in the early nineteenth century; and pressure on land for fodder for cattle and draught animals was competing with that required for food. Such ecological constraints were surmounted by the annexation of lands in other parts of the world, which not only supplied raw materials for industrial expansion, but also offered a refuge for migrations of the 'surplus' population of Britain, whether compulsorily, through transportation or as adventurers, the discoverers of new frontiers.

The subjugation of the territory of other people has always been central to the wealth-creation of the West, whether 'discovered' and confiscated from indigenous populations, as North and South America and Australia, or by military conquest and occupation, as India and large parts of Africa. This is why those prescriptions for 'development' issued with such solemn certitude by Western experts now are duplicitous and unrealizable. It is not that they do not have an answer to the depleted territories remaining for conquest. When

pressures similar to those in Britain at the beginning of the nineteenth century arose globally in the middle years of the twentieth
century, the answer appeared to lie in an extension and intensifica-
tion of industrialized agriculture. The means of this deliverance since
the 1960s has come to be known as the Green Revolution; based on,
not working with nature, but on the conquest of nature, with
enhanced purchased inputs of chemical fertilizers and pesticides.
This was to pump high productivity out of hybrid varieties of rice and
wheat. The Green Revolution is perhaps the proudest achievement
of 'development' strategies conceived as an answer to the danger of
mass discontent and uprisings in the Third World, which might
otherwise have installed governments hostile to Western interests. It
is also not true to say that industrialized agriculture was introduced
innocently, without awareness of its likely consequences. Vandana
Shiva describes, in *The Violence of the Green Revolution*, how in the
1960s, many Indian economists, and the prime minister, Lal
Bahadur Shastri, sought to resist the import of new varieties, which
would be costly to grow and would displace many small farmers.

It has recently become apparent that the achievement of the Green
Revolution has been at the expense, not only of soil fertility, the
contamination and exhaustion of land, poisonings of soil and water,
but also of the violence to human culture and dislocation of human
societies. Vandana Shiva makes the link between the ecological and
the social disruption of Punjub in the name of development; what is
now one of the richest regions in India is also the most violent,
tormented by social conflict, inequality and fear. This is falsely
ascribed to communalism: the real religious war comes from the faith
of those who imposed the alien technological fix on a society where
people of different faiths had lived peacefully together for generations. The West's belief in its 'value-free' science, and its economic
system based on reason and objective truth, has become the most
dangerous ideological mix ever unleashed on the world; and is the
more damaging for its vehement denial that it is any such thing.

Indeed, so profoundly rooted in this faith that further technological miracles are sought, in order to escape the limitations of this
particular 'solution' to the problem of hunger. Biotechnology is
promised as the most recent deliverer of humankind from the threat
of insufficient food. The Green Revolution was seen as a means of
transcending the constraints of nature, which were perceived as a
bringer of scarcity. It was intended to liberate humanity from subservience to its changeability and unreliability; and at the same time, to
bring peace and stability to those countries threatened by social
dislocation through poverty and insecurity. The latest promises of

biotechnology are of a piece with this earlier project; underlying them is the idea that nature is inimical to humanity, and that we can overcome its vagaries by the judicious harnessing of science and technology. Technology is seen as a substitute for both politics and nature, because it eliminates the need for agricultural reform and abolishes scarcity at the same time.

Industrial society has nourished the illusion that we can escape the rhythms of the natural world, of the seasons, of seedtime and harvest, almost, it seems, of birth and death. We can live free of its onerous limitations. The tangible pledge of this may be seen everywhere in the supermarkets of the West and Japan, where, in defiance of climate, season and common sense, it is possible, for example, to find baby sweetcorn and asparagus from Thailand, guavas and mangoes from Brazil, courgettes from Guatemala, pineapples from the Ivory Coast, starfruit from Malaysia, beans from Kenya, melons from Israel, cherries from Chile. What an expansive sense of freedom this gives to the privileged of the West, who feel that all the fruits of the earth are, literally, theirs for the plucking.

But even as increasing numbers of people worldwide are escaping what Marx referred to as 'the idiocy of rural life', it is apparent that the rationality and intelligence of urban life have also been exaggerated. The passage of people from direct dependency on the biosphere to dependency on the human-made environment, the 'technosphere', has come to be seen as a universal measure of progress. Indeed, rural people do not even have to migrate to become part of the technosphere; modernized agriculture, the Green Revolution, the new high-yielding varieties are actually industrial products that colonize the biosphere, moving out from the industrial centres to rearrange the agricultural and social patterns of living of those that remain. And in the process, they spread disruption and unrest: only the rich can afford the inputs; more and more poor and marginal farmers become landless, and are effectively evicted from their traditional livelihood; whether they remain as impoverished rural dwellers, or set out on the long journey to the city, they have still fallen under the influence of industrial society. The battleground has moved further back now, to the last dependants on the resource-base in the forests and fishing grounds and hillsides. This is why indigenous peoples have become at the centre of a particular struggle; for they ask whether there is really a space for alternative ways of living in the world, or whether all must be swallowed up in a single globalizing monoculture. They actually call the bluff of rhetoric of the West: can alternatives to its market economy be allowed to exist or not? Will all other ways of organizing human affairs be suppressed?

When we look at all the migrations, journeying and removals of people across the world at the end of the twentieth century, the most significant of all these epic migrations is not the passage through any national barrier or transcontinental frontier, significant though these are; it is the invisible yet fateful movement of humanity from the natural world to the industrial environment. Industrial society appears both a refuge and a deliverance. It is a transfer which, it seems, a majority of the world's people cannot wait to achieve. This is evident in the eager desire of the poor to gain access to the symbols and icons of Western manufacture. It is scarcely to be expected that there should be any significant resistance to this universal, one-way and apparently irreversible traffic, from farm to village, from village to city, from town to metropolis, from city to international megalopolis.

Yet there is resistance. It soon becomes apparent to many who have made that journey that this movement is at best ambiguous and often detrimental to their well-being. People realize that it means loss of control over crucial areas of their lives – growing their own food, building their own shelters, disposing of their own time in a desired mixture of labour, rest and play. It is the young who are most ready to trade away what seem to them unimportant, even burdensome, freedoms for the sake of the liberations inscribed in the very material presence of watches, radios, cars, motorbikes, jewellery, videos, music and fashionable clothing which are omnipresent on the streets of the cities. Since these items are so prominent in the displays of Western culture, this implies that basic needs such as food and shelter have all been effortlessly answered: the technosphere promises liberation from repetitive and humdrum activity. It promises leisure and rest from labour.

Yet older people evicted from the land often realize that the step they are forced to take is only the first one on a long road, where little by little, autonomy and control of their destiny will be surrendered. Of course, there is relief from the ancient subservience to nature, nature which is *not* kind, but often harsh, cruel and capable of inflicting great losses. Working with the intractable necessities of nature and not in opposition to them is frustrating, back-breaking and always to be started afresh, a labour of Sisyphus; but to believe that we can be emancipated from its laws remains, in the end, a delusion.

And in the initial stages, it does seem that the gains outweigh the losses: to go and work for money which you spend as you will creates

81

at first a wonderful sense of freedom. In the suburbs of Delhi, I met some refugees from rural Bihar, who had fled caste oppression, debt and landlessness. They were working as cycle-rickshaw drivers or steel-vessel makers in the factories of Wazirpur. The cycle-rickshaw drivers rented the vehicle – a large tricycle with a padded seat for passengers and a flimsy oval hood which protects against sun or monsoon rains. They rent the vehicle from the owner; their labour strains their bodies, as they pedal them over the rough slum roads or the modest gradients in Delhi's heat; their bodies glisten with sweat, their veins stand out, their muscles contract under the flesh. They are paid only two or three rupees by the poor who use their services. They may sleep eight or ten to a room for a price that will take up half their monthly earnings. The steelworkers likewise display their scars, where pieces of steel from unguarded forges have entered their body left a series of shiny scars, have taken away an eye or a finger, have disabled them for life. They are paid pitiful wages, a mere Rs500 (£15) a month; they must work a 12-hour shift. Yet all say that what they are doing is better than life where they come from.

This instant gain, immediate improvement, is often not sustained. It is only later that the true costs of such changes become apparent. Similarly, it is only now that we can begin to assess the real price paid for the wholesale relinquishing of the earth by an industrialized humanity; what has been successfully suppressed throughout the industrial era is now forcing itself on us: a world full of people skilled only in making money is actually a world of accomplished incompetents, who can do nothing independently of money, who cannot answer their own most simple and elementary needs, without buying in the marketplace. The ability to live in balance with the natural environment has been replaced by the knowledge of how to manipulate its technological substitute.

The industrial environment now seems destined to obliterate the biosphere on which it weighs with growing force. In the process, the technosphere pays tribute to what it is displacing, because within the false cosmos it creates, it mimics and reflects the world of nature; indeed, sets up an imitation of it. Industrial society has wrought an artificial shadow version of what it is snuffing out; an indication perhaps, that it is aware of the precious irreplaceability of what it is destroying. The complex webs of connectedness in nature are both imitated and mocked by the complicated networks of dependency in industrial society. When we hear talk of 'our complex modern society', this is both echo and repudiation of the fragile, interlocking relationships of the biosphere. The institutions of industrial society gesture towards, acknowledge their indebtedness towards what they have crushed. The language itself betrays the untenability of the project. Economic necessity becomes the defining edge of the 'real world', and the laws of nature are suspended in favour of profit and loss. The word 'resources' has come to mean, not the treasures of nature, not the infinite capacity of human beings to make and to create, but money. 'Survival' is perceived, not as preserving the balance of the biosphere, but as the ingenuity of individuals in procuring for themselves the money that will buy their daily subsistence. Subsistence itself is signified, not by the livelihood that results in self-provisioning, but a sum of money. Being 'independent' is a description of those who have a private fortune, whereas such people are, in fact, the most completely dependent of all human beings. No wonder the possession of riches makes people conservative and not conservationist: they want to conserve the social and economic order at all costs, even if these costs include the sacrifice of the earth and its resource-base. It is simply that they can no longer even imagine a life detached from the money-dependent abjection in which they live.

The proudest boasts of industrial society are always in some way a refraction of its power to imitate and to replace nature. Take, for instance, the claim that industrial society optimizes choice. In reality, the extension of consumer choice goes hand in hand with the extinction of biodiversity. As biodiversity shrinks, through the appropriation of germplasms by the transnationals, the patenting of seeds and the extension of monocultures with a narrowing genetic base, so the spread of items in the supermarkets of the West expands – twelve thousand different products are on display in any middle-sized supermarket. But the number of species that are daily becoming extinct, the strains of crop, protected and developed by farmers over countless generations, appropriate to the ecological niche in which they have grown, is reduced, lost and consigned to oblivion. The deeper meaning of the West's power to add value is its subtraction of worth. Vandana Shiva has described this process in the Punjab.

As the marginal lands and croplands are homogenized, diversity disappears. Genetic diversity in Punjab has been destroyed by the Green Revolution at two other levels – first, by the transformation of mixed and rotational cropping of wheat, bajra, jowar, barley, pulses and oilseeds into monocultures and multicropping of wheat and rice, and second, by the conversion of wheat and rice from diverse native varieties suited to different soil, water and climatic conditions to monocultures of single varieties derived from exotic dwarf varieties of CIMMYT and IRRI. . . . The destruction of diversity and the creation of uniformity simultaneously involves the destruction of stability and the creation of vulnerability.

Indeed, the whole dynamic of the industrial technosphere is one of growth and expansion, which itself is a caricature of the cycle of renewal and regeneration which occurs in nature. The 'real world' in which politicians and economists exhort us to live is itself a figment of the industrial imagination; and the prop of faith becomes more and more indispensable to hold our failing spirits to this increasingly sombre enterprise. But then, if 'development' was itself primarily a Western response to the threat of revolution and unrest in the South, now that those threats have been successfully contained, why should there be any more concern about development? If the whole idea is becoming more threadbare, this is because it no longer has much importance. The stage is cleared for a redefinition of the true purposes of the rich, which are domination and control.

The conquest of nature in the industrial project was always presented as being in the interests of transcending the bounds of natural scarcity. The promise of industrialism was that it would liberate humanity from the threat of poverty, famine and insecurity. Instead, what we have seen is once more an imitation of natural poverty by invented scarcities, artificially created feelings of, insufficiency, which lie at the heart of, and fuel the expansionism of, industrial society.

To be poor is an existential condition, in so far as we are all born with nothing and die with nothing. Poverty itself suggests a relationship with the natural world. Poor are those who must make a living directly from the resource-base of the earth; in this sense, indigenous peoples, tribals, subsistence farmers, all who live without taking more from the earth than they give back, those whose passage through life does not leave a net deficit of resources. Although this poverty can be catastrophic at times of natural calamity, flood, drought, failure of harvest, for the most part, this represents a rational austerity, a not joyless, but limited claim on the riches of the earth. Of course, people who lived for millennia in this way always took such precautions as they could against scarcity. They learned to husband and conserve what they had against all foreseeable disasters. Indeed, their beliefs, whereby the land and the waters and the trees were sacralized, helped to conserve the source of their renewable riches – the environment with which their lives were inextricably bound up. And that poverty was made more bearable by a wealth of tradition and custom; some of this severely practical, like the knowledge of where to find supplementary food in the forests, in roots, tubers and berries. But the poverty was also mitigated by a vast storehouse of memory, lore, stories, beliefs, an animistic faith, in which all living things participate in and have meaning for human lives; where gods and spirits, demons and fabulous creatures weave in and out of human existence, enriching, amplifying, consoling. Sacralizing the useful is another secret which industrial society mocks in its precursor: the object of all veneration is now money and what it will buy.

Those who pass the unmarked frontier of industrialized existence must incur another form of poverty, the multiple, artificial wants and lacks which come with its version of abundance. Impoverishment is the term more properly applied to those who have sundered dependency on the natural world for the strange mutations of poverty imposed by industrial society.

For this poverty is an artefact, a simulation of 'natural' poverty. Yet it is presented as though it were of a piece with the existential poverty which we imagine we have escaped. Those who have wondered at the persistence of poverty in even the richest societies have not always understood the nature of the dispossessions that occur at the point of abandonment of more direct dependency on the biosphere. For deepening industrialization strips away all the precious, incalculable means whereby people create culture, coherence, meaning for themselves; and they must then buy back all the substitutes and artefacts and consolations that can be had only for money. Industry offers its own restoratives to the impoverishments it inflicts. But those losses have not been incurred in the realm of anything that can be calculated in monetary terms. Therefore, in spite of the heaping up of things, the invention of new objects, devices, sensations, comforts, people remain with a gnawing sense of insufficiency. Even the richest people regularly complain that they do not have *enough*; indeed, they never can, for they are seeking to remedy injuries that cannot be made good in the sole area in which their search takes place. Wealth-creation merely compounds the pain. This is perhaps why there remain so much anger, resentment, unfulfilment and violence in the richest industrial societies. Indeed, the richer they become, the greater their sense of deprivation, the more urgent and driven the promptings to enrich themselves.

What has always been the birthright of all individuals in all societies – the gifts of meaning, the rituals, customs, practices, traditions, legends and lore of a culture handed down through time from previous generations, are all stripped away. And we are then offered 'freedom of choice' to buy back a caricature of what we should never have forfeited. The one freedom of choice we are not permitted is not to surrender them in the first place. Industrial society is a powerful generator of poverties, which fuel its chase after a form of wealth that can never answer them. Those poverties must be implanted subjectively, so that all human beings feel inadequate and impoverished in the presence of the endless promises of wholeness, healing and fulfilment of industrial society. No wonder we see anger, violence, breakdown, loneliness, addiction and impotence in the rich societies; although, of course, none of these things is apparent at the moment when human beings pass through the invisible frontier of industrial society. Turning their back on known forms of poverty, they do not know that they have a rendezvous with measureless and irremediable deprivations, which have neither name nor price. Indeed, the true price of things is not paid at the point of consumption. That is deferred, passed on, either to the future, or to distant, unseen and powerless others, in parts of the world distant from the places where people consume and enjoy with such conspicuous and showy unconcern.

And here is another anthropological peculiarity. All societies are, to some degree, concerned with the business of pollution and cleansing. These rituals, too, are central within Western industrial life. The pollution created by the intensifying industrialization of the world is conjured away, not primarily by pollution abatement technology, but by the efforts of busy advertising conglomerates, which promote all products as pure, desirable and innocent. Thus we see even the rites and ceremonies that all societies have practised in their desire to propitiate the forces of evil, reading signs and portents in the skies and fields and forests, repeated and mimicked in the technosphere. The singing of commodities and merchandise is the principal cultural activity generated by the West. What this means is that all the disagreeable circumstances that attend the production of things must be washed away. There must appear no pain, no blood, no exploitation, no sweat or suffering associated with their shining appearance in the shopping malls of the world. No one has been dispossessed, no one abused, no one unrewarded in their manufacture; indeed, they are scarcely even identified with manufacture at all; they are wafted into the display cases as if by magic. It also goes without saying that all other distasteful consequences of their production are also eliminated – the resource use and its depletion and damage to the earth, for instance. The insistence on the probity, purity and candour of all products is the function of the universal salespeople. They have the priestly role of making disappear from view all the costs that are an inconvenience or an embarrassment to an accounting system based solely on monetary gain and loss, which are the bounds of its known universe. Profit is all too palpable, but the real losses are swallowed up in outer darkness – the fate of the forest people's leader killed by the mercenaries of companies that want the gold that lies in the earth beneath their living-place; the death from AIDS of the wornout

servicers of long-forgotten urgencies of male desire; the militarization of areas where resources must be prised from the hold of those
who have prudently harvested and managed them for millennia; the
salvaging of economic dissidents – whether the street-children of Rio
de Janeiro or trade unionists in The Philippines; none of this must
tarnish the sanctity of the goods and services in the places where the
rich go in their hunger for a sort of salvation.

Everywhere, industrial society acknowledges its debt to nature; in
strange parodies, deformed mimicry and clumsy re-enactment of
that which it has effaced. Indeed, the defenders of universal industrialization make an even more overweening claim for the system
they promote. Having ousted the world of nature, they seek to show
that industrial society itself is a force of nature. Industrial capitalism
is presented as embodying 'natural laws': the laws of political economy are a reflection of the workings of human nature. Human
nature is fallen; greed and selfishness are the primary motors of all
human action. This idea takes a borrowed legitimacy from the
Christian doctrine of the Fall; but happily, the capitalist system knows
the means of harnessing these selfish characteristics and of turning
them into public good, by means of the creation of wealth. In this
way, economic necessity is not so much the usurper of the laws of
nature, but a working out of them through human institutions. It is
clear that industrial society sets itself up as a permanent substitute for
that which it has destroyed. Capitalism in this way becomes cosmos;
no longer merely one system among many, but the sole legitimate
one, occupying, as it does, the space which Creation itself once did.

The Unsustainable City: Bombay

Bombay appears to be a city constantly on the edge of collapse. The complaints of the middle class evoke a place barely capable, it seems, of supporting life. It is no longer possible to travel by train, because of the overcrowding. You can't travel by taxi either, because the traffic is at a standstill for most of the day. There are robbers and chain-snatchers everywhere. People are flooding into the city for the sake of easy pickings. It has become a haven for criminals, prostitutes and vagabonds. They should be cleared from the sidewalks. It gets worse from year to year, almost from day to day.

Yet the city doesn't collapse. Materially, it is sustained by the pressure it places for resources on an ever-extending hinterland. Bombay creates a widening ring of desolation around itself – including the polluted Arabian Sea. Its survival is at the cost of extractable surpluses from the countryside, which leads to an intensifying chemicalized agriculture there. At the same time, its industrial estates eat more and more deeply into the desertified landscapes along the dusty road to Ahmedabad, with its choking fumes, treeless dust and poisoned waters.

The slums of Bombay are seen by the rich as polluting the city. Yet slum dwellers are negligible polluters compared to those who live in the high-rise flats. The millions of bricks required for the construction of apartments are made from the topsoil of thousands of hectares of fertile fields within a radius of 70 or 80 kilometres of Bombay. With wood no longer available for the production of charcoal for the brick kilns, paddy-husks and vegetable matter are used for fuel, instead of being recycled in the fields, and this leads to a further erosion of fertility. The quarrying of limestone for cement has destroyed the watersheds for which the porous limestone rocks serve as storage reservoirs. With wood supplies around Bombay depleted, big builders were, until recently, obtaining much of their requirement from the Himalayan foothills. Now, that area also being denuded, they find it cheaper to import from other South Asian countries. One developer imports 10,000 tons of timber from Malaysia each year. The sand needed for the preparation of concrete has led to the dredging of several thousand cubic metres each day at Kasheli, which in turn has resulted in the erosion and loss of adjoining agricultural land.

Most of Bombay's water comes from artificial lakes constructed more than 100 kilometres from the city. Huge dams have been built for this purpose, which have displaced many *Adivasis* (tribal people). While the urban population – especially in the rich suburbs – receives an assured water supply for baths, fountains, lawns and private swimming pools, rural districts suffer severe water shortages. The sewage produced by those privileged enough to be connected to Bombay's municipal system is discharged into the sea, along with industrial pollutants and wastes. These have damaged and decreased the catch of the beleaguered fishing communities which still cling defiantly to the foreshore in parts of the city. Excessive nitrogen and phosphates in the sewage lead to a profusion of algae, but when these die, they kill much of the marine, mangrove and tidal life. Indeed, compared to those linked to the sewage system, the poor who defecate on open land are less polluting, for there, the wastes are quickly converted by insects into food for themselves and fertilizer for the soil. Vegetable patches brighten with vivid green all the available spaces in the city, especially between the railway slums and the tracks.

Every year, the monsoon causes floods in Bombay, sweeping away the homes and belongings of thousands of poor people. While Rs200 crores (over £50 million), with World Bank aid, are being spent on anti-flood measures in Bombay, this will help little, since the cause of the floods is not addressed: the covering of land by buildings, roads and concrete is so total that it prevents rainwater from seeping into the soil. It simply runs off into low-lying areas, where the poor live.

Agricultural products from the rural areas taken to Bombay represent an export of soil fertility, since the 'wastes' do not return to the village. Grass and oilcakes from the countryside feed the cows and buffaloes of Jogeshwari, which provide milk for the urban consumer, while the dung they produce pollutes rather than fertilizes. It is claimed that the industrial products of the city more than compensate for this draining and mining of the countryside. The theory is that what comes into the city is transformed into something of enhanced value. While this may be true in monetary terms, in reality the true costs are borne by the impoverished of the city, the environment and especially by the poor of the rural hinterland.

In this sense, Bombay – or any other major world city – is a symbol of the 'development' process. The creation of wealth involves passing on the real, as opposed to the merely monetary, costs elsewhere. How the earth and the people which have to absorb and deal with these costs respond, struggle, live and die, does not trouble those whose business it is to manage this increasingly devastating and destructive model.

The Place of Flowers:

Survival in the City

Pushpavihar is the home of some of the most disadvantaged people in Bombay, a city where over half the population live in slums and shanties.

Pushpavihar is at Borivali, in the north of the city, and was created in the 1960s by a handful of families affected by leprosy. Many had left their villages or had been driven from their homes by the stigma of the disease. Some had become tied to the wandering, mendicant existence which leprosy had imposed upon them. Pushpavihar was, at that time, a rocky barren place, uninhabited and beyond the city boundary.

It is built on a narrow ledge of land, between the railway line and some stone cliffs, which fall about 10 metres to a sluggish trickle of polluted water, which becomes a torrent in the monsoon. In this, the hottest part of the year, the waste-water from the huts at the very edge of the cliff blackens the rocks and collects in stagnant pools below. The people wash their clothes and children swim in this water, which is further contaminated by the effluent from a paint factory and the sludge from a buffalo stable on the edge of the slum. It is a sad environment; swarms of flies hang in the air; the smell of decaying vegetable matter pervades everything. The only amenity is a row of soaring pipal trees, which provide shade and cool the air; their roots force a way through the rocky soil, and at the base of some of them, little shrines have been constructed: a mosaic surface, a stupa covered with crimson powder, an effigy of Krishna.

Since the 1960s, other families have settled here. Leprosy actually offers the people some protection, which other squatter settlements do not have. Their homes are not threatened by the same violent demolitions, because the municipal workers are afraid of leprosy.

91

The community here – now 750 families, almost 5,000 people – is well organized. The *panchayat* (local community government) functions well, and is augmented by six other committee members who are elected annually. There is no crime in the slum and no police station.

In spite of this, the only livelihood open to the people is illegal – the distilling of dharu, or liquor. The prejudice against leprosy is so tenacious that no one will employ those known to be affected, and even relatives of patients are likely to lose their job if it becomes known that they live in Pushpavihar. Children get off the school bus before they reach home, so that their friends will not know where they live. At school, they often give a false address.

But at least this provides a place within the city economy. And there is money to be made out of brewing. The liquor is made in brick chulhas (stoves), constructed in the dried-up river bed, which opens, wide and shallow, beside the railway track. The dharu ferments in large zinc casks, behind a screen of hessian wound round bamboo staves; yellow bubbles of thick foam on top of the vat, bursting and seething under the hot sun. The main ingredients are jaggery (molasses), dal masala and other vegetable substances – orange peel, banana skins. Although the people at Pushpavihar deny that they adulterate the liquor, there are frequent scandals in Indian cities, when people are made ill, or even die, from consuming illegal liquor which has been strengthened, or poisoned, by the addition of battery fluid or industrial alcohol. The people say they can prove the purity of their brew: put a finger in the liquid and then hold it over an open flame: if the finger catches fire, the drink is pure.

Pushpavihar has, in spite of its oppressive environment, prospered in the past twenty-five years. Some people have added an upper storey to their home, or have rebuilt in stone and concrete, with tiled roofs. Geese, hens and goats forage among the wastes. In recent years, some non-leprosy families have made their home here, opened small businesses in the slum: fear of the stigma has been overcome by the opportunity for gain. There is a family of tailors from Tamil Nadu, a dry goods store, a food store where pekoras (snacks) are cooked in shallow iron pots.

Of course, the police have to be paid. They demand Rs175,000 a month, which is paid over by the committee to one individual, whose job it is to negotiate with the police. If he can get them to accept less, he is allowed to retain the difference. Recently, the police had begun weekly raids. It was discovered that the man designated to deal with them had failed to hand over the money. The community detained the man for twenty-four hours, a kind of informal people's justice, until he paid up.

Although the government runs campaigns to inform people that leprosy is not hereditary and that it is curable, there are no official programmes for integrating India's estimated four million sufferers into the mainstream. There are only a few charitable initiatives to rehabilitate long-term sufferers. Sara d'Mello, former headmistress of an exclusive girls' school, a job she gave up to work in Pushpavihar, says, 'Leprosy is a disease of the poor. It is not only curable, but preventable; but that would require a level of social, environmental and health care that is not within the power of any government to guarantee.'

Maruti Bhosle has been in the slum since the early years. To help establish the settlement, he travelled to Delhi and Bangalore, collecting money from other leprosy communities. 'There is a solidarity among leprosy sufferers, because they have had so little assistance from outside. We drew on their experience to help ourselves. There is money to be made from liquor, and that attracts people. Money doesn't have any stigma; nobody asks where it comes from, whether it has been handled by leprosy patients.'

The remoteness of Pushpavihar, in the social sense, means that although there is no shortage of money, there is a problem with lack of education and a sense of isolation. 'People may have a house with a TV, a fridge, they may have gold, their children may be in boarding-school, yet at the same time, there can often be malnutrition in the family, a lack of vitamins or iron. They rarely eat green vegetables or fruit. The struggle is on many fronts – overcoming the inertia of custom and habit, low self-esteem, as well as fighting the efforts of modern commerce to sell Western-style food – biscuits and soft drinks, which have no nutritional value. Western medicine is also widely advertised, and people demand injections as a cure-all. They depend on the drugs of transnational companies which are pushed by chemists with no medical training. Private doctors make a fortune, and no one ever challenges their diagnoses or prescriptions.'

For the first time, some young people are going outside the slum for training. Two young women are boarding at Sion Hospital, where they are studying nursing. But there is a high dropout rate from school. Formerly, no school would take children if they gave an address in Pushpavihar; but now, with a doctor's certificate saying they are not affected by the disease, the schools must take them. Even the municipal hospitals would not admit leprosy patients. Private doctors at least do not turn them away.

Many people here have endured terrible privations and humiliation. Naroli's story is not unusual. She buys dharu from the brewers and takes it to market. She gets up at 3 a.m., which is the only time when the water reaches the public taps of Pushpavihar. She fills the vessels for the day's needs, and then goes to Churchgate station to sell the dharu. She catches the train as it slows down (the driver and signalman get a small bribe for this service). Sometimes, the women fill an inner tube with dharu, and wear it round their waist, so that they will not be intercepted by railway officials and police. Naroli buys the dharu at Rs270 for 20 litres, and sells it for Rs400. Women have traditionally been used as carriers, because they are less likely to be beaten up by the police. Naroli can make up to Rs3,000 a month.

Naroli was diagnosed when she was thirteen. Her family did not want her to stay at home. She was sent to the leprosy hospital at Dharavi in Bombay. This was run by Christian sisters, who were kind to her but wanted her to convert. When her uncle visited her, she told him that since the family had rejected her, she would become a Christian. The uncle beat her and took her back to the village. Her mother and brother had gone to Bombay, and she ran away from her uncle's house to join them. When she arrived, her brother threatened to leave if she stayed. To save her mother from trouble, Naroli married a Muslim, who already had a wife and three children. The family and neighbours then assumed she had left home because she had married a Muslim, not because she had leprosy.

Naroli was badly treated by her husband. They had five children. Eventually, she took the children and left him. She came to Pushpavihar, and with the money she earns, pays for her children's education at boarding school. She is employed as a nurse by the community centre in Pushpavihar, but she still deals in dharu, which is far more lucrative; only now, she can afford to pay someone else to deliver the liquor to Churchgate station.

Early in 1991, Shekhar sent his children away from Pushpavihar to live with his grandparents in central Maharashtra. By doing so, he calculated, they would be spared the stigma of leprosy. When the monsoon came in June, it rained in the village for four days. The dam which was built at the head of the valley became dangerously full. The villagers were warned to leave their houses; but the grandfather, whose house was made of concrete, said nothing had ever happened to make him think there might be any risk to them. The oldest grandson, a child of ten, was afraid, and left with the neighbours when they evacuated their house. Shortly after midnight, the dam burst, and swept the whole village away. The grandparents, and two of Shekhar's children, a boy and a girl, were among the casualties. The ten year old is now back in Pushpavihar. His father is, on the surface, philosophical. What more can happen to me, he says? But he feels that he should never have tried to remove his children from the stigma that he bears; and sees what happened as a kind of retribution for his belief that he could overcome it.

Gita lived near Solapur in Maharashtra. When she was nursing her third child, she found white patches on her skin, and later, because leprosy destroys the peripheral nervous system and sensation is lost, her hands became deformed. She went to the *bhagat* (healer) to find a cure, but her husband said to her, 'You'll have to leave. Your life is over. Don't ruin four other lives.' She pleaded with him, saying it was not her fault. 'I don't know why you have leprosy. But you are a mother; if you do not sacrifice yourself for your children, who will?' He compelled her to go, but promised that he would look after the children, and would never take another wife.

Gita went to Pune, where there is a German-run leprosy hospital. She stayed until she was cured, and then came to Pushpavihar, where she has been for fifteen years. A few months ago, a boy arrived in the slum and asked for her by name. 'Are you Gita Kumar? I am your son.' She said, 'I have no children.' He said, 'I also thought I had no mother.' She wept, and all the neighbours wept with her.

Gita is not angry or bitter. She says, 'God is good to us. How many leprosy patients never see their children again?' Her husband had been true to his word; he had never taken another wife, but had brought up the children alone. The boy studied to the 12th standard and came to Bombay on his own. He has a job, at Rs450 a month, in the wholesale flower market at Dadar. When the father knew his son was going to Bombay, he said to him, 'I told you your mother was dead, but she is somewhere in the city if she is still alive.' The boy had searched for her, and finally located her. He went home to prepare the rest of the family and the neighbours before taking her back. Gita went; but only for a visit. She will not go back permanently. She says that her life is now in Pushpavihar. Her son visits her each week.

Khopade came with his wife from Pune fifteen years ago. Both were leprosy patients. He formerly kept buffaloes, but while he was undergoing hospital treatment, the buffaloes died. Because he had no earnings, he became a sign-painter. He was forced to abandon this too, because leprosy had affected his eyes and he could not see to do the fine work. He came to relatives in Bombay, and now follows the only livelihood open to him, distilling liquor.

While Khopade was in hospital, he used to teach the children, and he became known as Teacher. It was always his dream to become a schoolteacher. He is forced to do work which he finds repugnant, because there is simply nothing else available. Because he and his wife cannot have children – sterility is often a consequence of leprosy – they have adopted a little boy from an orphanage. Pankaj is four. Khopade is determined to give him the education he never had. To get the boy into school, he had to pay a bribe of Rs10,000. He says, 'It is no use people deploring the making of liquor, when there is no choice open to us.' Khopade is a Mahratta, the Maharashtrian warrior caste. He is proud of his origins, but says, 'We have become like the scheduled castes because of leprosy.' He says only adversity can abolish distinctions of caste and religion, as has occurred at Pushpavihar. The only positive result of leprosy is that it dissolves all such artificial barriers between human beings. 'In Pushpavihar, no one thinks of such things.'

It is a cruel fate that drives so many able, intelligent people into the liquor trade. Even so, thrown together by the chance stigma of leprosy, they have learned endurance and tolerance. If their long-term aim of integration into the mainstream is realized, it is impossible not to wonder whether they will take with them the wisdom they have acquired with such pain, or whether it will be submerged in the intractable hierarchies of caste and faith.

Industry in the Third World:

A Tale of Three Factories

Implicit in all assumptions of Western governments is that there is only one way for the rest of the world to follow; and that is the familiar path of the Western countries towards industrialization, the subsequent accumulation of wealth and its attendant well-being. It is, however, quite clear that the experience of the West cannot be repeated in the rest of the world. This does not deter its leaders from repeating that there is no choice for those countries called, with deterministic insistence, 'developing'. Western prescriptions for freedom mean the freedom to go forward in the only way of conceivable to the Western world-view; paradoxically, this absence of alternatives is seen as the surest guarantor of freedom.

What this means in practice is that the countries of the South must open themselves up to Western capital, investment and influence. This will not lead to forms of development prevailing in the West, but will merely institutionalize further the subordination of those countries to the power of the West, and its agents, the transnational corporations.

This is sometimes visible through the cloudy rhetoric of Western politicians. In June 1991, Lynda Chalker, Britain's Overseas Development Minister, announced that Britain was to allocate $80 million to help promote 'good government' in the Third World. She said that Britain has no ideological axe to grind. 'Our policy aims to ensure respect for fundamental human rights [which, it should be pointed out, are never so fundamental as to include the right to livelihood, and hence, of life itself], while increasing aid effectiveness and enhancing development.' Outlining what she considered to be good government, Mrs Chalker said there had to be 'sound economic and social policies', embracing the introduction of market forces and a strong private sector, as well as policies to tackle poverty and illiteracy. Some may call this conditionality,' she said sternly. 'I call it common sense.'

Western ideology, then, is common sense; universal and not even to be called into question. The most dangerous feature of such an ideology is that it does not recognize itself as such, and therefore appears to do its mischief in all innocence. Because it is not ideology, it can never take the blame for any of the consequences of its imposition. This is how the faith borne by an earlier generation of missionaries has been transformed into an equally messianic gospel. The only difference is that the old evangelists had only verbal descriptions of their promises of heaven; the apostles of Western economics have the shining imagery of their more tangible paradise inscribed in the inescapable transmissions of global communications conglomerates.

Obedience of the leaders of the South to these exhortations, conditions and dictates does not lead to the promised liberation of their peoples. What we see everywhere is an intensifying abuse of the South, whether its resource-base, its raw materials or its labour.

Woodard Textiles is in the Free Trade Zone on Penang Island in Malaysia. It is Japanese-owned, and the most automated textile factory in Asia. The cloth produced is 65 per cent terylene, 35 per cent cotton. Terylene is a by-product of petroleum. It arrives in the factory in great bales, whiter than raw cotton. The material has to be broken down, and this is done by a machine that sucks it through green metal tubes and transfers it upwards to the next floor. There are glass panels in the tube, and the separated material in its ascent looks like an inverted snowstorm. At the higher level, it is combed into hanks of thick twine and spun into thread. There is almost no human presence in this process. The machinery is German.

The management is particularly proud of the Mach Coning machinery, which winds the yarn onto cone-shaped spindles: great walls of whizzing, whirring bobbins, so automated that even when the thread snaps, it is repaired by a claw-like simulation of a human hand. Indeed, in this factory, it seems the hands have been swallowed by the machine and recreated in a gleaming metallic mockery of them. There is only one operation still performed manually, 'pulling out', which is done by women for M$16 a day. This, too, will soon be automated. When asked about the fate of the workers, management said they would be 'redeployed'; whether within the textile industry or not was unclear.

The most elaborate machinery is a Japanese winding-machine, which takes the thread onto the bobbins ready for weaving. The machine is about 20 metres long, and the pink plastic bobbins are speedily filled, lifted off automatically, and deposited in a skip at the end of the aisle occupied by the machine. The workers here are essentially machine-watchers, programmers of the pounding, sucking, puffing machinery, with its unearthly mimicry of human effort, stertorous, laboured, unceasing.

The warping shed also contains new Japanese equipment, adjacent to an older model. The new installation is encased in ice-blue metal, and produces the warp much faster. The product is sent on a roller to a frame, where a worker checks for flaws and breakages, and mends them manually.

In the weaving-shed, one person can look after forty looms. In Lancashire, a weaver traditionally oversaw six or eight looms at most. The sound is deafening, and the speed with which the cloth appears deceives the eye. Suction pipes of flexible plastic are strung on metal racks like a giant disembowelling: they promenade up and down the aisles, ingesting the whorls of lint and down that scud across the stone floor. Beyond the reach of these, women are employed as industrial gleaners, to retrieve all the stray wisps of cotton.

The temperature is overwhelming – 35°C. High humidity is required for the cotton so that it doesn't snap. There are four hundred looms; a vast acreage of furious activity, a violent rhythm of shuddering power. In one corner of the weaving-shed, there are some older looms, which produce only one third as much as the latest models; cumbrous, clattering things compared with the demonic energy generated by the new ones. The role of the workers is to monitor the looms, and to be alert instantly to any hitch or breakdown. When this happens, the maintenance staff – the most highly paid of the workers, many of whom have been trained in Japan – are called in to make good the defect.

It is a desolate place, strangely depopulated for a factory, even though the company employs over a thousand people. It has something of the aspect of a plantation – rows of identical objects producing a homogenized product, which diminishes the sparse and cowed humanity that must service them. The finished cloth goes for checking; it rolls across lighted screens, and each part is scanned for flaws by workers, who make a note of the nature of the imperfection. This is fed back to the maintenance teams, who immediately adjust the machinery that is at fault.

Finally, the grey cloth is folded and baled. Some goes for immediate export, the rest to local companies for printing and dyeing, some of which is subsequently exported. A fabric for Marks and Spencer is conspicuous in the display case in the foyer of the factory.

Workers here are still paid by the day, even after fifteen years service. They are also provided with a uniform. Some Japanese working practices were soon abandoned, including early morning exercises, because the staff did not turn up for them. Union members say the largest number of complaints comes from workers who have been abused by management, who compare their devotion to the company unfavourably with that of their Japanese counterparts. 'But the workers in Japan are paid ten times as much as we are. That's why the company is here.' Another worker observed that this is the second time in half a century that Japan has invaded Malaysia, 'but this time, they are using economic weapons.' There is, they say, army-style discipline here. The constant renewal of the machinery intensifies the labour. 'How can you increase output threefold without more and more pressure on the workers?' If they are uncooperative, they are moved to another section where they cannot cope, and then they will resign. Such practices are much resented by the workers.

The increasingly sophisticated machinery has led to a shedding of labour. A new policy offers retirement to the over-forties, with twenty-five weeks' salary in compensation. Many accept this, because they cannot keep up with the accelerating tempo of labour; they are clinging to work by the tips of their fingers in a work process that more and more dispenses with human beings.

The contrast with the Rubberworld factory in Manila is dramatic. This company operates under licence from Adidas, and the manufacture of both Adidas trainers and clothing is very labour-intensive. There are sixty separate processes in the making of a pair of trainers, and as a result, there is not the same frenetic activity as in the capital-intensive unit in Penang. Even so, the logic of the world market has its impact here, too. Since January 1991, there are only 1,500 workers on the permanent staff; the other 5,000 have become contract workers, which relieves the company of expensive responsibilities towards them.

Rubberworld was set up in 1965 by a Chinese entrepreneur, who had begun by selling perfume from a street-stall. He joined with others to create Rubberworld, specializing originally in making sandals, rubber cushions and car-seat covers. Orders came from abroad, and the company manufactured under licence from a number of transnationals. Sixty per cent of the output is now exported. Because of the foreign exchange crisis in the Philippines, the level of production has been reduced, and the number of shifts is down from three to two. The trade union here is recognized by management (in Manila alone, there are over 15,000 enterprises where there are no unions), but the union is concerned that the Philippines is being undercut by even cheaper labour in Indonesia and Thailand. 'The trouble is that we have old-fashioned machinery. However hard we work, we cannot raise output. But if they put in more capital investment, that will simply throw people out of work.' The last thing Manila needs is even more unemployment.

In any case, there is little chance of immediate investment. The company has 1.1 billion pesos of debt, and annually pays 24 million pesos in interest charges alone. There is competition from Reebok and Lotus in the Free Trade Zone of Bataan. The union leaders say that a global imperialism of power and wealth moves in and out of national entities at will. 'Countries are nothing to the transnationals. They form their own empires that are not inhibited by geographical frontiers.' This makes organizing across national boundaries more necessary, but more difficult.

At Rubberworld, the majority of workers are female, especially in assembly, finishing and sewing. There is a growing practice of sub-contracting outside the factory, especially trimming and finishing, which removes responsibility for pay and conditions from the parent company. The plant covers 15 hectares. It is like a small town. There are six units, long sheds, on either side of a tarred road. A conspicuous display-board announces which unit achieved the highest, and which the lowest, output as a percentage of target. Last month, the highest was 73 per cent, the lowest 57 per cent.

The workers are at benches in the crowded hangars, which have corrugated metal shades at the open windows, whirring fans and shadowless strip lighting. Even so, the heat and the smell of the rubber and glue are oppressive. The sole for the trainers is cut by hand with a knife heated on an electric element. The soles are attached to the uppers on aluminium lasts, and then bound together at high temperature in an autoclave. Between the sole and upper, an injection-moulding process inserts a mixture of rubber and PVC into the base of the shoe. This is liquid at the point of injection, and it solidifies as it cools. One of the components of this process – the PVC resin – is imported from the United States. A die press from Japan inserts the foam for the tongue, and fixes it to the upper; quarters, toecap, inside collar, overlay are added in sequence. Some of the materials can damage the eyes, skin and respiratory tract of the workers. Many others are employed sticking transfers and logos onto the finished shoes. One man has a pile of cartoon figures from the TV series *The Simpsons*: the boy of the family is a black-haired urchin, and he is saying from the side of each shoe: 'Underachiever and proud of it.'

The minimum wage for industrial workers in Manila is 118 pesos a day; few of the workers here earn less than 130 pesos. The shift is eight hours, with a 25-minute meal-break and a 15-minute coffee-break. As the shifts change, everyone emerging from the factory is frisked to prevent loss by pilfering. Even if a woman uses a shoelace to tie up her hair, this is an offence. If there is any theft, says management, the appropriate penalty is termination of service.

Lottie checks the collars at the back of the trainer; she earns 137 pesos a day. She has two children, and her husband sends money from Saudi Arabia each month. Abram, from Samar, one of the poorest islands in the archipelago, is embossing logos on the trainers. His family is in the province, and he sends money to them; he sleeps in a room with three other migrant workers. He says he tries not to think about the absurdity of embossing cartoon figures on shoes for privileged foreign children, when he could not afford such things for his own; indeed, he has to live apart from them, and sees them once a year. Rogelio comes from San Miguel in Bulacan, about 100 kilometres north of Manila. He is thirty-one, has three children, and formerly commuted weekly; but since the eruption of Pinatubo, bus traffic has been disrupted and he goes less often. Carla is in her forties. Formerly, she worked in the entertainment industry in Ermita, but as she grew older, she could not make a living. Now she earns 137 pesos a day stitching shoe-collars. The sewing machines at which the women work are from Mitsubishi. Sarah sews the tongue-pieces. She is from Leyte; her husband doesn't have a job and they have four children. He looks after them while she works, which he hates doing; but what choice do they have?

The rubber for the shoes is also kneaded at Rubberworld, rolled out between huge hot cylinders. The dust, steam and heat are overwhelming, and the workers must wear masks. They call this shed 'Saudi Arabia', because of the dust. The temperature is around 40°. Here, they earn 160 pesos a day, in compensation for a working life that will be abbreviated by the destructive conditions in which they labour. Altogether, Rubberworld produces thirty million pairs of trainers each year.

Much assembly and manufacturing work is sought after by Third World countries, because they provide livelihoods. But when, as at Rubberworld, so many of the materials, components and tools have to be imported, the value of the imports is almost equal to, or even exceeds, the value of the exported articles. The PVC resin, imported from Texas, is a petroleum-based material; the sewing machines are from Japan; the royalty is paid to Adidas in Germany. The peso is constantly devalued to make exports more attractive, but this makes imports more costly. Such factors can wipe out the advantages to the Third World countries of being used as assembly and manufacturing sites for the transnationals.

Furthermore, there is constant pressure on the unions – where these are permitted – to see the reason of management, whose own power is dependent on the subordinate role of the Philippines in the international division of labour. Even the most liberal of managements can only take them into the confidence of their own impotence in an increasingly integrated world.

Kamani Tubes. India, perhaps more than any other country, has until now resisted pressures of global integration; and although recent governments have capitulated to the remorseless tide of neo-liberalism, those who resist can still draw on indigenous traditions of self-reliance.

Kamani Tubes Limited at Kurla in north Bombay is a worker-owned co-operative, taken over in 1988 after years of mismanagement and neglect by its private owners. It makes non-ferrous tubes and rods, supplying a variety of industries. Using incredibly archaic machinery, and the skills and commitment of its workforce, it offers a model of what can be done in the wake of the disastrous indifference and profligacy of those who had brought the company to ruin. In the post-Independence era, the Kamani Group had been one of Bombay's major companies.

D. Thankappan of the Kamani Employees Union is one of the leaders of the pioneering initiative, and is working to extend the example to other companies written off by traditional commercial criteria. Thankappan points out that in India, only 9 per cent of labour is in the organized sector. 'In other words, 91 per cent are unorganized. And even that 9 per cent shows a decline of 1 per cent over the past ten years. You cannot organize in the traditional way in India, you cannot apply a Western hierarchial trade union model to the mass of unorganized labour. And in any case, in the last twenty-five years, we've seen the labour movement oriented only to the economic aspects of organizing, ignoring the social, political and cultural impact of work on people and their communities. In the unorganized sector, you cannot separate work from all the other aspects of life; all must be integrated into a single struggle. Such organizing involves existing trade union activity plus *something else*; and that means the social and cultural components of life, which have been taken up by the women's movement, civil rights activists, lawyers, journalists, environmentalists. The trade union viewpoint is that only the organized sector can protect the individual and put pressure on government. Yet they cannot do anything, because they are no longer a radical force; they have been bought off.

'What happened to Kamani is repeated with thousands of companies in India. When Mrs Gandhi came back to power in 1980, the policy of government baling out sick industries changed; and as a result, from 1982 to 1987, the number of sick units leapt to 24,000 a year, most of them in the small-scale sector. In face of this, what can the organized sector do? They can't pressure government to take over. Workers in the organized sector cannot influence more than forty constituencies politically in the whole country, and they are all only in city areas. On their own, they can elect no more than ten or twelve representatives to parliament. Government can ignore them. If the unorganized were more radical, it would be a different story. Because of its impotence, the working-class movement feels helpless to fight factory closures. That is why unemployment is rising. The government's "Exit Policy" can only lead to more widespread unemployment.'

It was in this context that the Kamani takeover took place. When it was first suggested, the organized trade unionists said, 'But you are making the workers capitalist' or 'How can a complicated industry be run by workers?' The union was accused of utopianism. It was unimaginable. But three years later, unions all over India are finding inspiration in the Kamani example, unions controlled by such diverse political groups as the Communists, Congress(I) and Shiv Sena. Legislation introduced in 1985 by V. P. Singh under the Rajiv Gandhi government made it possible; but the Kamani union was the first to find its way through the labyrinth of obstacles and bureaucracy to give it concrete shape.

'Trade unions have always believed it was management's job to run industry', says D. Thankappan, 'not the unions. And management believed their skills were beyond the comprehension of the workers. These set views have been eroded by the takeover. The Bombay unions have formed an organization called Workers' Solidarity against Job Losses and Industrial Closure. In Delhi, a Centre for Workers' Management was set up in April 1991. We have to demystify management. We are developing management courses in a participatory style, to train worker activists.'

Kamani Tubes now employs six hundred people. The Kamani Group started in the mid-1940s just before Independence, and was closely involved in national development infrastructure – transmission line towers, electrical installations. Kamani Tubes was established in 1959, providing tubes for sugar machinery, condenser tubes, air conditioning and refrigeration tubes. By 1963, Kamani enterprises ranked number 37 in the industrial houses of India. The founder, who was highly regarded, died in 1964. His eldest son took over, and he ran the company until his death in 1972. His brother inherited, and this led to a family crisis and quarrel, which ultimately ruined the company. The quarrel was over the sharing of the spoils. Money was transferred to a Swiss account by another brother, who then emigrated to the United States. Each brother who was in control of the various factories tried to siphon a maximum of money from each unit.

There was a Bank of India enquiry, after which additional finance was provided for the company, and it limped on until 1980, when it came to a standstill. There were subsequent disputes and lawsuits, a tangle between government, the banks, the family and the courts. In 1984, the company came to a halt once more. This time, power and water were cut off. No wages had been paid for fourteen months. The union eventually petitioned the Supreme Court. The family wanted to sell, but as there was no buyer, the union came under pressure to formulate an alternative, which it did. 'We asked, "Why can't Kamani sell to us?" Most lawyers thought we didn't have a case in law – owners cannot be forced to sell. But a Delhi lawyer drew up our petition to the Supreme Court. It created an important precedent, and was finally approved in September 1988.'

After three years, the workers are on 85 per cent of wages, about Rs1,300 a month. The most buoyant area has been orders for tubes for the sugar-refining industry. The factory itself covers several hectares, a compound shaded by trees and gardens, although the places where people work are dirty and oppressive, and the machinery is of great antiquity. Much of it is from Britain, imported as part of an aid package in the 1960s, with the help of Commonwealth loans. Even then, the machinery was already fifty years old, and had been discarded and reconditioned. The names of defunct manufacturers shine on worn metal plates – Fielding and Platt, Yorkshire Imperial Metals, Bullivant, Birmingham, GWB, Dudley. Some of the machinery was not adequately reconditioned. P. D. Nayar, former maintenance manager, who left the company in 1982, but returned to help with the workers' initiative, says, 'We have an extrusion press which we used for fifteen years. All that time, we were working below capacity, because there had been a fault in the repairs. We had been at a disadvantage all those years. Nobody cared, because after all, it was only material going to the Third World, they couldn't be expected to notice. We had it repaired properly and have improved efficiency. Our order books are full, there is work for nine months. There are no losses and no profits; we are just breaking even.'

The workplace itself arouses conflicting feelings. The space is filled with the shrieking and squeaking of archaic machinery: the heat and noise are reminiscent of descriptions of the nineteenth century in Britain: an eerie sense of visiting our own history. At the same time, there is a curious contradiction – what were felt in the West to be intolerable industrial horrors are seen here as the best hope of salvaging a decent living for the workers. The prospect of work, even in these conditions, is seen as the surest guarantee of survival.

Metal billets are cast from the required alloy mix and cut into slugs ready for the extrusion process. The furnace is pre-heated to a temperature of 800°; huge, bulbous containers, which emit enormous heat; and through the mouth of them a white-hot incandescence illuminates the glistening bodies of the workers. The slug is drawn from the furnace by individuals using a kind of forceps on a long pole, and is placed into the extrusion press, which punches out the core of the slug and then draws it. The extruded metal is expelled from the machine, a long red snake, which descends onto a metal chute, where the workers straighten it with hooked poles; the metal quickly cools to a dull grey. The tube then goes for hydrostatic testing, is steam-cleaned and electromagnetically tested. Finally, it is annealed to the required temper. These tubes, of diameter varying from 4 inches to a ¼ inch, are used to make pneumatic cylinders for pressure machines, radiator tubes, hand-pumps for deep wells.

Many of the workers are middle-aged or elderly. It has required great tenacity to stay with the company through so much uncertainty. Although the workers are skilled, there has been little updating of their abilities, just as there has been little enhancement of the machinery, although a spectrometer was recently acquired to reduce laboratory testing time, and some German machinery has been installed in the rod-making shed, which speeds up the process. But the workers remain vulnerable and exposed to dangerous practices: as the hot billet comes from the furnace in the rod-making section, it is handled by a worker wearing only an asbestos glove for protection. It catches fire briefly as he handles each one. Everywhere the sparks and the heat threaten the exposed limbs and torso of the workers. In spite of this, their commitment to the company remains; they know that the alternative would be unemployment.

J. K. Arvind is managing director. He insists that this role will be limited until the co-operative has formed into a stable and self-sufficient entity. His function is only transitional. He says that the non-ferrous industry has not changed in the last forty years, even in the West. 'The only difference is that in the West, people think they have to replace everything over ten years old, which is a criminal waste of resources. You replace stuff that is perfectly serviceable. The installed productive capacity of the world is twenty-five times greater than what is actually produced. It is clear that replacement of things has a purpose other than efficiency. The money wasted in this way could be diverted into more useful work internationally.

'Modern industry labours to increase transactions, so many intermediate processes that people lose sight of the overall purpose of their work. That becomes counter-effective – alienation of workers, lack of interest in what they are producing. This is where Gandhi was right – he perceived that minimal levels of interaction are best. The so-called international market is a big hoax. It has nothing to do with efficiency, even less with equity; it is a means of concentrating more and more wealth in fewer hands.

'We are the only unit with such a low cost of plant and machinery for our output. We want to show that you don't have to get into a competitive race for capital investment in order to make a living in the world, because that just throws more and more people out of work. If that can be done here, it can be done anywhere. I see no difference between India and the rest of the world – the international market plays on shortages that are deliberately generated by obsolescence, waste and dissatisfaction. In India, we have shortages through helplessness. The deliberate creation of them is far worse. It is a matter of concept: my car is a 1968 model. We are used to repairing and maintaining things in India, we expect cars to have a life of twenty-five years. The expenditure economy is replacing the conserving economy, and that is supposed to be development. It is actually a crime against the poor and a crime against the future of humanity.

'The consumerist mentality will not take off here to the extent it has elsewhere. I predict there will be a big fall in consumer goods here. For instance, once people have a TV, they won't rush to buy another. They won't replace them, because we're used to maintaining and repairing everything. Borrowing and spending beyond our means soon runs up against the spectre of real poverty.

'It is too early to say whether we will succeed at Kamani Tubes. We are starting to survive. The managing committee of the co-operative must become cohesive; we must resist takeover from someone else. I'm only a stop-gap defender against extraneous forces; when the co-operative can defend itself without me, I'll be happy. The eyes of many industrialists are upon us. They don't want us to enjoy outstanding success; moderate success they can live with. They want us to adopt their methods of management. We're not averse to that, but instead of giving the money to just one person, we will give it to six hundred fellows.

'Profit-making is not very important to start with; plurality in management and ownership is the crux of the independent co-operative. Our survival is the first concern. Making money is not the sole objective. You evaluate an organization on its life-span, not on an annual balance-sheet.'

Kamani Tubes is an attempt to escape the compulsions of 'rational-ization' in an irrational system, of 'modernization' in a world that has elevated wasteful and gratuitous change into high principle. It is the destructive and perverse logic of competitive global markets that evicts human beings from settled ways of life everywhere, destroys stable livelihoods and allows no rest to those disturbed in this way. Sufficiency and security must be submerged by driven forms of growth and 'development', which create a double prodigality – the squandering of both material and human resources.

Regenerating the Countryside

Ralegan Siddhi is a village in the Ahmednagar District of Maharash-tra, about 70 kilometres from Pune. It is in a rainshadow area, with less than 250 mm of rain a year. The surrounding landscape is bleak and barren; only a few trees in the water hollows and strips of cultivation, bajra and jowar. Decrepit villages cling to the empty slopes; thin cattle and pitiful shelters. The highway from Pune has helped to colonize this degraded land with industry, which has filled in many of the evacuated fields and abandoned farmsteads. The factories are substantial buildings and provide some employment for those who once subsisted on these arid hills. There are units making automobile parts, wire-drawing, plastics; incongruous superimposi-tion of industrial structures on a barren countryside – an image of 'development', and one that seems to contain the promise that we can live, by means of human ingenuity, quite independently of the natural world that we have spoiled.

Ralegan Siddhi appears in this human-made desert like a mirage. The slopes around the village have been afforested, the *kharif* (rain-fed) crop of the villagers is strong and tall – bajra (millet), sunflowers, vegetables; there are orchards of pomegranates, mausumbi, lemons and mangoes. The houses in the scattered village settlement are clean, whitewashed buildings, a mixture of traditional and modern. The ruins of the older village still stand – stone walls, dark, window-less reminders, overgrown with grass and flowers, of the time when Ralegan Siddhi was like its neighbours, a village without hope, a place to migrate from.

Until the mid-1970s, Ralegan Siddhi lost most of the limited rain-water that fell during the monsoon; the water simply ran off the rocky, treeless hillsides. It had become impossible for most villagers to support themselves. People had become dependent on money-lenders who charged rates of interest as high as 10 per cent a month. The income of most families was so low that they never got out of debt; and basic foodstuffs had to be bought in from outside.

Anna Hazare was born in a poor family in a neighbouring village. His parents had tried selling coconuts and flowers, but had been unable to make a successful living. Hazare went to Bombay as a young man and worked with the vigilantes protecting the poor against the attacks of *goondas* hired by landlords to harass them and drive them from their shelters. He joined the army as a driver during the Indo-Chinese war. Every year, when he came home on leave to his native place, he observed the deteriorating conditions, the degradation, not only of the land, but of the people also. There was only a primary school in the village, and the level of literacy was low. People were reduced to making liquor or breaking stones on the road, under the government's employment guarantee scheme for a few rupees a day.

The forestland had become infertile over generations, with the removal of the tree cover, erosion and drought. Most people had about 2 acres of unproductive land, and only a few were landless. During the mid-1970s, Anna Hazare had been involved in a road accident driving an army truck, and he saw in his survival a sign that he had been spared to perform *janseva*, service for his home-place.

He retired from the army and came to Ralegan Siddhi. He called together the youth of the village – about forty young people – and asked them how long they expected to carry on living as they did. By this time, the principal economic activity in the village had become the liquor trade, in illegal *bhattis*, or stills, which the people brewed for sale on the highway, in order to be able to buy food. At the same time, many of the villagers had become addicted to alcohol. The young men then called together all the dealers in dharu and explained to them that change was necessary and possible. The people themselves knew the work was degrading, but they said, 'How else are we to provide for our families? Nothing comes from our fields. What choice do we have?'

People had little faith that change was an option. Many young men had joined the army as an escape, but of those who remained, most had joined an older generation in becoming *bhatti*-operators. A few of them listened to Anna Hazare and tried to change their occupation – buying a few limes or onions for sale. Since the popular movement, the Maharashtra Gandhi Smarak Nidhi, had been working to get people out of the alcohol trade, a Gandhian recommended Anna Hazare's efforts to the Maharashtra government, and the government made a contribution to help diversify the village economy.

Some of the *bhatti* operators were able to buy a cow or buffalo to start a dairy business. But there were about half a dozen who could leave the production of alcohol, but could not overcome their own addiction. Anna Hazare and the youth of Ralegan Siddhi took the law into their own hands: the drinkers were tied to a pole in the centre of the village in front of the temple. There was no beating; just the public shame. Three were shamed into giving it up; between 1974 and 1976, drinking was stamped out in the village. Today, not only is there no alcohol, but no cigarettes, no *bidis*, not even *paan* (betel nut).

As alcohol was being eliminated, there had to be a practical demonstration of an alternative way of living. The principal means of this was watershed development, the construction of small check-dams and percolation tanks in the hills around, which would prove that the water could be harvested and used to make the fields fertile. There is now a carefully managed irrigation system; dazzling blue kingfishers and coloured dragonflies swoop over the canals, and most people make a more than adequate living from their land.

The next priority was education. There is now a flourishing secondary school, to which children from all the surrounding villages come. There is also a hostel for about 150 boarders. The school was built by *Shramdan*, which is community service. This means that labour is given freely by the villagers themselves; a practice that operated not only in the building of the school, but also in the construction of the percolation tanks and small-scale dams.

Before the school was built, the Minister of Rural Development came to see the project, and gave Rs500,000 (about £12,000). If it had been commercially constructed, the cost would have been Rs2,000,000. People helped with material, labour, carpentry, masonry; only a few specialist skills came from outside the village.

The teachers at the school are expected to live in the village, because the curriculum embraces not only the obligatory government programme, but also a much extended range of activities, designed to recreate a sense of the worth and value of rural life. Traditional farming practices are taught, as well as natural forestry and the richness and vitality of rural culture. The school is seen as a focal point for change.

Ralegan Siddhi is a special case, but only because there is no graft or corruption. The money that comes here is only what is due to all villages; but because of mismanagement and fraud, only a fraction of it actually reaches most communities. Limited government funds have been increased fourfold by the use of *shramdan*.

When people come together in a common purpose, to build and to create, their differences fade. There are about two thousand people in Ralegan Siddhi, a sizeable village. There are 325 houses, with 120 families from the backward classes. All castes mix here, eat together, worship at the same temple, attend each other's weddings. Inter-caste marriage has not yet occurred, but many feel that it is only a question of time. There are 'community weddings', whereby several couples marry at the same time: they can pool expenses, and not overspend on a single celebration. There is no untouchability. Twenty families from the backward classes have received loans to help them start some enterprise; people with particularly unproduc-tive land were helped to get wells, motors, pipelines to improve the crop yield. Even so, it was found that there was still not enough water in the well to improve the fields of some farmers, who after five or six years still could not repay the bank loan. The bank was going to re-possess the land, but because they were *harijan* families, the rest of the village came together in solidarity, and with *shramdan*, worked on the fields, brought the water from elsewhere, and helped them to use the land more productively.

As *kharif* (rainfed) crops, people grow bajra (millet), sunflower, mungphali (groundnuts); as *rabi* (winter crop), wheat, onions, jowar (pulses). Because water is the most critical resource, variety with a minimum use of water is sought. Sugar-cane is forbidden, because of the heavy demand it makes on water, although sugar-cane is, per-versely, one of the main crops of Maharashtra, in places where big landowners can pre-empt the water supply.

When Anna Hazare came here, only 60–70 acres were irrigated; now it is nearly 2,500; by means of small dams on the slopes, percolation tanks and check-dams at strategic points, the wells of the people fill up, irrigation is possible and there is minimal loss of rainwater. The prosperity that has come to the farmers is visible all around. The houses are built of stone, with cool, tiled floors and electric fans. Many people own a bicycle, a radio and even TV. The village streets are clean and free of garbage. The temple, in a room adjacent to which Anna Hazare lives, has been extended, a forest of pink and blue pillars, paintings of Hindu deities on wall-panels.

Anna Hazare says that government money is accepted, because that is the people's own money. But he will not accept anything from charities or aid agencies. When the Tata Trust sent a considerable sum, the villagers agreed to return it. He does not see the villages prospering on donations, but on self-generated *shramdan* and proper government funding. 'This should be every village's right, if they are not cheated by officials and bureaucrats. The people have created Ralegan Siddhi. Self-confidence should be restored to the people, *apnavishwas*. When people lose faith in themselves and their own powers, that is when degradation begins.'

The *panchayat* of Ralegan Siddhi are all women. The head is Shantabhai Namdev Mapare, who runs a general store, an open-fronted concrete building, with green-painted walls along which stand sacks of rice, cereals and pulses, tins of biscuits, soap and now, in August, *rakhi*, in preparation for the festival when girls and women will give their brothers bracelets as tokens of affection. The *panchayat* take decisions on the implementation of all government schemes and is elected for five years. Every two months the Gram Sabha meets, which consists of a member of every family in the village; in this forum, all people's suggestions and schemes are presented. Shantabhai was born in a neighbouring village, and came to Ralegan when she married. She says in other villages women have no rights, and it is unknown for the whole *panchayat* to be female. She believes women are more effective than men as agents for social justice. But in any case, she adds, there is little crime here. If people quarrel, they are brought together within the community. Both parties are called to the temple, and there is a discussion on who is to blame and which is the injured party. The wrongdoer's punishment is to ask forgiveness in front of the whole Gram Sabha. If, for instance, someone cuts down a tree in the village, the punishment is to plant a hundred new trees.

As we stand talking to Shantabhai, a *sadhu* from another village, Baba Garib Das from Jambli, in Pathurdi Taluka, stops in front of the shop. He says in his village they have also stopped tree-cutting and alcoholism, but as yet, they have found no work to replace the brewing of liquor. They now feel at a loss as to how to initiate more positive activities. He says, 'The flies are attracted to the light until the light goes out.' He has come to Ralegan Siddhi 'marg darshana', to be shown the way.

The school is an imposing building, painted cream and pink. Its reputation is growing as a place where children are not alienated from their rural roots. As a group of fifteen year olds come out of school, they say that they want to be community workers, agricultural workers, they want to help improve their village. Their energy has not been trapped into the feelings of inferiority that overtake so many villages, the sense that only in the cities do exciting things happen. Indeed, the teachers say that the cultural values that accompany mainstream education are urban, and undermine rural people's faith in themselves and in their ability to change or control their lives.

The school is run with almost military efficiency. Those in the hostel assemble on the parade ground at 5.00 a.m., and for two hours there is physical training, sports and running under the instruction of two retired army officers. After that, they have a glass of milk and sugar. After a shower, breakfast is at 8.00 – halwa and chapattis. The diet is carefully balanced – dal and lobia (beanstew) and jowar bread at lunchtime, and fresh vegetables and rice in the evening.

The non-government curriculum takes place from 8.30 to 11.30, when the essential learning takes place – village regeneration, agriculture; and the obligatory curriculum form 11.30 to 5. After that, they are free for 2 ½ hours, until dinner at 7.30. They study between 8 and 9, and bed-time is 10 o'clock. The school is original, in that the less able students get the most attention; the teachers say that the clever ones can make their own way. Those who do not have the same facility for learning need to be cherished and encouraged. As a result of this, there are now children in the hostel from Bombay, Pune, from Gujerat and Madhya Pradesh, as well as from the immediate neighbourhood. There is a wide range of sports, including kabbadi, khoklo, kusti, volleyball, running and football. The teachers say that the villages of India remain cut off, in spite of the spread of TV; most will know little of the problems of Punjab or Kashmir: their own labour and survival takes all their time. People do not really want to leave the village: it is despair and inability to make a living that have driven people from the villages; it is social injustice, casteism; it is debt and environmental degradation. In Ralegan Siddhi the sad procession of humanity in search of a better life in city slums has been arrested, at the only place where this is possible – at source. The young people, boys in Ghandi topee and girls in blue skirts and red hair-ribbons, radiate an intelligence and attachment to the countryside that have nothing to do with 'backwardness'. The next move is to start a college, where teachers can be trained; this will contribute to self-reliance, so that eventually, the young people growing up here will not have to go away to find meaning and fulfilment, but may find them in the renewed landscapes of the richness and variety of daily village life. The degradation of land goes hand in hand with the degradation of humanity, as Vandava Shiva observes of the Punjab. You cannot renew villages by mining and exporting their soil fertility, nor by urbanizing them. They have to be organic, functioning entities.

Shekhar Pathari runs a small hotel in the village, selling pekoras, snacks and tea; he is making jellabi, and as he works, he talks of the changes that have transformed the village since he was a boy. He had never dreamed that such transformation was possible. He has installed benches and tables under the verandah around the teashop;

some workmen are resting and taking a midday meal. Shekhar Pathari also has land where he grows vegetables; there is a pile of beans that he has just harvested. He has one son in the army, and another who works on his own piece of land. His two daughters are married and their husbands have come to the village, which is contrary to traditional practice.

Opposite the hotel, there is a row of five workshops, yellow-painted with bright blue doors. These were built as a project of the Gram Panchayat, to help those who remained below the poverty line. Ganpath was a labourer outside the village until a few months ago. Now he has a shoemender's shop. There is also a tailor, a carpenter, an electrical worker and a vegetable store. Further along the street are the abandoned walls and decrepit cavities of the old houses, which, it seems, nobody has wanted to restore.

In the village street, the women who have just harvested the green moog lentils are separating the pea-green pulses from ripe black pods. An elderly woman in a dark blue saree winnows the lentils; she pours them, a green cascade, from her sieve, into a basket on the ground; the black chaff and dust are carried away on the breeze, and the vegetables fall in a green pyramid in the basket. The pods will be fed to cows and buffaloes.

There are no big landlords in Ralegan Siddhi, and no sense of social injustice. In the small post office building there is a branch of the Bank of Maharashtra, which grants loans to the people. Twenty villages have branches in Ahmednagar district; but in Ralegan Siddhi the repayment rate is significantly higher than elsewhere. The little office is just a desk behind a grille, a pile of dusty ledgers in which all entries are made by hand.

In the temple *chowk* (courtyard) there is a fig-tree, and the pole where the drunks were tied. The pastel-painted dome of the temple dominates the square. Anna Hazare was awarded the Padma Shri medal by the president in 1990; a year later, he threatened to return it because of corruption. When Hazare first came here, the temple bell had been sold and the pillars taken for the bhattis. Now, nothing is ever stolen from the temple, and the door is left open night and day. The temple was also reconstructed by *shramdan*.

Even the poorest live in properly constructed houses, in a crescent behind the stream, small brick shelters, with little concrete terraces in front, and shaded by fig-trees. The people here are landless. They had previously left the village to do labouring work elsewhere, but they came back when they saw the transformation that had occurred. Their houses were also constructed with the help of the better-off villagers. The landless work making jharn brushes, which they weave

115

from dead palm leaves peeled from the trunks of the trees. One family can make fifty of these in a day, and they are sold for Rs5 each. Parvati, a woman in her thirties, came back to Ralegan Siddhi, because she knew there would be a house for her. She has planted a chickoo tree, beneath which she weaves the palm leaves, while the young children play on the concrete square.

Congress-grass has invaded the area, wiry stalks with tiny white flowers. This is not an Indian species, but was imported with some seedlings from the United States, and has now spread over wide areas of Maharastra. It is toxic to cattle. The fields are full of ripening crops; around the margins, pumpkins, red peppers and tomatoes. Bajra is ready for harvesting; sometimes called 'bulrush plant', it has cone-shaped heads, with thick stalks and broad leaves. An onion field has just been transplanted, and the yellow heads of sunflowers in bloom shake in the warm wind. Tamarind trees provide shade, and wild flowers – the white lilies and the pale bells of dhatura – attract violet and black butterflies. All plots of land are privately owned, and each family decides what to grow; only sugar-cane is prohibited. There is solar street-lighting, there are solar pumps, heaters and cookers.

There have been limited plantings of subabul, which will be grown for making agricultural implements, for furniture and housing; and in front of the school there is a ceremonial row of ashoka trees. But most of the reforestation has been a regenerative, natural forestry, including babul, which grows commonly here, neem, the twigs of which are used as toothcleaners, nilgiri and mango, papaya.

Of the achievement at Ralegan Siddhi, Dinesh Kumar of the Centre for Science and Environment in New Delhi says that free labour of the villagers saves the biggest single cost of development programmes. 'Out of every 100 rupees, labour takes about 70, materials 20 and transport 10. When you have voluntary labour, one major element of corruption is eliminated. Officials and contractors employ ghost-workers, which uses up large sums of money. When villagers work for themselves, that 100 rupees effectively becomes 170. What happened at Ralegan Siddhi could occur elsewhere if corruption were cut out. In that sense, it is a very hopeful example.

'There is no doubt that without Anna Hazare there would not have been so spectacular an improvement. He has been a good leader. Indians do look up to leaders, so long as they speak the people's mind and are not imposing something on them. The village was transformed, first of all by watershed work; secondly, the moral transformation of the people, the giving up of liquor and collective labour programme. Then came the fight against corruption. If this had been done at an earlier stage, it would have collapsed.'

Of course, there is a problem with the discipline with which Hazare carried out the changes. 'Hazare is a mini-Gandhi. He has no assets, is not corrupt. He travels everywhere by bus. He has no longing for power. Local leaders don't seek power, which is why it is right that local initiatives should be fostered. There have been attempts to hijack the work by politicians, the BJP among others. He went on a *maunvrat*, a silent fast earlier this year [in 1992] against corruption. In Ralegan Siddhi, as with Chipko, the women have always been at the centre of the changes. Where men are involved, they always have their own priorities. Yet the sufferers of environmental degradation and economic loss are women. Women think up new means of achieving justice. Hazare went to the women and said, "If there is more family income because you now have water, where will the money go?" The women said, "Not to us." The women took the decision that there should be no liquor shop. Men go out to work, but it is women who must walk up to 10 kilometres for fuel or water. Men migrate and women are left to cope as best they can.'

Ralegan Siddhi is an oasis of human-made regeneration in a human-made desert. It seems that we have to destroy the earth in order to prove that it is essential to our well-being. 'The West is now cleaning and patching up its own environment, and in the process, destroying other people's. This is environmental colonialism – blame the poor, ask them not to develop, and at the same time, take their resources for the further polluting development of the West. What is happening is that in the West, the environmental movement takes the conserving crusade upon itself; and it is left to an unchanged economic system to do the exploiting. And the poor suffer. The experience of Ralegan Siddhi shows that it doesn't have to be like this. It could be replicated in any, in all, the villages of India.'

SEED, RAJASTHAN

The road from Udaipur crosses the degraded Aravali Hills, many of them bare of trees, others with a thin cover of toor and kikar, planted along the contours to prevent further erosion. Some of the hills are bare stumps of jagged red rock. Beside the Zinc Smelting plant just outside Udaipur, it is impossible to distinguish between the ruined natural topography and the human-made heaps of waste.

By February, the land is looking parched; many of the brooks have dried up; a bleached landscape, with thin grass burnt to a pale straw, the trees faded by a coating of dust. The terrain is bleak and stony, eroded beyond productive use in many places. Where there is irrigation, there are vivid patches of cultivation – wheat or sarson, a lemon-coloured oilseed. In the sun-drained landscape, the most vivid colours are in the turbans of the men and the sarees of the women, who, under a heavy headload of fuelwood, sway gently beneath their sarees of crimson, orange and scarlet, as dazzling as the occasional shower of cerise bougainvillea spilling from a whitewashed wall.

A fork in the road beyond the little town of Kanor, some 85 kilometres from Udaipur, separates the villages of Seed and Setwana. Setwana is reached by a bumpy track, about half a kilometre from the road. Here there are a hundred families, a population of about six hundred. The village is distinctive; not so much because it is conspicuously richer than those around it, but because it is well tended, clean and fragrant, and exudes an air of more than usually purposeful activity. The houses are built close together, each raised on a hardened mud base, of stone, coated with mitti, or earth, which when it dries reflects a hint of rose colour in the pale sun. The roofs of the houses are latticework of branches, and on this, hand-made tiles which are fabricated in the village. The walls of the houses are thick to keep them cool. Some of the houses have verandas to provide shade; these are propped up by rough pillars of wood, bleached white as bone. The cattle stalls are well stocked with fodder and straw, stalks of sarson and bunches of ripe gram, from which children have eaten all the seeds.

The occupations of the people are very visible. In a small brickyard, a family are making roof-tiles and bricks. They mix the dark, rust-coloured earth with water, shape the tiles with a deft movement of the hand and leave them in the sun to dry before hardening. Mud is used mainly as a coating for the walls, which are made up of layers of flat stones. The village potter sits at his wheel: a circle of stone about six inches thick, with a hole into which he inserts a stick to make it spin. He then throws a shapeless handful of wet clay onto the wheel; as it revolves, his hands caress the mound until it changes its shape, now a vase, now a jug, now a broad-topped open vessel, now a slender-necked container for water. In the street, a man is making string from bark, with a crude charka which he turns to toughen the fibre as he draws it. Elsewhere, a bullock cart is being made; the crude wooden spokes of the wheel are inserted, the platform with its shallow sides that will hold the firewood, children going to school, dung, sarson, vegetables, a load of fodder overhanging both sides so that it completely blocks the main road and nothing can overtake it.

Around Setwana and Seed, the landscape changes dramatically.

Amid the monochrome desolation, there are islands of vibrant green, patches of wheat, hillsides reforested trees now 6–10 feet high, grass, oilseed, fruit trees, mango and papayas. Twenty years ago, the whole area was arid, rocky and uncultivated. It was a poor, tribal village, whose people had been unable to make a living from the deforested land, and who had no other livelihood than brewing dharu, illegal liquor, from mahua flowers, and stealing. The process of dispossession had begun with the British and continued after Independence, as the state government simply sold to contractors the forests on which the people traditionally depended. The resulting denudation had destroyed and degraded the traditional life-ways, as it had obliterated the once richly forested landscape. Many of the older men, dignified and respected elders now, tell how they would waylay and rob strangers of their clothes for a few rupees, had been addicted to drink, regularly used to beat their wives and children.

The community has been regenerated through the influence of Gandhi and of Vinobha Bhave, a Gandhian and social reformer, who was the initiator of the *bhoodan* movement, whereby rich landlords were persuaded to distribute their surplus land to the poor.

Rameshwar Prasad has been one of the principal actors in the transformation. He tells how, when Vinobha Bhave visited the district in the late 1950s, he had gone to hear him speak. The meeting had finished, so he followed Bhave to where he was lodging, and asked his advice on regenerating the village and the life of its people. Bhave had said, 'Work for your village yourselves; do not depend upon the government or expect them to do anything for you. The villages of India are self-reliant in food; make them become self-reliant in as many other ways as you can.'

Thirty years later, Seed has become a model of self-governance. The community is registered under the Rajasthan Gramdan Act, a unique piece of legislation inspired by Bhave, which gives executive and legal powers to the *gram sabha* (the village council, which consists of the entire adult population). The *gram sabha* has full control over the land within its boundary, even land that formerly came under the purview of the forest and revenue departments.

The restoration of the village commons has been perhaps the most spectacular achievement, particularly at a time when so much of the commons of India are being privatized and compelled into the destructive necessities of the market economy. The *gram sabha* has divided the village commons into two categories – that where grazing and leaf collecting are banned, and that where grazing is permitted, but where tree, and even leaf-cutting, are prohibited. Even trees on private land can be cut only if the *gram sabha* decides that this is absolutely essential for the economic survival of the family.

The *gram sabha* elects an executive committee (*karyapalika*), and a chairperson (*adhyaksh*), and there are six committees which oversee different spheres of activity – crop loans, forestry, nursery development, water resources, disputes and development. The committee consists of representatives of the whole community, and women are equally represented.

In Seed, in the small concrete shelter where the committees meet, some of the members of the *karyapalika* have set up a shrine to Gandhi and Vinobha Bhave. They make an offering to me of village-spun thread, a coconut and a rupee coin. They place the red chandan on my forehead; and then offer me the aluminium plate so that I can pay homage with the chandan to Gandhi and Bhave, by making the red print on the glass covering their portraits over their forehead, and garland them with the holy wool.

We sit on a handwoven mat, as they explain how the village committee works. Seed has legal powers to plan its own resources, to implement its decisions, and to judge and punish when its rules for conservation are infringed. Records are meticulously kept of all disputes – who has cut wood, damaged trees, stolen food, where they come from, the proceedings of the hearing, and the outcome. Over the past ten years, the committee has raised more than Rs5,000 in fines from those who have come from other villages to cut trees, to graze in forbidden areas and even to steal leaves. Rakhava was the first president of the executive committee. He tells how the police never come to Seed or Setwana, because now there is no crime. If there is any dispute between members of different families, a special meeting will be called – if animals have eaten crops or trampled growing things – and everything is resolved within the village.

The people have become vegetarian. Those who keep goats and sheep sell them in the market, some of them going as far as Bombay. 'We live by the teachings of Gandhiji, *gramjivan*, village life. We have the control of our fields. We decide collectively what to do. All people have the same quantity of land.'

Lalooji is the village forest guard, a particularly important role, given the central importance of reforestation. He keeps a constant vigil over the afforested hillsides and writes down the name and place of origin of anyone he finds cutting grass or stealing leaves. When the monsoon comes, the grass now grows waist-high. When this is cut, the villagers use it as fodder. It costs them Rs11 for one bullock cartload.

The village covers 1,000 acres. Most families have about 5 bighas of land, almost one acre each, so most of the area is common land. The reforested area has sturdy trees of palas, bans, khejra, harsiya, sagvan. Rameshwar Prasad says, 'It is easy to cut down and destroy. It is much harder to build up and conserve. But this is what we have done. There is still some derelict land. It belongs to the last remaining private landlord of the village, who has abandoned it rather than return it to the village commons.' Even in the dry season, small yellow and purple flowers grow in the substantial shade from the trees; birds have returned, nightingales and weaverbirds, as well as wild animals and butterflies.

The crops grown here include not only makkhi, jowar, moong and vegetables, but many of the traditional pulses, adjvan and udid, which have been decreasingly produced in India because they are poor people's food. They do not have the market value of wheat or rice, but they are more nutritious. On the roads around Setwana, some people have strewn their freshly harvested adjvan and sarson; as the carts and vehicles run over it, the wheels separate the seeds from the stalks, which saves elaborate threshing. Women then winnow the seeds in shallow baskets.

Since the people's afforestation programme began, the water table in the area has begun to rise again. There have been severe droughts in Rajasthan in the 1980s, but people now say the rains are also returning; certainly in the past few years, the rain has been more abundant. The variety of growing trees is an attempt to regenerate the forest in as much of its earlier diversity as possible – saghwan, kher, karanj, sisal, sirara, timru, babul, nim, amle, pipal.

There are no landless people in Seed or Setwana. Caste has become secondary to the common endeavour of social improvement. As the children come out of school, they place their hands together and say in greeting 'Jai jagat', 'Peace to the world'.

Complete self-reliance is not possible, and the village has to import some basic necessities. This is not a rice-growing area, because of the aridity. There is no longer a *ghani* (oil-press) in the village. Some villagers have electricity, but for the most part, kerosene lamps are used. There is no shop selling the products of transnationals – Hindustan Lever soap, Colgate Palmolive toothpaste, Nestlé's Complan, Cadbury's chocolate – as in so many other villages.

In an unjust system, it is a constant struggle to preserve equity. The biggest problem now, says Unkalal, is *arthik vikas*, economic development. The question is how to improve the living standards of the people. The community is now good, the sense of collective work established. Now they are discussing the meaning of economic development. They do not want to import more than is necessary into the village, nor extend the cash economy into areas where this has no

121

place. They do not want to incur debts, as the government of India is now doing, and what is worse, dressing it up as a matter of high principle. They recognize that that way ruin lies. They have seen it at the local level, and they are shocked to see that this is now the policy of the government. Unkalal says that he, too, has become vegetarian and no longer drinks. He has four children, who are proud of the achievement of the village. Progress, he says, is not something that you see happening in the world, it is what takes place in people's hearts.

Many women have to travel long distances outside of the village for fuel. The *gram sabha* will give permission for dead wood to be cut within the area of the commons, but no living tree or leaf may be touched. Some of the women burn gobar, cow-dung, but this is limited because this is more properly employed as manure for the fields.

In Seed itself, fifty-five families benefit from lift irrigation, which means that wheat can grow even in the dry season; this was constructed partly from government funds, but also by *shramdan*, or voluntary labour. The cultivated fields are protected by toor fences, quickset spiky hedges of dark green cactus. There is a small nursery plantation, rows of mango saplings and red-leaved shoots of bhas, which are almost ready for transplanting into the reforested area. In the village street – it isn't really a street, but a series of spaces between the houses – people sit in the somnolent afternoon. Some women are building an extension to their house: a solid wall of slate and stone, cemented with earth. Inside, the houses are cool and sweet-smelling. There is no corrugated iron in this village, and inside, very little furniture – a bed and bedroll, some aluminium vessels, but many locally produced clay pots and containers. The houses, people say, will last a hundred years. They are eminently suited to the environment; indeed, are an emanation of the environment itself, emerging from the pale, pink earth. The contours of street and house are smooth, without jagged edges, the colours muted by dust and chaff. The serenity of the scene is, for once, not deceptive: the environmental harmony is reflected in the social peace here. The children take the buffaloes down to the stream, where they stand in the water; the horns of the cows are painted green, yellow, crimson. On a bullock cart, a woman with a fever is being carried to the health centre. The children come out of school, running across the fields and carrying their satchels with a strap around their forehead.

There is no role here for the *patwari*, the government land official. The people keep their own records, and all transactions occur only with permission of the *gram sabha*. Of course, Seed alone cannot reverse the destruction and barrenness of the Aravalis, but here, a model of what can be done when the community has control over the use of its land has created an oasis of fertility and hope. There is still a shortage of water in Seed, and fodder remains insufficient. Today, one third of land in India where trees and grass could grow is under government control. Almost half of this is degraded. Under existing laws, even if villagers in those government-owned areas were to plant trees on ruined forest or revenue lands, they could, in theory, be sent to jail.

Only local initiatives operating together can begin to restore the enormous waste and degradation of land in India. No technological fix coming from outside has done half as much as the people themselves, where they have control over their land. Those who propose further industrialization for India will only compound the problems of land exhaustion, mining of the resource-base, erosion, lowering of water-tables, more destruction of the agricultural base of the country. The people here know there is no escape from the biosphere. Indeed, living within its constraints and disciplines gives to the people of Seed a freedom that is lacking in the other villages of the region.

Rameshwar Prasad says, 'You should go and do this in your village.' I say that my village is a suburb of south London. He smiles. 'You can still make a *gram sabha*. And even if not, you can make *Gandhidarshan*, live by Gandhi's example.'

Death of a Socialist:

The Chattisgarh Liberation Movement

Bhilai, in Chattisgarh, the poorest part of the central Indian state of Madhya Pradesh, is the site of the largest steel plant in Asia. Together with its ancillary industries, it employs 100,000 people. The plant is now thirty-four years old, a Soviet–Indian collaboration, which sends its pollution over the countryside, blighting the tamarind trees on the Raipur–Bhilai road, and filtering the sun through a perpetual industrial cloud. The core workers of Bhilai have regular employment, but for those on the periphery, and in the private industries that support the vast steel facility, work is casualized, dangerous and poorly paid; factories where women are locked in for the night so that they cannot even use the urinal; opencast iron-ore mines where, when a worker is killed under a rockfall, the first concern of the owners is to cover up the death to avoid paying even minimal compensation. The people of Chattisgarh remain poor in a part of India that has some of the country's richest resources – iron ore, dolomite, coal, copper, uranium, as well as forests of teak, sal, mahua and tendu.

The workers of the Bhilai plant were organized originally by AITUC, the union of the Communist Party of India; but it was indifferent to the conditions of the casual workers, who form a majority of the labour force.

Shanker Guha Niyogi came to Bhilai from West Bengal in 1961. He joined the steel plant as an engineering apprentice. While working and studying for his BSc, he founded the Blast Furnaces Action Committee. As an engineer, he knew how to bring the whole plant to a standstill, and was dismissed in 1967 on security grounds. He went to Bastar, a tribal area of Madhya Pradesh, and worked in the fields, grazing cattle and selling them for meat in the city, by-passing profiteering middlemen and earning for the tribal people a decent livelihood. He later worked in the dolomite mines, where he married one of his co-workers, a tribal woman whom he called Asha, Hope.

During Mrs Gandhi's Emergency, in the mid-1970s, he was arrested and spent thirteen months in jail, because of the newspaper he had started in Bastar. At that time, many workers had broken away from the Communist Party union, and had formed what is now the Chattisgarh Mines Sharmik Sangh, the union identified with Niyogi. In 1976, he came to Dalli Rajhara, to the iron ore mines, where the workers were being paid Rs3.50 a day. In the early period, the union doubled the wages, but Niyogi was dismayed to find that in spite of the financial gains, the living conditions of the miners and their families had not improved. Much of the increased wages was going to the liquor shops. The next campaign was to reduce the consumption of liquor and the profits of the liquor barons. This was the first time that a trade union in India had allied itself with social reform in this way. The women were the principal players in the liquor campaign. It brought Niyogi into conflict with the liquor mafia, which also had its links with politicians. So not only the contractors who cheated the casual labourers, but also the management of Bhilai and the liquor barons and politicians, were added to his list of enemies.

For thirty years Niyogi fought for the social and economic uplifting of the oppressed and exploited people of Chattisgarh. From the mid-1970s, he evolved his vision of an alternative to the existing system, which would avoid enslavement to technology, would halt ecological ruin and exploitative work, elevate the status of women, devise appropriate means of enhancing rather than supplanting human labour. The movement went beyond the work of any conventional trade unionism, and embraced those released from bonded labour, slum dwellers of Raipur, farmers, workers in the nearby cotton mills, child workers, women deserted, beaten or abused for the sake of dowry. Several hundred thousand people become part of the Chattisgarh Mukti Morcha (The Chattisgarh Liberation Front), and today, the red and green flag is flying all over the region.

The flag dominates the town of Rajhara, where the earth has the highest iron content of any in India. The dust has turned the rivers red, and transformed the trees into rusty metal sculptures. A perpetual hot wind of rusty powder is stirred up on the terraces of the denuded hills, from which the trucks and trains swiftly remove the rich ore from the place where it is produced. The machinery for extracting its wealth efficiently is reminiscent of the Rhondda Valley in the late nineteenth century.

Rajhara is a frontier town of about 100,000 people; buildings chaotic and improvised, shacks, slums, cheap hotels, vendors and cart-pullers, ox-carts and buses with people clinging to sides and sitting on the roof. At the end of the day, the miners are going home, faces and clothes stained with the rusty element of their labour. The wages of miners have now reached Rs80 a day, the highest in India. They pause to buy tomatoes and aubergines, peas and cauliflowers from the vegetable vendors on the dusty margin of the road; sweet Nagpur oranges and claws of ripe bananas. None of these things was within their reach fifteen years ago. Now, their houses are improved, clean and tiled, the wretched hutments have been swept away. Everything speaks of a dignified sufficiency.

Tonight, however, there is tension, a suppressed energy in the air. This is Republic Day weekend, and tomorrow, all over Chattisgarh, there will be marches and demonstrations of the red–green movement; a protest against the inertia of the authorities in tracing those who, on 28 September 1991, murdered Niyogi in the modest hut where he slept, by firing six bullets through the open window.

The previous evening around midnight, he had left his friend Rajendra Sail, a human rights worker with the Raipur Churches Development and Relief Committee. Sail had asked him to stay, for it was common knowledge that Niyogi's life was in danger. A few days earlier, he had met the President of India, and speaking to him of the repression and retrenchment in Chattisgarh, had said, 'Do the people have to use AK rifles before anyone will listen to them?'

There had been warnings of a conspiracy against Niyogi. An anonymous letter from a well-wisher in Bhilai had been handed to the police in Rajhara in April 1991. No action was taken. Three months later, a second letter was received, with the warning that it would happen soon. All had been finalized. The name of the killer was known, as were some of the influential individuals involved in the conspiracy. This letter was also handed to the police, with a covering letter from the union office. No action was taken. After the assassination, the police issued a statement, saying they did not know his life was under threat. The Criminal Bureau of Investigation, the highest investigative authority in India, has implicated some of the leading industrialists, liquor barons and politicians of Madhya Pradesh. The face of the actual assassin is on posters, a hired killer called Paltan Mallah. A reward is offered for information as to his whereabouts. He is probably dead by now, eliminated by those who hired him, so that the chain linking him to the powerful is broken.

Rajendra Sail came to Raipur in 1977, as a civil liberties activist. 'I was interested in investigating this question of what development with social justice is. And I saw these ideas transformed into living experiments by a Marxist. But of course, he was never a traditional ideologue. He was a mixture of Gandhi, Marx, Mao; he believed in openness, flexibility, experimentation.

'I went to look at the mining areas to see for myself. The first thing you notice whenever you go to mining areas in India is the children who will gather round as soon as a stranger comes. And they are always pot-bellied, with runny noses, dry hair, wearing only ragged pants or nude. Here, the first thing that struck me was that the children were different. If they were not wearing clothes, this was because they did not want to wear them. They looked healthy and clean, their hair was combed and oiled. They were all going to school as well. Indeed, government schools which had no teachers – because teachers will not come to such areas – were being supplied with teachers by the union. Another thing: when you go to the mining areas, you will see that women wear no petticoat – just a saree wrapped around their body. Here, they were wearing blouse and petticoat and sandals. Their hair was clean and combed, and they wore jewellery. The men also looked cleaner. They were not in the teashops and liquor shops. The people's houses were not very good, but they were clean; not shanties but huts with tiled roofs and kitchen gardens. I talked to the women about the anti-liquor campaign. What difference had it made? They said, "Earlier, we did not know what we would eat or when. Now we eat when we want to." That is a powerful statement. They showed us they had rations stored for ten days.

'Then we went to the shopkeepers. Is the story of the success of the anti-liquor campaign true? Yes. How do you know? We had a lot of debt, but now that has been reduced. If there is a defaulter, we go to the trade union offices, and report to Niyogi; he'll pay the money from the union, or he'll get the defaulter to pay us directly. Money is now spent on food and clothes.

'Then we went to the banks. They said, "We now have small savings accounts, from Rs300 to 3,000." The workers told their own stories. Most had come from the neighbouring areas. At the Bhilai Steel Plant, there were then 72,000 workers. Less than 10 per cent of them came from Chattisgarh. This was a big issue: employment through industrialization had been the promise to Chattisgarh; but the industries had brought in all their key personnel from outside. Most Chattisgarhis were working as manual mineworkers or contract labourers. They stood to lose most if the mines were mechanized. They had been able to reclaim land that had been mortgaged, or had purchased small plots of land for themselves and their families.

'Niyogi attracted a number of scientists who worked on a semi-mechanization programme, but not mechanization that would throw people out of work. The balance between technology and human energy must be right in India. The Steel Authority of India adopted this scheme. But now once more, with the new economic policy, pressures for increased mechanization are intensifying once more.'

The Chattisgarh Movement has always been non-violent. Inspired in this respect by Gandhi, Niyogi created a movement, open, without exclusions or limits, which integrated the work and social and cultural lives of the people. A fierce solidarity was forged here of a kind that has become all but extinct in the West. One of the proudest monuments is the hospital, built by the labour of the workers of Rajhara, staffed by committed doctors and nurses and serving all the people of the surrounding areas. Next door to the hospital are the union offices. The union hall has been turned into a shrine to Niyogi. His portrait and his chair have been garlanded with marigolds and strewn with crimson rose petals. Workers come in small groups each day, and stand in silence in front of the light that burns in the shrine.

On the walls of the union office are the shoes and work-tools of those killed in the first police shootings at Rajhara on 2 and 3 June 1977. Eleven people died at that time, including a pregnant woman and a teenage boy. There have been other shootings against agitating workers, as well as against people protesting at the molestation of a woman by a member of the Central Industrial Security Force while she was gathering firewood. In 1984, police opened fire when Niyogi formed the Bagal Nagpur Cotton Mills Union. This is, in fact, the oldest industry in Chattisgarh; it had seen the first trade union in the area, formed by Thakur Pyare Lal Singh, advocate and freedom fighter. It was here, for the first time in India, that police fired on striking workers in 1924; the first death was that of a tribal, Jaharu Gond.

Chattisgarh, however, had had its martyrs long before then. In 1856–7, Veer Narayan Singh mobilized peasants in the interior forest area at a time of a great drought. When landlords refused to open their granaries, he went with an army of tribal people to loot them, promising that they would return what they had taken in a better season. He was hanged by the British in 1857.

On the day before Republic Day, the police presence around Bhilai and the surrounding towns is concentrated. They are turning back people arriving in buses, trucks, cars and even on motorcycles for the march. In spite of this, 25,000 people are on the streets of the city, with about 6,000 in Rajhara. They walk through the towns and industrial villages in dignified, solemn silence, exhibiting the discipline and restraint which even the industrialists of Bhilai concede was one of Niyogi's greatest contributions to the productivity of their factories. The women carry the tools of their labour, with food and water tins on their heads, a barefoot procession of injured humanity, setting in movement plumes of rust-coloured dust, so that they appear to be walking in the clouds. The people at the roadside watch them pass with respect and sympathy.

Attempts by the industrialists to exclude, damage or smear Niyogi had been persistent over fifteen years. They had used all means, legal and illegal, to silence him. In 1990, they had used the Externment Act against him. He was externed from five districts in Chattisgarh. This was a British Act (known as the Bombay Act), used against freedom fighters, who were harassed by being excluded from certain districts. The Act was first used against Thakur Lal Singh, who was forbidden to enter the mill area. But because the railway station was not then legally part of the state where it was located, he would come by train and hold his meetings on the station platform at Ratnand-gaon. But the Act had never been used before to exclude anyone from *five* districts. Of course, the Internal Security Act is still in existence now. This was intended for use against hardened criminals, but is used increasingly against social and trade union activists. Rajendra Sail says, 'We filed a writ petition, and the High Court granted a stay. In the notice served by the state government on Niyogi or the externment proceedings, it said that "As part of a large-scale destabilization plan of the movement, he married a tribal girl and named her Asha, in order to win the hearts of the workers." He had been accused of many crimes, including attempted murder. He had been in jail many times. For two months early in 1991, he was imprisoned for failing to appear before various criminal courts, and his bail was cancelled. Until that time, the courts were giving him leave of absence. And while he was in prison then, one of the big industrialists implicated in the case had used his absence to enter into an agreement with AITUC, to replace Niyogi's union, which was then on strike. The company placed advertisements in the paper, urging the workers to return to work, promising them many benefits. They did not go back.'

Finally, the High Court of Madhya Pradesh released Niyogi, and commenting on the order, the judge said, ' It is an injustice to keep a well-known labour leader behind bars on such grounds. He is work-ing for the downtrodden sections of the people.' He was shown in the reports as 'absconding', in one case, on the day when he was actually meeting the prime minister. It was after this that the externment proceedings were initiated. People had tried to prevent him from coming to Bhilai in the first place; they tried to throw him out. When that failed, they killed him. Rajendra Sail says, 'After the failure of

129

the externment attempt, I said to him "What next? The government's attempt to throw you out has failed." He said, "There is no other way but bullets." '

I was able to meet many of the beneficiaries of Niyogi's work in the Chattishgarh region. He has been supported by a number of non-government organizations, notably the Raipur Churches Development and Relief Committee in Raipur. Chattisgarh has seen the highest number of bonded labourers ever released from bondage at any one time in India: after a Supreme Court ruling in 1988, almost five thousand were freed in Chattisgarh. Many of them immediately became members of Niyogi's union.

The system of bonded labour in Chattisgarh was called the *kamia* system. The *kamia* is the adult male labourer. The wife of a *kamia* is a *kamiana*; a teenager a *katia*, a child a *pejoli*. Although the Bonded Labour Abolition Act was passed in 1976, there are an estimated five million still in bondage in the country. The Act defines and describes various forms of bonded labour. There are four criteria in determining bonded labour: (1) that the individual has taken a loan or advance; (2) in return for that loan, his or her labour has been mortgaged; (3) he or she is not free to go to work elsewhere until that loan is repaid; (4) he or she receives less than the minimum wage, or no wage at all.

Under each or any of these conditions, a person is bonded labour. In Raipur district, six thousand have now been released. Government officials who came here originally reported that there was no bonded labour. Social workers and activists drew up a petition in 1983 naming 683 labourers, who were then released under an order of the Supreme Court. In 1988, a further petition to the Supreme Court was followed by the mass release of more than four thousand people.

A unique feature of Raipur has been the rehabilitation of the affected people, some of whom had inherited their bondage from a father, or even a grandfather. Rajinder Sail says, 'We have combined struggle on the streets with action in the courts; including dharnas in Delhi and Bhopal. Most rehabilitation has hitherto been a partial or total failure. After their release, many people had no alternative means of survival. Here, nearly all have found employment. The pressure has come from below, from people's own power and strength. Membership of the union has given a powerful thrust to their campaign. The scope for corruption in the rehabilitation has been cut to a minimum. We kept a diary of corruption, and the money has been, in many cases, returned to the cheated labourers by the corrupt officials. The scope for corruption is there, because the government allows a monetary sum to be paid for rehabilitation purposes (Rs6,250 – about $250).'

The Raipur Churches Development and Relief Committee (RCDRC) submitted a scheme to the Supreme Court, which then requested the government to give them freedom to experiment. They have trained 472 former bonded labourers, some of whom have gone to school for the first time. Multipurpose polytechnics have been established all over Chattisgarh, where the released people are given training in technical skills, in economic activities that will provide them with a livelihood. The people spend six months at the polytechnics. The rehabilitation money is an ex-gratia payment of Rs500 and Rs5,750 for bullocks or land development. Each is also guaranteed a place to live. 'We fought for that. If the labourer was living in a house belonging to the landlord, he could not be turned out. It is a condition that anything mortgaged shall revert to the labourer. There are also facilities available under the rural employment programme and government anti-poverty scheme, so they can benefit in a number of ways.'

But this is the first time in India where former bonded labourers have been unionized. The union is organized by representatives, 280 of them, each representing 20 people – 5,600 people. 'We are often asked what they have gained. We have tried to make the dream come true of giving voice to the voiceless, hope to the hopeless, power to the powerless.'

A dozen or so representatives have come to Raipur from the surrounding areas for a course at the RCDRC centre. Some of them had never seen a railway before their release; had rarely left the land of their owner. Some had been in bondage for three generations, simply because their grandfathers had taken a loan of Rs200 fifty years ago. 'People have said that those seeking release from bondage are only looking for rehabilitation money,' says Rajendra Sail. 'But the hunger for freedom is greater than the greed for money.'

Some of the people were paid only two tamis of rice a day; that is 1½ kilos. Value is measured here in rice: 20 tamis make one khandi. Twelve khandis is equal to about Rs400 (about £15). Some of the bonded labourers were given a small piece of land by the landlord to cultivate their own produce, but they were always given the least productive land; then when they had cleared and improved it, made it yield , the landlord would take it away and send them to some other piece of worthless or degraded land.

'If you do something wrong', says Hemsingh, 'you may be fined out of the produce you have grown. If you are absent, even for a day, for sickness or a family celebration, you must send a substitute to do your work. If you don't, the landlord will have to hire someone who is not bonded and pay at the rate of a free labourer, which is 5 tamis a day; and the bonded labourer will have to repay the landlord those 5 tamis. The landlord also has the first option on the wife's labour, and if he says so, she must give half a day's labour free. Whenever the master calls, the labourer must be available, from the early hours of the morning until late at night.'

The people tell how their ancestors used to live in symbiotic subsistence with the forest. They built their own houses and depended on the forest for a livelihood. When the forests were felled and the people could no longer survive in the traditional way, they were forced to take loans and enter bondage. Once this happens, they will never be free again. The landlords have sold the forests for timber; and that resource having been exhausted, they turned the people into slaves.

Sudhu Ram tells how, at eighteen, he took over his father's bondage. He studied until the 3rd standard (age nine), and then worked looking after the cattle. During the growing season, he had to bathe the animals and feed them while the adults were toiling in the fields. His sister was at the beck and call of the mistress, washing utensils from early morning until midday, then returning at 2 until sunset. They would eat two meals a day – pasia, the cooked leftover rice mixed with water and left to ferment; and then at midday only chapati and roti, with rice and dal in the evening.

If the *kamia* ran away, even to a distance of 25–30 kilometres, the landlord would find him. If he was found to have been employed as free labour by anyone else, a traditional court hearing would be held, and the employer, if it could be established that he had knowingly employed a bonded man, would be punished. If there was no work in the house of the landlord, he would send the *kamia* to another farm, and the wages earned there, at free rates, would go to the master. Even if government work was available, the wages would still go to the landlord.

'Even free labourers got only 4 or 5 tamis of rice, so they were not much better off,' says Daya Ram. The landlords used to describe the relationship with their labourers in lyrical terms, as a homely and beautiful understanding. 'If I throw him out', they would say, 'he would die of hunger. We, too, are poor. We could not survive without bonded labour. With us, they have work all the year. If they were free, work would only be seasonal, and they would starve when there is no work.'

'When we tried to become free', says Hemsingh, 'they said we were disturbing the peace. When the People's Union for Civil Liberties

filed writs in the court, they were accused of destabilizing the countryside. It was said that they were financed by "foreign money"; they
were trying to "make conversions to Christianity".'

Hemsingh remembers how, when he was a child, he would watch
the landlord beat his father for any small wrongdoing. Work never
ceased; ploughing, sowing, carrying mud on their heads, building,
clearing stones; while women had to fetch wood from the forest,
cook, bring water. When we asked Hemsingh what was the difference
between being in bondage and being free, he said, 'Now I am happy,
because I work when I want to. In bondage, you are only paying off
the interest on the loan. You never get to pay any of the principal,
and that is how you remain chained.'

Reshambai tells how her husband was a *kamia*, who worked from
dawn till 8 at night. One day he fell sick. The landlord came to the
house and said, 'Why is he not at work?' 'He is sick.' 'Then you come.'
Reshambai went in his place. They gave her a hoe to dig the earth and
maintain the irrigation canals. 'I did man's work; compost, looking
after the animals. When I came home, I had to work, feed the cattle.
We were afraid of being released at first. The landlord threatened he
would throw us out, and since we knew nothing else, we did not know
what would become of us. We could see only that there would be no
work or wages. For one year I worked in place of my husband. Then
he was released in May 1988, and was trained as a cycle repair man.
He fell ill again and I took him to hospital. I had to sell our utensils,
everything that had been bought with the rehabilitation money. We
had no land; four of our children work in the fields as day labourers;
three others are in school.'

Dayaram learned tailoring when he was released after eight years
in bondage. He had become indebted for Rs400 and 8 khandi of
padi. Now he is earning Rs15–20 a day. He makes and stitches shirts,
trousers, blouses, sarees, underwear. He has been able to buy a watch
with his earnings. He is also building his house. With the rehabilitation money, he bought a pair of bullocks. For his sister's wedding, he
took a loan of Rs2,000, but now has the means to pay it back. He has
bought brass utensils worth Rs450. Although he is landless, his
grandmother has two acres of land, which are farmed by five
brothers. He says, 'I now work in my own time, I have no fear that the
landlord will come and drag me out of bed. Work was a burden to me,
but it no longer is.'

Some of the released labourers have occupied government land,
where they can build a small house and grow basic foodstuffs for
their own consumption; mostly small plots of about one acre. Much
of this land had been barren and unproductive. Kanto share-crops

one acre, which yields 20–5 bags of padi each season (one bag is 75 kg, half rice, half husks). He has one pair of bullocks, which he bought with the rehabilitation money. He cannot remember when he became a *kamia*.

Meghnath has taken over 2.5 acres of government land. He is now struggling to gain the titles of this land which he has brought into productive use. Some released labourers were given the deeds to land, but they were not told where the land is, so they cannot use it. The issue of land rights is the next phase of the union struggle. Useless forest or revenue land can provide them with the space to farm to provide themselves with basic security. They say, 'Zamin ka faisla zamin per hoga' – the decision of the land will be made on the land itself; what they mean is, there is no point in going through the courts, because that will go on for ever.

In spite of the record of Chattisgarh, there are still people in the region in bondage. Government officials come, they are bribed by the landlords, and they go away to report that bondage has been eliminated here.

Raipur is one of the major cities of Madhya Pradesh, and has the chaotic vigour of any fast-growing city. Its development has been accelerated by its proximity to Bhilai: the conurbation draws people from all over the drought-prone and degraded areas of central India.

A 1981 survey showed that there were 87 slum areas in Raipur; five years later, there were 146 slums, and by 1992, well over 200. The formation of slums is overwhelmingly because of migrations of people from Orissa, which is adjacent to Madhya Pradesh and second only to Bihar in its poverty. There has also been continuous migration from rural Chattisgarh. In Madhya Pradesh, the administration which preceded the present BJP, legalized the landholdings of people in cities. This was, on paper, a very radical Act. It says that a 50 square metre piece of land should be regularized in favour of the landholder. They were to be given *patta*, land-deeds, on a 30-year lease; and this was to be done irrespective of the claimed ownership of the site they occupy.

In Raipur there had been wholesale demolitions and evictions in 1982–3, following which, a number of slum dwellers' organizations came into existence, and these joined to form the Citizens' Rights Forum. These groups filed a writ petition in the High Court, with the result that a stay was granted in May 1983, effectively halting demolitions. The stay is still in force, but the case is still going on nine years later. The slum dwellers are not hopeful that the decision will ultimately be in their favour. Alternative sites and rehabilitations have been promised, but this means, as the evictees from dam-sites, slums and forests have learned, inadequate, barren land, without amenities, transport or livelihood. Second, the work of the slum dwellers demands that they should remain on their present sites for the sake of the jobs they do. The People's Union for Civil Liberties is now arguing that the right to livelihood and the right to shelter are also basic human rights. Since India claims to operate a 'welfare state', it is the duty of such a state to supply housing, welfare and basic facilities. As the state has failed to provide any of these necessities, the state is not entitled to take them away from people who have provided them for themselves.

Nothing has been given by the government. The people have worked on their own initiative, mobilized their own money, by mortgaging utensils or wedding jewellery to raise Rs500 – 1,000, and they will sit by the roadside, earning the money honestly to ensure a living for themselves and their children. Then the government says they are an obstruction and a public nuisance. 'How do they become public?' asks Rajendra Sail, 'Who is the public? The argument in our petition is raising the question, "Do I have a right to sleep on the railway platform if the state cannot provide for me and I cannot provide for myself?" The right to life overtakes all other rights. And right to life means life in all its fullness, it is not the life of an insect. The right to life is enshrined in Part II of the Constitution of India.

'In 1986–7, in spite of the Act being in force that legalized the holding of the occupant of the land, what happened? I was arrested on false and flimsy charges, for obstructing government officials, abusing and threatening to kill them, because I had been opposing demolitions and the uprooting of people.

'I was bailed out, but it wasn't until 1990 that I was acquitted. We decided to fight the case. They had seventeen government officials as witnesses, and the Deputy Superintendent of Police. What they are doing now is instigating criminal cases against social activists and civil liberties workers. This taints them with being common criminals. It is an abuse of the law and also a godsend to real criminals, both those who endanger other people's lives and corporate and industrial criminals. The tactic is one of constant harassment, and is very time-consuming. Some people may have to spend 50–100 days a year in court, so their work is effectively immobilized. Some activists have 30–5 cases against them, just as Niyogi had.'

India has much legislation protecting juveniles, the rights of the workers, bonded labour, but these Acts are only implemented when there is agitation from below. Only when people are aware and organized can they begin to claim what is theirs by right.

'We have the Madhya Pradesh Slum Development Board funded

by the World Bank. Kashiramnagar was an improvement area under the aegis of the World Bank. Relocation affects the lives of people in ways that do not enter the calculations of the World Bank. What do they know of the consequences of their "improvements"? None of their experts or officials ever has to live there. The houses they built were fine, but they disrupted the lives of the people. It doesn't look like a slum now; but the women are the worst affected, because they now have long journeys before they can continue their livelihood. You take a bidi-roller. When she lived close to the place which is the source of her work materials, she could earn maybe Rs8 for an eight-hour day. Now she has moved 5 kilometres from there, to where there is no public transport. So what happens? She must travel a long distance on foot. If she does not reach the bidi [cigarette] factory on time, she does not get her raw material; if she returns the work too late, they will not accept her quota, because their day's quota has already been filled. She must take a rickshaw part of the way to get there more quickly; 2 rupees each way – that is half her day's earnings gone.

'Other women are working as vegetable vendors in residential colonies. They now have to return home on foot late at night. There is the risk of rape, abductions. They are afraid. We conducted a survey in Kashiramnagar; all the girls under eight had stopped going to school in the families who had been relocated. Over half the older girls had dropped out, because of the insecurity of walking. Boys can cycle; but the impediment to the girls' schooling, together with apathy of parents towards the education of girls, discourages them completely.

'The fruit and vegetable vendors get a loan of Rs300 a day. The loan is actually Rs250, but they are charged Rs300, as that is the lender's commission. If she sells it all she can earn Rs25 a day. When she has moved away from the vegetable market, the dealers will say, "We don't know where you live, how do we know you will come back in the evening?" And then, in Kashiramnagar, all the able-bodied people are away in the daytime. The whole community remains insecure for young girls and old people. There are break-ins and molestations; such things had been unthinkable in the slum.

'The World Bank development had provided a public toilet. They were charging 25 paise a time for upkeep and maintenance. In a family of four, that is one rupee a time, several times a day. That means spending a significant portion of the day's income to perform natural functions. Men and women would go to the fields; but of course, there are no fields around Kashiramnagar, so that is a matter of some difficulty. The people have no option but to use the ground

136

around the residential colonies. So the people who lived there started throwing stones at them. The women's organization met the Collector. "You cannot charge people for this." The Collector was not aware of the situation. He reduced the charge to 10 paise a time. That is still unfair. The Mahila Chattisgarh Jagriti Sanghatna (Women's Awareness Organization) led a protest and a hunger strike. Women were jailed; one woman gave birth in jail. She called her daughter "Jailibhai".'

One of the oldest established slums in Raipur is a small settlement near the wholesale vegetable market, Lenditallab. This was originally an area of water seepage and is owned by the municipality. It is a community of about five hundred people, in huts of mud, wood, metal, none higher than about 5 feet. Being close to the market is convenient for the women vendors; but the waste and refuse accumulates on the ground adjacent to the slum. The structures they have built are solid, but cramped and insanitary. Families of eight or ten people sleep in one room, with an earth floor, the kitchen separated only by a mud wall. The cooking fires fill the huts with choking smoke; there is no ventilation. The scarlet embers make the interiors of the houses hotter than ever; and in this part of central India summer temperatures regularly rise over 40°C.

Most of the men here are cycle-rickshaw drivers. The red and green flag flutters from their vehicles, and flies over many of the houses. The work of driving is arduous and backbreaking, and rarely yields more than Rs20 or 30 a day (40–60 pence). The work is uncertain, because there is extreme competition. Most have taken a loan to buy the rickshaw. Many of the vehicles stand idle, a tangle of black-painted metal, with a plastic seat for the passengers, sometimes with a threadbare canopy to protect the occupants from the rain or sun. Some of them are proudly maintained, painted with flowers, pictures of gods, gold and silver paint. Others are rusty and broken down. The only other work open to men is construction; if they are trained masons or carpenters, they make a better living, but those who are unskilled are worse off than rickshaw drivers. Some women also work as construction labourers, others work in small garment or plastics factories, but the majority are domestic servants.

I asked them, in a family with four children, how much do you need each day to survive in the city slums? After some time, the people agreed that Rs50 a day was necessary for a decent life; some felt that Rs40 was enough to survive. 'If you want vegetables as well as dal with rice every day, you would need Rs50.' The word *khana*, food, means rice to them; and that is the measure of eating properly. In the morning, most eat pasia, which is leftover rice soaked in water overnight so that it swells and ferments slightly. At midday, they eat rice with chilli and perhaps one vegetable – *brinjal* (aubergine), *kobi* (cauliflower), which cost Rs3–4 a kilo. In the evening, there will be dal with chapattis. On Sunday they may eat meat – goat or chicken. For people doing heavy manual labour, an adult should eat 1 kilo of rice a day. Women who work on construction, or who carry headloads greater than their bodyweight, eat the same as men.

What is development, I asked them: 'Vikas, kya hai?' They said, 'We don't know, we've never seen it.' 'Development', said one woman, 'is the money that goes into the pockets of politicians. If the government will give us security of tenure of the land, then we do not mind moving; if we get one room per family, we will go; at present some of us are sleeping two, three families in a room.' Another woman says, 'The government does not want to give us accommodation, because they believe we will sell it and come back to the place where we have been staying. They think we want the money only. The government is befooling us. They may give land to one person, and on paper say they have given to fifty. Paper houses are even less use to us than those we have now. In Kashiramnagar it is true that some people have sold their houses, but they are not doing this for greed, they are doing it from necessity. They are afraid of the anti-social elements where they stay. Here, in the slum, everybody unites at times of suffering; when there is illness and death and pain, people are helped by the support of the community.'

The people have been here for twenty-five years. Why did they come from Orissa in the 1960s? 'There is no farming there. It was a place of drought. There was no foodgrain. Traditionally, we were weavers. But because there is weaving by machine now, there is no work for us. There was skill and beauty in what we made. We took pride in it. But if we were to do that now, no one would buy from us, because they do not want traditional cloth, they think our work is old-fashioned. We came from Orissa because the land had become unproductive. Our language is Oriya. There we were happy. Here, we are not happy, but we can eat. Anything is better than hunger, so even if unhappiness is the price you pay, you will pay it. Unhappiness is the price of survival. We cannot go back, because there is no water. Even if land were given to us, we could do nothing with it. Drought was caused by deforestation.'

The home-place is still evoked with tenderness; and the work of weaving with regret. Both their landscape and their skills have been degraded: only their dignity is not impaired. And it is this stinging sense of loss that has driven them to find strength and succour in the Red–Green Movement.

In Lenditallab, as in the other slums of Raipur, child labour is an integral part of the family economy. The CMM has also been trying to reach the children. On Republic Day, some of them gathered in the RCDRC to reclaim a few hours' leisure from their stolen childhood; and they paused to reflect on their life and labour. Some are the principal earners in their family; others are making life a little easier for their families; some are working desperately to survive. Dhani is twelve. His mother works ironing clothes. His aunt makes *agarbatti*, incense sticks, and he works three hours a day with her. For this he gets Rs5 a week; he gives it to his mother. Mina is a domestic servant of fourteen. Her father is a sweet vendor and her mother a domestic worker. She earns Rs150 a month, which she gives to her mother; occasionally she is given a few rupees to spend for herself. Narayan is fourteen, and works in the stores of the company that supplies the hospital with cotton, dressings, scissors, etc. He works from 11 to 9 each day, and gets Rs350 a month. From 7 in the morning until 11 he goes to school; he is in the 8th standard. When he finishes work at night, he returns home to study. His father is a rickshaw driver from Orissa, and earns Rs10–20 a day. Narayan is studying hard because, he says, he wants to be a policeman.

Papu Ambade is from Gondya in neighbouring Maharashtra. He is in the 7th standard, aged about 13, and works in a soap factory for Rs50 a week. His father is a construction worker and his mother a bidi-roller. His job is to label packs of soap and detergent. He goes to school in the morning. When he finishes his studies, he says, he would like to become a doctor, although he knows the chances are slim.

Pramila is a small girl, with a serious face; a determined child of eleven or twelve – she is not sure of her age. She earns Rs80 a month as a domestic help. Her father is a rickshaw puller, and she has three younger brothers and one sister. Her jobs are cleaning and dusting, shopping, serving water to visitors, minding the children. She is given some snacks where she works. Her hours are 8 to 11 a.m., and then from 1 p.m. till 5. She has been working for two years.

Rajah is fourteen. He is apprenticed to a tailor, learning skilled work. He receives only Rs5 a week. He works from 8 to 10, then goes to school until work starts again at 4.30 and continues to 8. His father is a sweet-maker. Amjad, twelve, makes paper bags. His father brings home the paper, and the family work together at home. Amjad doesn't know how much his father earns from this, but he is given 50 paise a day. Santosh, twelve, makes *agarbatti*, rolling them, which is the toughest job. Many women who roll *agarbatti* have completely erased the creases in the palms of their hand; their palms also become black. It takes Amjad two hours to make 1,000 *agarbatti* sticks. His mother makes 3,000 a day, and the pay is Rs1 per thousand. At 2 Santosh goes to school. Salim is ten, a bidi-maker. He helps his mother; without him, she could not make up the daily quota of 200. Salim goes to school from 7 till 12, then makes bidis until 5.

Sitaram works in a hotel, so small it has no name. He washes plates and cups, serves pekoras and samosas. He is thirteen. He works from 7 in the morning until 5, and has a half-day off on Sunday. He is paid Rs25 a week. His father is a rickshaw driver. Sukhnami is ten; a solemn and severely exploited child. He works in a vehicle repair shop, holding the metal panels as the older boys and men hammer them into shape. He earns Rs10 a week; his mother is a wage labourer on construction work. Sukhnami works from 8 till 1 then from 2 till 10. His father was a rickshaw puller, but he fell ill. Sukhnam had to work, and cannot study because he is so tired when he comes home at night.

The labour of the twenty million or so child workers in India is essential for family survival. To talk of doing away with the evil is not possible while the lives of the poor are so insecure. The present government of India has placed its faith in more 'liberalization', which means doing away with even the nominal laws that fail to protect the weak. In the process, even greater burdens of exploitation and loss will be imposed on the least defended. It is this work which the Chattisgarh Mukti Morcha has addressed; and for that Niyogi died.

In the atmosphere of struggle and resistance that has been generated around Chattisgarh, many brave initiatives have been taken, some of them unique in India. One of the most exciting and original has been the work of the Women's Movement of the CMM. Shashi Sail is editor of *Awaz Aurat Ki* (Women's Voice). 'Because of the tribal cultural background, the women of this region are less bound by the traditions that have hindered many Hindu women. They are more militant here, and strong in all the popular movements. In the women's organization, we are taking up larger social issues – dowry death, rape, harassment within the family, and here in particular, deserted wives. Culturally, a second wife is acceptable here, but only with the consent of the first wife. How that consent is won is often questionable. The men start keeping both wives, and after a time, evict the first wife. Deserted women are a growing problem. We had to evolve a way of dealing with it. Legally, it is not an offence to evict the first wife. The courts cannot help in redressing the problem of the abandoned wife. So we developed a way of using the community.

'We have invented the *mahila panchayat*, or committee of women. This is a new experiment, which started two years back. It is made up of women from the village, neighbouring villages, with two or three representatives of our women's organization. The *mahila panchayat* is formed on an ad hoc basis, to deal with individual cases, as they arise. It is not a permanent fixture. The *panchayat* will determine the facts of the case, prepare a report, and then conduct a public hearing in front of the concerned community. In Raipur City, parties from both sides will be invited to make their depositions; and then afterwards, there will be a report and recommendations. These are then discussed openly, and it is the community's burden to decide whether to implement them, and if so, how best to do it. There has been success in almost every case. The *mahila panchayat* lasts for the duration of the case only, so there is no accumulation of power to any individual.

'One deserted Sindhi woman, Raj Kumari, was abandoned after ten years of marriage. The husband remarried and brought his new wife to the home. We took up the case, with a series of protests, dharnas, hunger strikes, posters to help raise the issue of wife desertion, and after seeking help from the law courts and administration, we got nowhere. The girl was sitting outside the house with her eleven-year-old daughter. We said to her, "That is your house, go back in there." Meanwhile, the *mahila panchayat* was formed. There was an open hearing in March 1990. Family members, women's groups, youth groups, neighbours, lawyers took part. All came and deposed their evidence. There had been a long battle in the court. All the documents were studied thoroughly and published. Then, in the evening, there was a public meeting of the community. The report of the *mahila panchayat* was read out. The recommendations were that (1) no violence should be inflicted on Raj Kumari or her daughter. She had been beaten, drugged and abducted, and then left at her mother's house. (2) Until the divorce, she will stay in the house. After the divorce, she will move out. (3) She should be paid a monthly maintenance of Rs1,000, because the family in question was quite well off. After the public meeting, three thousand women took her in procession to the house, and she went in. She has not been beaten, but has been treated politely, even though they do not maintain her economically. So that is a success. It is a kind of popular justice, tempered with mercy.

'In the most recent case, a woman was murdered in a village for the sake of dowry money. This was in October 1991. The village is in the interior of Chattisgarh, and the woman's father-in-law, who was guilty of the murder, sought to suppress the case. Unless the police are informed, they never come to hear of it. When the police did finally come, there was no information about the case. There was simply a dead body found decomposing in a field. The police said it

was a case of suicide. Even the newspapers do not carry an insignificant item about an insignificant person in an insignificant village in
the depths of Chattisgarh. This was in Abhanpur Block, Torla
village, about 20 kilometres from Raipur.

'When we tried to get information, there was a wall of silence.
"What can you do now?" people said. "The girl is dead, you can't
bring her back." We had to do a lot of work before the women
recognized that a terrible injustice had been done to another woman,
and that they should act.

'We formed a *mahila panchayat* of nine women: two from our
organization in Raipur, others from seven villages around. The
mahila panchayat talked with people from the villages, with young
people, women, in order to get information. We spoke to police
officials, and asked them, What have you done, what is the case you
have made? They had made a report out of the information they had.
We convinced them what they had was wrong and insufficient, and
we offered them knowledge we had gained.

'On 20 December 1991, there was a public meeting in the village.
Before the meeting, the women went on a procession, over three
hundred women. At the beginning, there were no men. We set out,
chanting slogans, and began our way around the village. Because that
village was new to many of us, we did not know the way. One young
man came forward and showed us which way to go. There were many
children in front of the procession, both girls and boys. We stopped
at different places, to tell the people what we were doing, and why we
were doing it. After about 3 kilometres, we went back to our meeting.
By that time, there were as many men as women.

'At the public meeting, the *mahila panchayat* report was read out,
and the recommendations made. These were (1) that the man who
had committed the murder should be socially boycotted, and (2) that
the dead girl's husband should not be allowed to get married again.

'The social boycott became a big issue. You already have the
community *panchayat*, of course, and if something is wrong, it is the
work of the community *panchayat* to take up the issue and impose due
penalties. Our *panchayat* is specifically to deal with issues relating to
women – its very existence has social and legal implications. After 20
December, further meetings were held to decide how to implement
the social boycott. The idea of the women was that people should not
share with the family the cooked vegetables, the fuel dung-cakes,
should not give them *agi*, fire, because not all families have matches,
and usually they take a lighted straw from one house to another. The
family should not be permitted to be present on special social
occasions, like the ceremony of naming a child. We discussed with the

Sahu community, to which the man belonged, and asked what the community *panchayat* was doing to redress this wrong. The family involved were poor, landless labourers. The girl's family were also poor and landless, and the father was sick. For the first time in the history of the community *panchayat*, a women's organization was invited to attend, and our report and ideas asked for. On the basis of our recommendations, they decided on a boycott by the Sahu community also, and that was a big punishment. They have gone further, and decided to debar the family from community meetings up to the District level. Only they have the power to do this.'

It is a very delicate issue, because of the non-legal status of the *mahila panchayat*. It has no power to give a judgment, but can only make recommendations. The police case was weak. Suicide was not plausible. On 17 January 1992, women besieged the police station and protested against the attitude of the police. 'What had been decided by the community was sufficient punishment; it really doesn't matter if the law does not punish. But people were shirking their social responsibility when they said the law will take its course, that it is not our concern, it is not a matter of community action. Even if the police had arrested the man, he would have been released on bail.

'We cannot take up all cases, but we take on those that show the worst abuses, or where there is a matter of precedent, where the community can take some action. There is always a social dimension to any crime, and this aspect should be dealt with at the social level. Women are concerned by rape, desertion, drinking, gambling. We have hit upon an idea, the idea of the *panchayat*, which is culturally acceptable, so we are not making any excessively radical departure from the culture, although it is a departure and it is radical. We are loyal to the existing *panchayat*, and cannot defy it. But because the idea of a *panchayat* is rooted in Indian experience, it has met with a tremendous success.'

Since the death of Niyogi, new members have come to the trade union movement. Shock and anger have strengthened the resolve of the Chattisgarh Mukti Morcha. In one Raipur industrial estate, where the workers of only one company were affiliated to the red–green flag, there are now twelve whose employees have joined.

The present context of India is, however, against them. It is not purely fortuitous that Niyogi should have been murdered at this time. India committed itself to 'liberalizing' its economy, following the prescriptions of the IMF, World Bank and GATT negotiators. In order to service its $70 billion international debt, and to compensate for the loss of its former Soviet market, it is desperate to be competitive in world markets.

This means that the price of its cheap labour must not be compromised, no matter what the cost of maintaining this competitive advantage.

Many social activists and human rights workers met in Nagpur, in the neighbouring state of Maharashtra in February 1992, to create a national movement of solidarity with the people of Chattisgarh. They are asking whether the assassination of Niyogi is not perhaps the supreme act of a 'liberalization', designed to remove any defence of some of the most abused and exploited people in the world. Does the much trumpeted death of socialism now mean that it is also legitimate to do away with socialists, as they so brutally did away with Shankar Guha Niyogi?

Subsequent events in Chattisgarh suggest that this judgement is by no means far-fetched. An industrialist, Chandrakant Shah, had been arrested in connection with the death of Niyogi. He mysteriously 'escaped' from police custody in May 1992, and no further action had been taken. There remained over three thousand retrenched workers in the Bhilai ancillary industries; the issue of the contract system had not been addressed.

It is significant that the Chattisgarh Mukti Morcha had wanted nothing more than the implementation of the labour laws of the country, and justice for what was, after all, a murder. Scarcely revolutionary or extravagant demands. Talks had indeed been organized, between the Chattisgarh Mukti Morcha, the local industrialists and the Labour Department of the Madhya Pradesh state government, but these had dragged on inconclusively. Not surprisingly: it is no accident that the existing labour laws of the country are a point of contention with India's external creditors. Liberalization of the economy does indeed mean sweeping away of such modest protection as the organized sector in India has enjoyed.

On 1 July, a demonstration of Bhilai workers was organized. The workers obstructed railway traffic at Bhilai powerhouse station. The CMM president had sought an assurance that the administration would resume talks. At 5 in the evening, the police opened fire, killing – according to official figures – sixteen people; activists and workers put the figure at closer to fifty. Many of the injured said that after the shooting, and under instruction of the senior police and administration officers, dead bodies were removed from the tracks. 'It was a gruesome sight,' said one eyewitness. 'Policemen were seen throwing the dead bodies onto trucks.' The police later were pressuring the hospital to release injured people, and arresting them as they were discharged.

Since then, the workers dismissed for belonging to the Chattisgarh Mukti Morcha have continued their vigils, dharnas and protests, with the calm dignity they owe to their dead leader. The Chattisgarh Mukti Morcha, far from being deterred by an economic climate hostile to them, are seeking to extend their activities into other parts of India.

Migrants and Refugees

The West has become obsessed with the distinction between 'political refugees' and 'economic migrants'. The former category requires evidence of a 'well-founded fear of persecution in their own country', according to the United Nations Convention on Refugees; the latter are merely seeking a better life, and therefore must not be allowed to pass through the increasingly impermeable frontiers that shield the rich from any necessity to share their privilege.

This distinction was first tested by Britain in Hong Kong, on those who had fled Vietnam. The last major colony of Britain was serving, as so many colonies had before, for policies destined, like the migrants themselves, to be repatriated.

When the boat-people were first found adrift in the South China Sea, they were greeted as heroes who had broken out of the prison-camp that was Vietnam. Much media time (that curiously intense and extra-temporal chronometry) was spent on their courage and endurance. At that time, Vietnam was still being punished for its victory over the United States, and was treated as an outlaw state. The invasion of Cambodia only intensified its isolation, and since the West was then backing the resistance groups inside Cambodia, the most significant of which was the Khmer Rouge, it required some moral agility to depict Vietnam as more malign than the rump of the Pol Pot regime. The boat-people, therefore, only confirmed what we knew – that life in Vietnam was intolerable.

It was only later that the refugees from Vietnam became an embarrassment to Hong Kong. As a result of the numbers, the squalid conditions in which they were held in Hong Kong, the consequent disorder and riots, they were criminalized and stigmatized. Hand in hand with an increasingly urgent need to be rid of them, Vietnam was seen to be rehabilitating itself, so that the Hong Kong authorities would be justified in returning them to the benign, open arms of a repentant and liberalized Vietnamese government.

Indeed, a common reason for refusal of refugee status to individuals was found in the fact that large numbers of Vietnamese people had been mistreated: 'because involuntary transfer to New Economic Zones was accorded to hundreds of thousands of Vietnamese, the Applicant was not singled out because of his father's anti-Communist record.'

The moral acrobatics required by such a shift is apparent in the reports to the Hong Kong Security Secretary from the Refugee Status Review Board on those to whom refugee status has been refused. A report on Do Giau declared:

> It should be borne in mind that the Applicant never gave evidence in court and thus his allegations of persecution by the Vietnamese authorities have never been fully tested until now and found to be wanting. . . . In view of these obvious facts, coupled with recent assurances given by the Vietnamese government at the United Nations meeting in Geneva, 1991, that none would suffer persecution who returned to Vietnam – such assurances having been accepted by the international community – this Panel can find no valid reason which could justify its recommending to you the recognition of this Applicant as a refugee *sur place* within the proper meaning of that description.

Similarly, in the rejection of Tran Thi Van, who claimed to fear persecution for her religious belief, the Panel concludes:

> Madam Tran endeavours to give the impression that she and her family were singled out and harassed to abandon what she claims to be her faith. She does not substantiate why this special treatment and harassment should have been applied to her as opposed to others in similar circumstances to herself.

The Panel declared that 'her replies were unconvincing and contradictory'. They added: 'Both members of the Panel happened by coincidence to be practising Catholics, and it was apparent that the Applicant had little knowledge of the Catholic faith.' They concluded they were dealing with 'the exaggerated and sometimes untruthful claims of a simple woman who may well have deceived herself believing she was persecuted for religious reasons.'

Indeed, the tone of the reports is reminiscent of that of early nineteenth-century magistrates condemning working-class criminals in Britain to deportation for life. ('The prisoner evinced no trait of ferocity, but was possessed of a calm and comely demeanour; in short, an appearance well calculated to conceal a criminal heart.') These magisterial judgments have a curious resonance and correspondence with those of a Communist system which labelled them 'bully landlord class', 'third generation anti-Communist', 'family with wicked family history'.

This pilot essay in racist exclusion might have been a blueprint for an increasingly xenophobic Europe. The British government announced in July 1991 more stringent controls on those seeking political asylum. Figures were issued, showing not only that there had been a significant increase in the numbers applying for refugee status, but also to support the claim that many of these were 'fraudulent'. This gave legitimacy to an outburst of fury in the popular press: the opportunity to denounce the poor of the earth as cheats, crooks and shams was too good to miss. Asylum-seekers were no such thing: they were migrants in disguise, liars and opportunists, taking advantage of Britain's humanitarian tradition, abusing our hospitality and tolerance, etc.

The language of the reporting betrays the real world-view of the rhetoric. The words used were flood, tide, waves of would-be immigrants. Tides, of course, must be stemmed, floods halted and the surge checked. It is clear that we are in the presence of a natural catastrophe; one of those that are so conspicuous a daily occurrence in the unhappy countries of the South. The image of flood leads naturally into that of 'explosion' of population. 'Britain must not allow these islands to become a soft touchdown for the footloose masses of the world,' said the *Daily Mail* sternly. We are already at a Malthusian 'nature's banquet, at which no place is set for the poor'.

The migrants 'slip through porous frontiers', they 'con' and 'trick' and 'cheat' their way into Britain. They are bogus, phoney, they employ a catalogue of ruses, tell falsehoods and lies; thereby demonstrating that the moral character of those we once ruled has not improved since we 'gave' them their independence.

The Times pointed out that Britain's 'influx' is scarcely one tenth of the total who are 'rattling the doors of the whole EC', but went on to add that 'since the world-wide evidence of human rights observance in the last five years is one of significant improvement, the pressures would appear to come from economic rather than political motives, aided by cheap flights.'

Amnesty International's report in 1991 scarcely supported this sunny view of human rights: human rights abuses continued, and often got worse, in 141 countries. More than 100 countries tortured and ill-treated prisoners, and thousands disappeared or were executed outside the law in 29 countries. Further, even if asylum were granted to all at the time of the peak number (fewer than a thousand a week), it would still take a hundred years to add five million to the population of Britain.

And this brings us to the real reason why the West has such a horror of 'economic migrants'. There is no doubt that the isolation of Vietnam, for instance, although partly of its own creation by its adherence to a sanguinary and discredited ideology, was severely compounded by the withholding of aid and by an international outlawry that more to do with a continuing punitive response to its humiliation of the United States than with any Western horror of tyranny. In this sense, the role of the West in the production of economic misery in that country was not negligible.

And so it is with most countries from which 'economic migrants' come. For those people are seeking that 'better life', of which the West is such a tireless champion and promoter, and images of which it beams around the world with ubiquitous insistence. Indeed, the West is at pains to reassure the whole world that everyone can attain its level of affluence, if only they will carry out the prescriptions and advice issuing from the Western financial institutions, the IMF and World Bank.

Economic migrants, in reality, frequently bear a quite different and unwelcome story from the places which they flee. The truth is that the Western way of wealth-creation has depended on pressing the whole world into its service. The Western experience is not replicable. The prescriptions of the West are actually a formula for impoverishment and loss to the world's poor. The 'irresistible migratory pressures' to which the British Home Security referred are in large measure imposed on the world by an economic necessity wholly within the control of the West. Much of the injustice, and the ensuing abuse of human rights of those who resist in the Third World, comes from the abuse of people who are protecting from a greedy world-system their land, their habitat, their forests, their coastal or riverine resources, where they have lived for millennia. The seizure of fish, minerals and timber or other export commodities is, more often than not, in the interests of earning foreign exchange, in order to service bottomless debts to the West.

This is the suppressed connection between the sharp division that separates 'political' from 'economic' migrants. Those who have lived under the tyrannical logic of Western economics (that supreme generator of opaque, impersonal violence, in which the absence of flesh-and-blood torturers or military personnel cleanses it of all responsibility for their sufferings) are the same people now 'rattling the doors of the EC'. Indeed, economic forces have themselves become, as it were, the secret police of capitalism, dispossessing, impoverishing, expelling from livelihoods, evicting from habitats with as ruthless an efficiency as the agents of malign totalitarianism. What could be more understandable than that people should seek to escape from them?

If Britain is not to become 'the dumping ground for the impoverished of Africa and the Far East', then the countries of the South should cease to be the dumping ground for obsolete and dangerous technology, trash culture and junk economistic ideology. For these are the root of so many of the sad upheavals, reluctant leavetakings from the homeplace, the sunderings and violent disturbances that leave the poor no space to live with a decent sufficiency, which is all they are looking for. The real answer to 'economic migration' is equitable development, a secure home which does not become the site of starvation, social dislocation, resource wars and environmental degradation.

Life of Migrants

Those people described by Western governments as 'economic migrants' are often as unhappy with their exile as they are necessary to the economy that affords them a grudging livelihood. Many migrants are sustained by the dream of the return; and few people can be in greater need of dreams than those who have exchanged the landscapes of the south Indian state of Kerala for the grey Victorian terraces of south London.

Jain and Prakash have been in Britain for ten years. Their fathers both worked in the docks of Singapore and had British passports. The families came here when their fathers retired, even though this meant disrupting the boys' studies. This was less of a wrench than it may sound: one of the problems of Kerala is that there is a surplus of graduates in this most literate part of India. (Kerala was the first state to achieve 'total literacy' in 1991.) As a result, the educated unemployed are a major issue in Kerala, and something like one sixth of the people of the state are now abroad.

In 1990, Jain and Prakash returned to Kerala for the first time. Memories of the little town where they grew up, Chirayinkil, 40 kilometres from Trivandrum, the state capital, have become more poignant with the passage of time. Apprehension tempered the excitement of going home. The role of returnee is a complex one. It is important to be prosperous and generous, to justify the desertion; but care must be taken not to diminish the home-place, not to comment on the pace of life, the static quality of the culture or the dust in the main street. Nor must emotions be allowed to take root there too strongly: real life still means the factory where Prakash is now foreman, and the company making air-conditioning for cars, where Jain is now employed. At the same time, little of the deeper costs and pain of migration must become apparent to those who remain; the irreversible journey must never be permitted to look like a mistake.

Chirayinkil is a town of a few thousand people; surrounded by palm-trees and meandering inland waterways, which make this coastal strip of India so spectacular. The palms meet above the roads and the railway tracks in sombre arches, which form outdoor Gothic cathedrals. This year's rice crop has just been transplanted in strips of acid green which cut sharply into the darker shade of the palms. The soft landscape, where palms are relieved by plantations of cardamom, rubber and cashew, and patches of ancient forest, conceals the fact that this is one of the poorest states in India. 'Everything produced here is exported', says Dr Thomas Isaac of the Centre for the Study of Developing Societies in Trivandrum; 'the many varieties of banana, cashew-nuts and coir, prawns and cuttle-fish which go to Europe and Japan; and above all, the people, who have become diasporic.'

Keralans can be found in the Gulf, North America, Australia, Germany, Singapore; and in Britain, mainly in Croydon and East Ham. It is harder now to find work abroad. Many who went to the Gulf and were displaced by the Gulf war have not had their contracts renewed. Some over-extended themselves in the construction of new houses of brick, marble and ceramic tiles. Some of these have now been abandoned around Chirayinkil; wild flowers grow out of the cracked masonry.

As soon as they arrived home, Jain and Prakash exchanged their suits for the dhoti which, in Britain, they wear only at home. Their delight in rediscovering the tamarind and jackfruit in the neglected gardens, the coconuts which, for 2 rupees, a dark-skinned local boy will climb and throw down from a height of 100 feet or more, the relatives and friends who still recognize them in spite of the long absence – all this is clouded by the sombre realization that the return is only an interlude. For the moment, it is thrilling to open up the house that has stood unoccupied – and unvandalized – for several years; disturbing the lizards, spiders and mice that had made their home there; sending up the dust and removing the planks from the well with its water still sweet and uncontaminated. They meet the friends who have not gone abroad or east to Madras, north to Bombay. One is giving 'tuitions' to the children whose eagerness to learn will produce yet another generation of jobless graduates. One man is saving up to acquire the documents needed to go to the Gulf – Rs25,000 for a passport and No Objection certificate, and to appease a vast unofficial bureaucracy of agents and middlemen. Another is content to stay here, because he has work in his father's mill, where oilseeds are pressed.

Chirayinkil in the heat of the afternoon has the oppressive languor of all small towns from which many able people have departed. The warm breeze plays in the palms, the buses raise eddies of red dust; a black umbrella used as parasol protects old men with their bent legs and coarse shopping bags. Prakash says that nothing has changed. He walks along the dusty margin of the narrow metalled road, just as when he was going to school; past the station, where the trains from Quilon and Trivandrum draw clusters of vendors and sightseers; past the rows of shops, where the owners stand behind glass counters with their display of Britannia biscuits, Lux and Lifebuoy soap, Colgate Palmolive toothpaste, Cadbury's fruit-and-nut chocolate. There are new shops too, selling TVs and videos, washing machines and electric light-fittings.

Since Jain and Prakash went away, the impoverishment of their home state has worsened. One day, we visited a coir works just outside the town. Coir is the shell of coconut, soaked in water for three months, beaten into fibre and then spun into rope. A row of women sit individually under the shelter of a single palm leaf, propped up by stones and bleached ghost-grey by the sun. Each holds a wooden mallet, and she takes the shells from the stinking water which has softened them, and beats them on a stone anvil. They will earn Rs11.40 a day (about 25 cents), if they crush 200 shells into fibre. Many work with small children beside them, some of whom imitate the actions of their mother, beating the earth with their fists. The water sprays a muddy, foul-smelling juice everywhere; and as the women work, their outstretched legs become covered with small pieces of fibre, so it looks as though they are grotesquely hirsute. When the fibre is ready, it passes to the drying shed. Here, only men work, and they are paid twice as much as the women. The fibre is dried by hot-air machines. The drying shed is full of dust and small pieces of fibre. The temperature is over 40°C. Suresh, who has worked here for five years, suffers from chronic respiratory disorders and is never free of a cough. He says health is a luxury which the poor cannot afford. Livelihood undermines life, but what can he do?

The fibre is then wound into loose bundles under the palm-trees. It is spun into rope or twine by women, by means of a large metal spinning wheel which is turned by hand. The women must run at great speed with the bundles of fibre, and the wheel twists it into a firm, taught twine. This is exhausting work, and the women are paid Rs15 a day. The people walk to their work in the coir yard, some from a distance of 10 kilometres or more. They start at 7 in the morning and finish at 4. The final product of their labour is used for matting and baskets, and these are exported, mostly to Russia, Burma and Germany.

The coir workers are among the lowest-paid in the state. There are around 250,000 of them. Their work could be eased by automation, but Kerala already suffers from a rate of disemployment through technology that far exceeds any corresponding employment-generation. Jain and Prakash look at the scene beneath the trees in awed silence. The fathers of both young men started work in the coir yards of Chirayinkil when they left school. It was only recruitment by the British for dock-work in Singapore that rescued them in the 1950s. But for that, Jain and Prakash might also have begun their working life here.

There is the same story of displacement by technology with the fishing communities all along the coast of the Lakshadweep Sea, from Pondichery to Kanyakumari. Traditional catamarans and dugout canoes have been rendered uneconomic by mechanized trawlers, which have depleted fish stocks and disrupted the fragile marine ecology of the region. The government has, after many years of struggle and organization by the fishing communities, banned trawlers during the monsoon. But the fishing people have been hopelessly impoverished by their inability to compete with industrialized fishing. Tajan, who works in the fishing villages, says that it is in fact the mechanized sector that is breaking down before the traditional fishing methods – the trawlers are energy-intensive, they use increasing horsepower and bigger boats so they can cover more ground; they have been decreasing the size of the mesh so that the small fry are caught and thrown away, thereby undermining their own future catches. 'Traditional fishermen know the ecology of the shoreline. They warned that indiscriminate trawling would destroy the natural reefs in Kerala. Trawlers are an investment, not a livelihood. We have been constructing artificial reefs in the past few years: fishermen knew that objects dropped into the sea attract fish; during World War Two, a ship sank off Anjengo, and became a fishing ground. They have a better understanding of ecology of the Arabian Sea than marine oceanographers, because these have all been trained in the West.'

Tajan says they are working for marine reform, just as farmers work for land reform: the sea belongs to the fishing people, not to absentee landlords. 'A development that pushes money into productivity and efficiency, disemploys people and uses up resources in the process is not development; it is terminal stupidity.'

Fishing families live on the foreshore, the *purambook*, government-owned land adjacent to the beach. Their shelters are pitiful, sometimes simply woven palm-leaves bleached by the sun. The boats go out in the early hours – three or four in the morning – and return the following afternoon, sometimes with a catch worth no more than Rs100. We visit the village of Vettukad, just outside the Trivandrum boundary. This is a Christian village, one of the richest parishes in Kerala. It is a place of pilgrimage, because some mentally afflicted people were cured here forty years ago. In the shadow of the imposing parish church, beggars and sick people sit, a frieze of still, silent supplication. Formerly, all here were involved in fishing, but now there is much unemployment. The men have always been drinkers in these villages, because of the long hours at night on the cool water. When they came back to land, they continued drinking; and now that their occupation is gone, drinking is the only reminder of it. The diet of many fishing families now is tapioca and the inferior fish they cannot sell. In the local market, carrots are Rs5 a kilo, onions Rs3, brinjal Rs4, bananas Rs6 or 7, plantain Rs4 and tapioca Rs2½; but the depressed incomes can barely afford even this basic fare.

Nearby there is a hugh titanium plant, which is the biggest employer in the area. It discharges sulphuric acid directly into the sea; a cloudy yellow stain spreads over the surface of the water, where the men bring in their catamarans; their nets rot in the inshore waters. Attempts to upgrade the boats here by means of Yamaha outboard motors have led, not to improvement, but to even greater indebtedness. The motors need constant repair, and the quantity of fish caught cannot meet the repayments on the bank loans for the motors.

When the tide goes out, a greyish crust forms on the sand, and the smell of sulphur is overwhelming. A quarter of the jobs in the factory are reserved for the people of the area, as compensation for the pollution. The children run out onto the shore, chanting 'aceed, aceed' in English. A man comes out of his hut and says that the worry of living here has turned his hair grey.

There is an even more dangerous pollutant from the plant, and that is radioactive waste. The technology of this plant is banned in some countries, notably Japan. There have been a number of leukaemia cases in the area; but because radioactivity is invisible, and poverty all too palpable, the people are not prepared to agitate against the plant; they live under the greater terror of loss of the jobs that at least assure some income in the impoverished coastal strip.

It is an historic irony that the fishing people, like the landless agricultural labourers, the coir workers, those who clear away waste-matter, dispose of dead cattle, leatherworkers, remain outside the caste system. The function of the Untouchables has been to manage the resource-base in a sustainable way. The real generators of pollution are the rich, the owners of industrialized trawlers, the makers of synthetic rope and nets that displace traditional artisans. Those who are believed to be polluted by their work are, in fact, custodians of the environment. 'Development' means that they are being robbed even of the opportunity to carry out this essential labour.

The irony of this is not lost on Jain and Prakash. They are both from Ezheva families, former Untouchables, who were lifted up by Sri Narayan Guru. They were keen to visit his memorial at Aruvipuram, a rocky promontory overlooking a broad, fast-flowing river. Here, Sri Narayan first set up a temple for Ezhevas, where previously only Brahmins had worshipped.

What the two young men learned from their visit was the ease with which they could fall into the rhythms of their childhood; but also that there is no function for them in the economy of Kerala. Their sensibility has been reshaped by Western industrial society, almost stealthily, without their being aware of it. They could not go back to the lassitude and underemployment of the beautiful, melancholy little town. Both prepared themselves to go back to Britain, determined to make enough money to be able to come home permanently – in another ten years perhaps – to start a small business, create a place for themselves, build a new house.

Even the visits to relatives have a strong undertow of sadness. Prakash visited the family of his brother's wife. Of the five children, three are in the Gulf, and the only daughter in London. Sushila's mother looks at the wedding video over and over again, to bring the daughter she hasn't seen for eight years a little closer.

And then Prakash has to visit his sister's husband. He is living in Madras, and has been refused even a tourist visa so that he may go to see his wife and children in London. He finds it incomprehensible that the British government should have singled him out for discrimination. It is difficult to explain to him that this is government policy, not the indifference of his relatives. An arbitrary and mistaken decision by an official that the marriage was contracted for purpose of migration has hardened into an issue of high principle; as a result, husband and wife and child must live in separate continents. The oldest child is now six years old. When the husband comes home to Chirayinkil from Madras, he daren't go out, because everyone wants to know why he is still in India, while his wife and children are in England.

It is evening in the square around the Sarkara temple, shrine to Sarkara Devi, banisher of evil. The compound is an open space, banyan trees with matted aerial roots, and pale sand made pink by the sun's reflection on some towering mounds of cumulus. People are bathing in the tank beside the temple, cool water the colour of copper in the dying light. Others make their offerings of coconuts, ghee, sandalwood, bougainvillea, garlands of marigolds and jasmine. As the light fades, the temple buildings turn gold in the sun's afterglow. Palm leaves chatter in the wind and shine like silver. Tomorrow, Jain and Prakash will put away the dhoti and take out the suits from their cases, ready for the flight back to Colombo and London.

Jain had his passport confiscated at Colombo, because, he was told, the officials suspected it was forged. It wasn't returned to him until he reached Immigration at Gatwick. He was then asked to name the nearest railway station to his home in London. Prakash was detained and searched by customs. His suitcases were slashed and ripped apart. They thought he might be carrying drugs. There is a long, weary wait before they are allowed to go home. Next morning, they must both be at work by 7.30. The first day of the next ten years.

Dispossessings: The 'First World'

There is, it seems, no stable state of development, or of 'being developed', in which the evictions and uprootings we have seen do not occur. The creation of wealth is at war with stability, security and sufficiency. Far from the richest countries being exempt from these visitations, they are the scene of some of the most relentless mobilities and upheavals. The same relentless processes mangle and disfigure humanity there as drive indigenous peoples from their habitat in the South, and send the children of farmers to squat in city slums. The only difference is that the victims of development in the rich world are not accustomed to see themselves in that way. They have before them the miseries of the poor of the earth, and are constantly expected to be grateful for the dispensation that spares them such a fate. Perhaps this is why people in the West have internalized economic necessity: they have learned to identify the rise and fall of production with the elations and sinkings of the human heart; they scarcely distinguish between the buoyancy of markets and the dilation of their own spirits; they make heroic efforts to read their own happiness in the indices of economic success. Indeed, we have become a new techno-peasantry, no longer seeing signs and portents for our own lives in the sky, trees and stars, but superstitiously seeking salvation and meaning in technology, progress and higher levels of consumption.

Even our alienation has been privatized. That is to say, the sense of impotence, pain and violence that is an integral part of the experience of millions of people in the West, cannot be named, has no conduit for public recognition. These things must resolve themselves within the narrow compass of the lives of individuals. Socially determined wrongs seek their remedy through private escape; which, doubtless, helps to account for the addictions, breakdown of families, the loneliness and cruelty of Western society. The million people in the prisons of the USA, the 28 million crimes reported in 1990, the tramping homeless in the boarded-up doorways of the abandoned city centres, the 10,000 who die each year from gunshot wounds – casualties of the undeclared war against the poor – are never seen for what they are. They are, of course, a small visible part of the externalized costs of development; but they are presented to the frightened citizens of the West as though they were the consequences of the actions of flawed or deranged individuals. So many deranged individuals! The celebrated Western cherishing of the individual has another purpose: it is to make people absorb, infinitely, the cruelties and violence inflicted in the name of 'development', although it isn't called that domestically in the rich countries. It is called economic growth, or wealth-creation, or progress or getting rich.

It is the cloak of tainted and unquiet privilege that conceals from the people in the West their kinship with those in the South, the underlying samenesses and correspondences in their daily experience. Fear of losing what they have has another side – the longing for liberation.

THE EARLY 1990s

For the second time in a decade in Britain, we are seeing a significant 'shake-out' of labour. Many of those unemployed this time are the same people who had dutifully 'priced themselves into jobs', the very service jobs that were promised as the salvation of those who had been compelled to bow before the necessities of 'structural adjustment' in the early 1980s. This time, however, there are also new groups being evicted from the labour market; and their relationship to the victims of the earlier wave of redundancy and disemployment is significant.

The early 1980s saw the loss of function and purpose of a generation of workers in heavy industry. It was a destructive, corrosive experience for those who became depressed and prematurely old, waking up in the early morning, sweating because they had momentarily forgotten that there was no longer any mill to go to, and that the factory had become a site of mangled metal and crushed brick. Some of those people killed themselves. I remember the family of one man in Lancashire, who showed me the note he had left: a few lines apologizing for his own superfluousness to the system that had discarded him. Others saw their marriages fail, the bonds of kinship and affection dissolve. Some gratefully took to the poisonous consolations of alcohol, illness and psychic disintegration. It was a cruel time, when people were displaced and ousted from settled ways of life which, until that moment, had seemed to them to guarantee them a permanent place in industrial society.

Many of those now redundant were recruited in the 1960s to the 'caring society', which was seen at the time as a pledge that the old brutalities of mass poverty and unemployment would never occur again, and would certainly not lay waste a whole generation, as had happened in the 1930s. Their role was, they had imagined, to heal and soothe the casualties of industrial society. Those who have found themselves deprived of function in the last decade of the century are people in social work, education, charity, the health service, public administration, planning and architecture. Many had implicitly believed in the creation of a better world, for the making of which their skills were indispensable.

And what makes the relationship between the two groups even more poignant is that many were themselves the children of the old industrial workers. They saw themselves as perpetuating the values of the welfare state, for which their parents had striven in great pain and sacrifice, and the absence of which had made their lives – especially the lives of women – unnecessarily harsh and burdensome.

Already during the 1980s, the professional workers now being marginalized had become more and more disaffected from the excesses of the neo-liberal certainties of the Conservative government, which was about the conservation, it seemed to them, of nothing; but was a time of violent, forced change. Their original scorn at the policies of Thatcher had soon turned to incredulity; later to outrage, anger and finally, a kind of numb submission to the inevitable. It was a time when Disgusted of Tunbridge Wells became reconciled to the social order, Placated of Tunbridge Wells; and his or her place was taken by Disgusted of Camden Town or East Dulwich. They were constantly appalled by the latest policy statement, the most recent cuts in public expenditure, the latest emanation from free market think tans. They were shocked; everything that happened was disgraceful: 'I can't believe this is happening.' They clung to a set of archaic moral values that was being jettisoned; and they could not adapt to the rigours of a rehabilitated free market. In a way, their experience was a repeat of that of a very different social group marginalized in the 1950s and 1960s, the returnees of empire, who lived out their twilight years in the amenity of Cheltenham or Torquay, ritually bemoaning the long decline and the incomprehensible social landscape of the country they loved.

But however horrified they were, for the most part they kept their own jobs during the first recession of the decade. Many have found it unbearably painful now to return to their very elderly parents and confess that they, too, have been made redundant, and from the very jobs which were seen as a guarantee of a security which their families had never previously known. It might be felt that they ought to have been better armed against the experience; but of course, so many of them (I mean, of course, of *us* – there is no point in claiming a spurious distance from something that affects me so closely) had believed that we had opted out, settled for the consolations of a well-rewarded job, even if it did seem curiously disarticulated from the sense of high purpose with which we had entered it. We retreated, uneasily, into private life, professing disgust with politics, a revulsion against ideas of social progress; and unable to understand why the caring society in which we believed should be attended by so much violence and cruelty, so many addictions, the ruin of structures of kinship and neighbourhood. Although it was distasteful to us, there seemed little point in holding to notions of improvement in any area other than the economic. In a way, we had already secretly conceded the case of those we still thought of as our opponents.

But now, even that tenuous and unstable job security has been swept away. Many of those unemployed now are in their forties and fifties, and are as defeated and depressed as the old industrial workers were in the early 1980s. ('I shall never work again,' people of forty had said then. 'I'm on the scrap-heap,' one 37 year old said to me in 1983.) There are few calamities (apart from injury or sickness) that can befall human beings that are worse than loss of function, especially when they know what they have been doing is of social value. And the old industrial workers knew that their lives were bound up with the making of material necessities; just as today's redundant knew that their concern was with human values, with healing and helping the weak and vulnerable. That such areas of manifest goodness and utility should turn out to be irrelevant to the majestic sweep of wealth-creation is a deeply scarring experience. In the early 1980s, I met many people bereaved of their purpose. They closed the front doors of their modest terraced houses in shame, and sat beside gas-fires turned to a tepid flicker in the draughty room, incapable of grasping why people like themselves, who had been schooled to labour, deferred pleasures and scant joys, people who had had so little, should nevertheless still be capable of being deprived of something so vital in this late season of their lives.

It still comes as a shock to realize that we have been taken up, used and then discarded by our society. We have received compulsory instruction in its power to appropriate the energies of people, to flatter and cajole them for as long as they are needed, in order to ease periods of awkward and violent social transition, and then to expel them when their services are no longer required, or when the dangerous, transforming moment has passed.

For some of us, it is not an entirely new experience; indeed, it has even a certain familiarity. When we were in university, for instance, in the late 1950s and early 1960s, to be working class was itself highly fashionable; was to be courted and urged to amuse our peers with vignettes of northern life; was to exude a patina of glamour which those from more exalted social strata found – inexplicably to us then – exotic and desirable. A form of flattery, the better to absorb and neutralize us, perhaps, to attach us more securely to a system from which we, like our sometime recalcitrant working-class forbears, might have remained irremediably estranged.

The feelings of being socially valued increased during the 1960s, when we became teachers and social workers. People often said to me at the time, 'You're a social worker? I think you people are wonderful. Of course, I could never do it myself, perhaps I'm too sensitive, but I do admire what you do.' There could be no greater contrast with the obloquy and humiliations to which social workers are now exposed by Conservative politicians and the popular press.

Since then, both the working class and the caring society have been disgraced, and those tainted by any association with either have become deeply unfashionable. The miners' strike, perhaps more than any other event, dispelled any lingering glamour; the working class, or rather what was left of it, had proved itself once more to be the violent, perverse and disruptive rabble which it had appeared in the early industrial era; it had reverted to type. And what could be more unambiguous than the fall of social workers, who are now blamed for all the social ills which they themselves, in a more innocent time, thought they could cure?

But that isn't the end of the story. In the late 1960s and early 1970s it was, briefly, interesting to be gay. Those of us in that minority who knew how to amuse and entertain were taken up as emblems of other people's liberalism. That was an even more short-lived period of approval, and the fall from grace even more abrupt than our eviction from either of the earlier desirable groups; a process hastened in the 1980s by the appearance of AIDS, and the reassertion of popular cults of machismo, which found their supreme expression in the heroic male iconography of the Gulf war.

There was one other experience that called for our energies to be employed once more. That was in the early 1980s, during the first flush of Thatcherism, when it looked as though the period of transition on which the Conservatives had embarked with such insensitive gusto was going to be distinctly bumpy. It was a time of mass daily redundancies and inner city riots. There was a clear possibility that it might all end in violence and disaster. We were useful once, not only to absorb the intensified workload placed on those of us working in the health and social services: our betters were also quite keen to learn anything we might have to say about the formation of a permanent underclass, from which they were anxious to separate the mainstream. At that time, it was possible to write about the poor and the transformation that was changing the sensibility of the successful working class. We possessed something that they wanted, and that was information; our assessment of the task that lay before them, and the likely resistance they might expect to meet.

But now the transition is complete, the awkward moment safely negotiated. There is no longer any threat to the existing order. The only alternative has itself been vanquished, exorcized. Socialism is off the agenda, domestically and globally. The market reigns supreme. The West has won. There is no longer any need for dissent. Hence, the time has come for silencing, for marginalizing, for side-lining. We have become unpersons, by means of that most delicate and violent of suppressions, by being deprived of a livelihood.

These multiple and repeated expulsions have their cumulative effect; repeated blows to a sense of worth and value, a denial of skills, a repudiation of insights and energies. I have, perhaps, been more fortunate than many, because I have been able to find great strength and support in the struggles of many people in the South; not as a form of escapism from the more opaque and intractable problems of my own society, but precisely because of the parallels and similarities with what we have experienced here. If there is now only one global system, of which we are all inescapably a part, then we should expect to see convergences, correspondences and echoes of the same experience across cultures, regions and races of the world. And this is, indeed, what is happening. Everywhere, people are being displaced from their environment, disturbed in settled ways of life, and by the same processes that rob us also of security and continuity. Indigenous peoples, tribals and forest people are being ousted for the sake of their resource-base, required by an omnivorous market economy to earn foreign exchange. In the West, it is the human commons that have been enclosed and privatized, and sold back to us as service, and as this happens, supports of neighbourhood, ties of blood and kinship are swept away. This is the open secret of our relationship with the children of rice farmers in Thailand, the evicted dwellers on the commons of India, the fishing communities of Malaysia or

Kerala. Economic forces are a kind of universal army of occupation; and we must all incline to their coercions.

It has become a source of great self-congratulation to the West that there is no longer any overarching ideology to oppose the patterns of development which it is now free to dictate to the whole world. This means that the existing overarching ideology must now go uncontested. Indeed, it fills *totally* the vacuum created by the absence of alternatives. The market system is to be the universal means of deliverance of all the suffering peoples of the earth, whether they like it or not, and no matter what violent discontinuities, what unsustainable practices, what damaging consequences it may bring in its wake.

We have already seen some of the effects of this in the West. In the 1960s and 1970s, we saw that areas of human experience previously considered to be beyond the reach of the market system could readily be turned into marketed services and commodities – indeed, the caring professions themselves marked the passage into the money economy of things that human beings had always offered each other freely. The 1980s was the decade in which what was not marketable was shown to have no worth. The 1990s will go further and show that what is not marketable does not exist. The power of the market, unchecked and unresisted, becomes a tyranny like any other concentration of power. Indeed, precisely because it is the most dynamic and forceful feature of our lives, there is no source of moral resistance strong enough to contest its domination of society. The supreme, triumphal emblem of its success is perhaps the shopping mall, to which all other social institutions now seek to approximate themselves. Thus, cities become halls of merchandise, adjacent to which people happen to live. Airports are shopping centres, at which aircraft call from time to time. Hospitals are franchise outlets, where people are incidentally healed or not. Churches are bazaars, in which people also sometimes worship.

The ceaseless movement of peoples all over the world, the evictions and removals and transformations are all in the name of the market economy, whose extension and expansion is now the only serious project on earth. It represents a vast colonization, or recolonization, one to overshadow all previous conquests. This is why the fate of the former miner, in the bleak functionless pit village, is the same as that of the tribal family, forced from their home and squatting in the fetid slums of Bombay or Manila. The displaced fishing communities of Langkawi or Goa are subject to the same forces that make families homeless in the Bronx or Hackney; the people under the bridges of London or Paris with their fires and bottles of drink are the sisters and brothers of those under the motorways of São Paulo and Mexico

City. Indeed, as the logic of the global marketplace expands, people in Bombay or Seoul will be competing for work and money with the people of Marseilles or Naples, or even Moscow. We must expect to see a blurring of distinctions between First and Third Worlds.

But while our experience remains fragmented and unconnected, we shall remain impotent and alone, unable to name our common suffering, let alone act together against it. Yet this is why these times are less gloomy than they might otherwise appear to be. So much is becoming clearer, despite the efforts of those who would render our own experience impenetrable to us, who would promote incoherence and call it pluralism, preside over the spread of powerlessness and ask us to bless it as the highest freedom.

Women Who Stay

In the West, rising material standards of living over the past half-century also serve purposes other than the well-being of the people. The relative prosperity is always fragile; and it masks the impoverishments and losses in realms other than the economic, within our own experience. While we jealously cling to our privilege, and a poor, hungry, wasting world looks reproachfully on through the one-way mirror of our TV screens, we are also subject to multiple dispossessions, precisely in the private lives to which we believe we have retreated, the shelter from a public realm which becomes increasingly incomprehensible and threatening and beyond our control.

We are, to some extent, all victims of development. Wisdom comes from recognizing the boundary between socially determined wrongs and irremediable existential evils. This is a frontier which has become blurred in rich Western societies, where individuals are supposed to take responsibility, not only for their own actions, but also for socially induced evils, like poverty and unemployment, and even for all the tribulations that life itself brings: it is now regarded as the duty of the individual to take care of sickness, loss, old age and infirmity, which have become other people's business opportunities.

It is a paradox that part of the 'externalizing' of economic and social costs of development has been through forms of 'internalizing' them: that is to say, individuals, especially women, have absorbed, secretly, privately, unspeakable burdens of social shame, disgrace and sorrow. These, too, need to be counted, before we can make any realistic assessment of profit and loss, advantage and penalty, gain and impoverishment, in our lives.

My mother had summoned me to her deathbed so many times over the past twenty years that it seemed inconceivable that I would be absent when her death came. I had heard her voice, countless times. 'Come quick. I need you. I'm dying. It's the end.' And always, obediently, I had gone. Sometimes she had forgotten that she had called me, and looked at me as though to say, 'You don't usually come on Wednesdays, what's wrong?'

I was in Uttarkhand in north India when she died. The feeling that I had deserted her was strengthened by what I learned from the women of the Himalayan foothills. For they said it was always the men who leave. The men go from the marginal farm, the village, the forest, into the city. What is usually presented as male enterprise and intrepidity is seen differently by women. Men are more easily defeated. They walk away. They do not stand and fight the daily war that is waged against the poor at the level of the resource-base, of the familiar home-place.

In a quite different context, my mother had been like the women of Uttarkhand. She had remained. She had endured and overcome the devastation of her life, had salvaged from it some dignity, even a quiet heroism.

The youngest of twelve children born between 1880 and 1905, there had been little scope for individual choice in the working-class streets around the shoe factories of the Midland town. All had worked in the factories, and all taken their marriage partners from neighbouring families. Later, my mother would say, wonderingly, 'I thought you just got married and that was it. You didn't stop to find out if you would get on together.' Marriage prescribed roles: a good husband gave his money to his wife and didn't drink; a good wife stayed at home and made meals out of bones and pot-herbs. Certainly no one looked far afield for a partner. The working-class culture was a formidable arranger of marriages.

She soon learned. She had always loved reading; and her husband, who had never read a book, allowed her to read to him one night. Self-taught, having left school at fourteen, she knew long passages of Dickens, George Eliot, the Victorian poets; but she chose to read *Coming Through the Rye*. When she looked up to see if he was enjoying it, he had fallen asleep. She said, 'That was when I realized how lonely marriage can be.'

But not as lonely as it was to become later. He had been a slaughterman before marriage, and they opened a butcher's shop on a new estate at the edge of town. But he would not be tied down. He wanted to be on the move. He took a job driving a lorry that carried bricks from the brick-fields of Bedford all over the Midlands. He was an attractive man; the photographs show crinkly hair shiny with cream, a seductive smile wrapped around a cigarette that always hung from the corner of his mouth; a flower in the buttonhole of his suit. He began to stay away, days, weeks at a time. What my mother referred to as his 'fancy women' was something of a hyperbole: the snapshots show them to be quite ordinary, even downright plain. 'A bottle of pop', she would say of them, 'a blonde with a navy-blue parting'. She had one miscarriage early on in their marriage, but no other pregnancy.

Early in 1938, her sister came one day and told her that his lorry had been parked outside the doctor's surgery every night for two weeks. Nothing could be done in that town without being observed. The community imposed discipline and conformity, and extended its protective care only to those who complied with its ungenerous vision of right and wrong. It had developed extraordinary skill in detecting irregularities of conduct, especially if these were sexual. Sid had been ill, it appeared, for months. He regularly went poaching and caught rabbits by the sackful, which mother sold in the shop for a little extra money. To those who asked what was wrong with him he said he had become infected by a diseased rabbit.

But it was syphilis, which had reached the tertiary stage. By the time it was diagnosed, there was already tissue loss to the roof of the mouth and nose. The treatment would be long and drastic, indeed would take several years. He was prescribed daily injections of arsenic and mercury. My mother was terrified that someone would find out. Their livelihood would be finished, because he could no longer work. Every day, she would empty the buckets of mucus and waste that came from him. The stench remained in her nostrils till the end of her life. At the same time, she served in the shop, exchanged pleasantries and gossip with the women of the estate.

She was already well into her thirties, and sexual intercourse with her husband would have been impossible, even if it had not already ceased. It seemed to her that she would remain childless. One sunshiny day, as she stood washing up at the kitchen sink by the open window, a man came and asked her for some water. He was working on a nearby building-site, where a palatial road-house was being constructed, with lounge and winter garden. There was to be a big car-park, he told her enthusiastically, because in the future people would drink in style, a far cry from the austere street-corner pubs which, until then, had been their only escape from the redbrick houses of correction of industrial life.

He was a craftsman and a socialist. He introduced her to the work of William Morris and Bernard Shaw, and in return, she gave him *Mill on the Floss* and *Middlemarch*. She decided on their first meeting that she would have a child with him. In the event, she had twins. I don't know what agreement she had reached with her husband. I imagine she promised to look after him until after he recovered, and after that, gave no pledge. She soon learned, however, that her lover was no more dependable than her husband. When she became pregnant, he withdrew to the bleak refuge of his own joyless though comfortable marriage, and told her she was on her own.

She waited until her husband was restored to health before she divorced him. By that time, my brother and I were eight. It was still an enormity for a working-class woman to divorce her husband in the 1940s. Many of the customers came to retrieve their ration books, clearly unable to deal with people who permitted themselves the frivolous dissolution of such solemn bonds. Others, less sophisticated, withdrew their custom because it was still widely believed that menstruating women handling meat caused it to go bad. If only they knew, she said grimly. Some men on the estate thought that a divorcee was by definition a woman of loose morals, and therefore available. Accordingly, they leaned on the counter and propositioned her over the faggots and pork sausages.

At times, she would say to me and my brother, 'Ah, if you only knew!' She hinted constantly at something dark and unsayable, and although we might have attributed this to parental mystification, part and parcel of a strategy to make us more tractable, it nevertheless filled us with anxiety and foreboding. Such allusions were the only relief she allowed herself over thirty-five years. Perhaps they made her feel a little less alone; they certainly attached us more closely to her through the fear they aroused in us.

Occasionally, we would arrive home from school and find the man we subsequently discovered to be our father sitting beside her on the sofa in tense silence. We resented him. He was there when I passed the 11-plus and before I went to Cambridge, soft-eyed, anxious to celebrate. He was there when my brother started his apprenticeship, and there to mark its completion. We did not understand this obtrusive tenderness from someone who had no connection with us. He clearly wanted to take part in the rejoicing over our achievements, although he had wanted no part in the daily drudgery of our care.

As for our mother's husband, we grew up separated from him by the distance of his shameful illness. He slept alone in a room which we were not allowed to enter, a chamber of prohibited and rancid maleness. He used his own plate and cutlery. He rarely touched us. Our model of being male came to us across an immense space. My mother's bitterness towards men did little to reconcile us to our gender. She used to say, 'I've had to be father and mother to you as well.' It was a fierce, expiatory, overprotective love, saturated by her own guilt and unhappiness.

It seemed to me a pity to have had two fathers and to have known neither of them; a bit of a waste really, since I had such a fragile sense of my own sexual identity. To make it worse, the separation of the men in her life was mirrored in her relationship with her twin boys. I think she feared above everything the possibility that we might combine against her. To forestall this, she kept us apart, as she had kept her husband and our father apart. We grew up as strangers to each other. Our personalities were constructed by her in such a way that we were mutually incomprehensible. I was clever, he was slow. He was handsome, I was ugly. He was well behaved, I was trouble-some. He was practical, I was supposed to be 'creative'. As it turned out, he had inherited his father's craftsmanship, and I his radicalism. But what could such beings possibly have in common? We grew up estranged from one another in the claustral intensity of our narrow family group; and so effective was it that it has persisted all our lives. She praised us endlessly to outsiders, but never to our faces. She also complained to each about the other. 'He'll never amount to anything. He hasn't got a ha'porth of common sense. He'll never get anywhere. He'd better learn to hold a brush properly, because sweeping the roads is all he'll ever be fit for. He isn't sharp enough to give handbills out. He's a great dream of delight.' But she gave us to understand that each was the preferred one; and this was perhaps the best way of keeping us apart. We savoured, in secret, our superior status, not knowing that this was part of a competitive separation destined to last a life-time.

When she told us, she was already seventy. She spoke to us separately; but for once we were united in our response that she had done the right thing. But as soon as she had parted with her secret, she began to shake. It was as though keeping it had been the principal thing keeping her together. She was diagnosed has having Parkin-son's disease, but she said, what did the doctors know about such things? She also suffered from agoraphobia, and became afraid to go out of doors. Her life was already limited to the daily walk into town from the little terraced house where we lived with her sister after the divorce; her only outing was to the market square, to exchange gossip with acquaintances around the trestles laden with locally grown apples and tomatoes. But even that ceased. Soon, she would no longer leave the security of the house; then of the room, and later, of the chair and bed placed next to it. Illness became her last refuge, her identity.

She had lived in dread of going into a home; but that is where she finally went, rigid with arthritis and yet shaking uncontrollably. It cost the state £350 a week to keep her there. The private room looked onto a golf course, landscaped, an instant garden of hypericum and cotoneaster; a room with floral curtains and matching watercolours on the walls. She looked round and said, 'When we were kids, we had orange-box furniture and sacks at the window, because other people were making money out of us. The only thing that's changed is the scenery.' She hated the thought that her infirmity and dereliction should be someone else's business opportunity. But in spite of her loneliness she had a considerable capacity for attaching people to her. The women workers in the home used to gather to her room, to complain, to confess, to cry, to tell of their secret worries, their breaking marriages, their children's success. Perhaps they sensed they were in the presence of one whose supreme gift lay in the keeping of secrets.

She had always appeared to me a sombre woman, puritanical, always anticipating the worst. I feared that she would die as she had lived, in struggle and in anger. I dreaded that she would seek our company in death as she had sought our unknowing complicity in her life. But it wasn't so. She had a chest infection that failed to respond to antibiotics, and within a few hours, she was dead. They were giving her a cup of tea; she appeared to die; but then raised up her head once more to take her last breath. An easy death, they all said. A lovely way to go.

Having been away, I felt a need to see her. Her body was in the undertaker's chapel of rest. They had dressed her in a white gown with silver embroidery and lacy cuffs, raiment really, a going-to-heaven wear of her childhood Sunday school hymns. She would have hated it, just as she had always hated the crematorium where the funeral service was conducted, built in the 1930s and given as a 21st birthday present by the owner to his son, because he had foreseen that burning was the coming thing. Perhaps it was the gulf between appearance and reality in her own life that gave her such a lively sense of social incongruities; and this has been one of her many gifts to me. Although she had ceased reading many months before, she kept her two favourite books close to her; they were *Bleak House* and *Mill on the Floss*.

Although I had been preoccupied, almost obsessed with my relationship with her well into maturity, I felt neither guilty nor overwhelmed by her death. I thought of the women of the foothills of the Himalayas who had stayed to fight the destruction of their environment; and I thought of her kinship with them, who had remained to fight the inner desolation of her life. I am grateful for these insights into the same endurance and creativity of women of different societies and cultures; women who remain and remember, where men run away and forget.

Britain's Third World:

Cornwall Undermined

A council house in Troon; a small estate on a grassy promontory overlooking Camborne in Cornwall; white painted cubes cool in the clear Cornish light. The house has a fleecy carpet, there is a stereo, a television and video; a cabinet with painted china birds, a comfortable three-piece in chocolate brown. The late sun pours into the room and the cigarette smoke uncoils slowly. A cat lies on each windowsill.

A curious anomaly: we are talking about poverty in this comfortable and pleasant interior. And in spite of the possessions, it is a real poverty. Tessa has just had to borrow £2 from her neighbour Lorraine, so that the children can stay to school dinners tomorrow. She owes Lorraine £50 for money she borrowed to redeem her furniture from the bailiffs when she had not paid the poll tax. Altogether it cost her over £200, including court costs, for a poll tax bill of £77. Lorraine herself has debts of about 'two grand'.

Tessa has divorced her second husband, and Lorraine is now on her own. 'You could count the happy marriages on this estate on one hand.' Why do our relationships seem so fragile? 'Money. It puts a strain on you. You start to argue. More people break up over money than anything else.'

Another curious thing; money is seen as both the cause and the cure for this sickness of the heart and spirit that leaves so many women on their own. 'Men walk away,' they tell you. 'It's the women who stay, the women who pay off the debts, pay the bills, face the hardships, go without for the children. Men can't put up with what women have to bear. They walk away scot free.'

Tessa is in her thirties, with two children; a woman with strong and independent views. 'Two weeks ago, I looked out of the window and saw two blokes coming up the path. When I got down here, they were already inside. I'd written to them offering to pay off so much a week; mind you, I got a bollocking because I didn't put a stamp on the letter. They took the washing machine and the stereo and the microwave, which they damaged. I had to find £88 poll tax, £44 court fees, £128 and £4.50 a day for storage charge. They said, "You've got a lot of nice stuff in here." They were gifts and presents. They said, "I should get your little girl out, you don't want any unpleasant scenes in front of her." "There won't be any scenes unless you make them." '

'I get £64 family credit, I'd saved £33 in pennies and five pence towards the children's Christmas. I had to borrow. I was working, but I gave it up because I was sick. I was working in a nursing home, domestic work, cleaning, getting £47 a week. £2.35 an hour. I loved the old people.'

Lorraine was working as a care assistant in a nursing home, at £2.90 an hour. 'I've got these debts, rent arrears. I was taken to court, I offered £10 a week, they took £15. There were my kids and his kids, and he had a lot of family who favoured his. It didn't work out. I ought to have known, a guy who had "BOLLOCKS" in Indian ink all down one arm.'

Tessa says, 'I came here happily married to the children's father, but we split up after four years. I was married again; that lasted six months. He pinned my son against the wall, a ten year old, and threatened to knock his fucking teeth down his throat. He called my daughter, who was eight, a slag and a prostitute. He was younger than me, but jealous. If I talked to anybody else, I was having an affair with them.'

Lorraine was in court because she worked without declaring her earnings. 'I was paying the babysitter, so none of the wages I was getting came to me. I got reported by the bloke I kicked out. I was done for fraud. I said to him, "It's the kids you're hurting, not me." They said I'd been overpaid by £470. After he'd gone, he broke in a few times, ripped the mattress up, my clothes, carpets and curtains. The police won't do anything. He's on a suspended sentence, but still he can pester me and they won't stop it. He got a pasting, he accused somebody of having an affair with me, and he got himself put in hospital.'

Tessa says, 'I have a clothes party once in a while, because with the 12½ per cent commission, you can buy a few summer clothes. I don't have perfume of jewellery parties.' The children come in, wanting to play with make-up. They have some nail-polish. 'On your toes only', say the mothers severely, 'not on your fingers.' Tessa's present boyfriend is working. He is earning £45 a week, car-valeting, a full-time job. 'If he didn't take it, he'd have to go to a jobclub, and he'd be made to take something for benefit plus £10.'

Camborne was, until the mid-1980s, the centre of tin-mining in Cornwall. The stone fingers of chimneys point upwards everywhere, garlanded with ivy; and the ruins of the pump-houses are the size of abandoned churches. The earth has subsided under the tunnelling beneath: it is a regular occurrence for holes to appear, for houses to be made unstable; recently, a big hole appeared in a garden in Gunnislake, swallowed up by a mineshaft. Houses are boarded up, precariously balanced on the verge of disappearing into the honeycomb of adits and shafts under the town. Old miners tell how they have been able to hear the Camborne town clock chiming above them as they've worked.

Many are bitter about the haste with which the mines were closed. There is no shortage of tin; it is simply that the price collapsed in the mid-1980s, and the government refused any further subsidy. It has taken the heart out of Camborne. Camborne–Redruth have one of the highest levels of unemployment in the country. The deskilling of another workforce: their children the inheritors of strange new poverties that come with an absence of function or purpose. In the town streets at weekends, the young people line up as the nightclub turns out, facing the police and waiting for something to happen.

Dennis worked at Crofty Mine. 'It was a family,' he insists. 'I had two wives. I was married to the pit before I was married to my wife. I loved the mine. It talked to me. I finished up as charge-hand at Crofty. Before it went automatic, the bosses were the same as we. Look at this town now, it's like a frontier town. I voted for the Conservatives. I thought the sun shone out of their backsides. Not any more.'

His son, Steve, lives on the Treswithian estate. He thinks himself lucky: Jenny, his wife, writes him love-poetry. They started their married life in a caravan, where, in winter, the weather was colder inside than out. They then rented a cottage at the Beacon, the highest part of Camborne, from where you can see the bay of St Ives and Penzance. 'I was going to drop with the baby, two weeks away', says Jenny, 'and I came home one day and found the door was locked. The landlord had defaulted on the mortgage and his house was repossessed. The rent we'd been paying him – £280 a month – hadn't gone to the mortgage.' 'When I found out what happened I went bananas. I was gonna go and drop the guy, he was an ex-marine, you know, sound as a pound type. If it hadn't been for Jenny and the kids I would have done. We couldn't get into our own house. When we did get in, they allowed us just three hours to pack up everything; we went in at 9.00 and had to be out by 12.00. The bailiffs nailed the windows and doors. We had nothing. No nappies. All we had was what we stood up in. It took four weeks before we could get our stuff.'

'After that, we went into council bed and breakfast for three months.' Steve had done 2½ years at the same mine as his father, but left just before the wave of redundancies were announced. 'I was laying tracks, digging gutters, laying pipes to carry the ore away from the face. I was getting good money when I was twenty. I left to do better work, site clearance, but that only lasted a few months. Since then I haven't worked. That's six years ago. I'm a skilled tyre-fitter. I have been offered a job at £60 a week, but I can't afford it. I always say I can't afford to work.'

Jenny says, 'We lived in a damp, wet caravan. Our child was bronchial and asthmatic. We were told by the doctor and the health visitor we had to get out. We went to stay with his Dad, but we had to ask him to throw us out, because the council said that leaving the caravan, we'd made ourselves intentionally homeless. The owner of the van was a dog-kennel owner; the dogs lived warmer and drier than we were. The nearest shop was 2 miles away.'

Steve says, 'As it is now, we get around £140 a week, all told. If I got a low-paid job, I'd lose a lot of the benefits I get. I'd rather earn a wage; you get satisfaction knowing you sweated for it. I can cook, I do a lot of the work round the house. I keep myself together decorating and making improvements. We'll get there eventually. We got a loan from the social fund for the baby. I resent this area being a holiday and retirement area. They forget we live here. As far as the government is concerned Britain ends at Plymouth. They could have kept the mines open. I know guys who've gone to Nova Scotia, Canada, South Africa, Australia, if they have their certificate in blasting or drilling. If I had mine, I'd go too. My best friend went to a gold mine in Nova Scotia.'

Like so many before them. In the graveyard in Troon, the stones commemorate Cornish people who died in Australia, California, Cuba, Nevada, and Pachuca, in Mexico, where Cornishmen were involved in silver mining. 'Wherever in the world there is hard rock mining, you'll find Cornish people there.' Cornwall is the only county in England to have a population lower now than in the mid-nineteenth century. Camborne–Redruth have the languor of all small towns from where able people have departed over decades; 'Life down here is all right once you get used to it. There's two speeds in Cornwall, slow and stop.'

Pauline's mother died three months ago. She says bitterly, 'On her death bed, she was counting her money to see if she had enough to pay her poll tax.' She was granted attendance allowance one week before she died. She said, 'I had to go without for twenty years, then when I'm dying they give me money.' Pauline says, 'She lived on a packet of cup-a-soup, an orange and a Weetabix for a week.' Pauline's grandfather founded the Labour Party in Camborne. He went to jail in the General Strike: 'People couldn't afford to buy milk, and the ice-cream merchant was buying it all up cheap to make ice-cream. My grandfather overturned all the churns, and all the milk went down the street. He said, "If they won't give the milk to the poor, nobody else is going to have it." He did fourteen days in Bodmin Jail for that.'

Pauline is a fighter; in constant pain from a motorbike accident, when her son took her out on his new motorbike and took a corner too fast. She had a fractured spine, and has also had several operations for cancer. She has three sons in the army. They have been in Northern Ireland. She says, 'My boy's best friend, a Sikh boy, was lured with another by a woman into a house for a drink after the pub closed. She said to them, "Wait on the couch while I get a drink"; and they were machine-gunned, as they sat there, by two men. The boy's head was blown off.'

In Cornwall they say if low wages and no unions were the key to economic success, we'd be the most booming place in Britain. 'We've done what we were told and now look at us'; a service economy, daffodils, nursing homes and tourism. As it is, Camborne has one of the highest rates of unemployment in the country. Mining skills lie neglected, a generation grows to futility and absence of satisfying work.

The main street of Camborne is lined with empty shops, dusty windows and flyposters for long-gone fairs and concerts. Many shops have been taken over by charities, windows displaying faded albums of Our Wedding, Diana and Charles mugs and lurex string-paintings. The decline of the shops has been quickened by the new Tesco store, which occupies the site of the former principal employer in the town, Holman's Engineering, which specialized in Mining equipment and provided work for several thousand people. The company was taken over and asset-stripped, and the rump of it is now owned by a transnational. The Holman mansion is now a nursing home. 'The big stores have not only killed the small shops, they're also destroying the livelihood of smallholders in Cornwall. Farms used to supply small shops; but they can't do it on the scale the big stores want. A cauliflower grown in Cornwall now has to travel back via London and Birmingham, and costs three times as much,' says Kevin Austin, who runs an organic food shop in nearby Falmouth.

Crofty is the last mine working now. The Wheal Jane was closed in the 1980s, the pumps turned off and the mine flooded; so that even now the price of tin has risen again, the mine cannot be reopened.

Redruth, with its grandiose nineteenth-century buildings, is a town left with archaic industrial buildings on a scale too large for its present size; the viaduct, the clock tower and monuments to the industrial inventiveness of the Cornish: the first building lighted by gas in 1792, the first locomotive tested in 1784. The town evokes its industrial past, when there were over a hundred mines around Redruth–Camborne, with smoking chimneys, horse-drawn traffic taking wood, coal, ore, the balmaidens, women who broke the rocks, crushing the ore for tin.

But today's reality is the secondhand shop run by Chris Mayall in the shadow of the industrial dereliction. 'People come in to sell small things for one pound, 50 pence. A woman came in with a plastic bird; she wanted 30 pence to buy milk for her baby. Some of the things are pitiful, you have to offer something, although it's junk. You're not getting stuff for £50, you're talking about pennies. The lack of personal and public transport means that a lot of people cannot even get to the offices to claim the benefits that are theirs by right. My own son and nephew, they pick daffodils, pinks at this season, get £10 or £11 a day. One lives in a caravan, the other in his van. People become travellers because they have nowhere to live. Some of the caravans on disused mine areas are shanty towns. A bed-sit here costs £55.' Chris Mayall is extending the shop with information about communal activities, green products, a car-share system, tools for self-reliance and recycling. 'Traditionally in Cornwall they make and mend, they never throw anything away. In one way it is easier to live an alternative lifestyle now – we are no longer regarded as nutters; but on the other hand, it is getting harder, because animosity is being whipped up against the Greens – look at Dan Quayle's description of "extreme environmentalists as the new Communists".'

Cornwall is Britain's Third World, the forgotten part of the country. Some of the caravan sites, the trailer parks, are reminiscent of squatter settlements in the South.

Boscarn Park is at Pool, midway between Redruth and Camborne; close to the old pump house and chimney of a disused mine; behind it ravaged hills and disused workings, covered at this time of year by wild flowers – willowherb and cornflowers and toadflax. Behind, there is a cement works, which blows perpetual dust onto the site. There are twenty-one homes here, mostly mobile, metal and wood, arranged around a cul-de-sac, some with fences and little gardens; but nearer the entrance to the site, the vans are parked very close together so that there are only 2 or 3 feet between them; the site is littered with glass and recycled material, wood and old furniture; and unsightly tin sheds, which the council installed as outside latrines.

Caroline Richards has seven children and forty-two grand-children, mostly living on the site. Her caravan is close to two others; outside there are some green moquette chairs, an overflowing dust-bin, rank, coarse grass; clean washing dances on the line and catches on the bushes nearby. Inside, the caravan is spacious; a sofa and chairs, a TV and stereo; an outsize birthday card on the wall, a mirror with tarnished metal curlicues, a plastic chandelier, a picture of an idealized country scene, children's toys. A video called 'Blood Sport' on the sideboard. She makes sweet, strong tea, which she offers in fluted rosy teacups. Although there are only twenty-one vans , the site contains nearly two hundred people. Caroline wears a necklace of old coins, a yellow and black dress, and remembers the time when they really were travellers, going round in pony and trap with her parents, making and selling clothes pegs and paper flowers; they used to burn the old wooden waggons when the owner died; these were ornate and painted in primary colours. Caroline was fourteen when they came to the site; they settled because her brother was dying of leukaemia. They worked as rag and bone people, and made a living out of scrap metal and iron. Boscarn Park has a reputation in Camborne. 'Don't go there', people tell you, 'they're all criminals.' The people who live here are proud of their gipsy origins. 'We all bleed the same way', says Caroline, 'we all die the same way, how can flesh and blood be any different?'

Sophie is Caroline's daughter. Her husband, Philip, is now on a return-to-learning course, improving literacy and numeracy. He worked eighteen years for a market garden firm, and now has been four years without work. Philip is not a gipsy; he grew up on a farm. For ten years they lived in Redruth away from the site. Sophie says, 'The worst thing about living here is that we're too close together. If anybody goes to the lav, everybody knows about it; you can hear what people say to each other, there's no secrets here. That's why we went to live away. But Philip got into a fight , he was beaten up and lost the sight of one eye. With the criminal damage money, we bought a house, but when he lost his job, we lost the house and moved back here.' Sophie would prefer to live in a house, mainly, she says, for the children's sake. Her son's best friend is not allowed to visit him because of where he lives. 'But the family is here. We might quarrel and have our fights, but as soon as anyone comes from outside, we stick together.' From outside it is mainly the police who come. 'We're not angels, but we get blamed for things we haven't done.'

Robert has been in Exeter jail a few times, starting with stealing milk for the children. 'The gorgies (non-gipsies) call us diddicais and worse. We're gipsies and proud of it. We have a tough life, but we have freedom the gorgies don't have.'

Robert has separated from his wife, and has kept Craig, the eldest boy. He is not working now, because, he says, it is a full-time job being a parent and getting it right. He is pleased to spend his time taking care of his son.

'Do you feel poor?' I asked. 'We do feel poor, because we have to go without. We never go out for a drink, we have to buy the cheapest foods. I spent £40 today', says Sophie, 'and that will have to last a fortnight. Philip has a goat, and he will sell the kids at £10 each.' Philip sits on the sofa, taking the cigarette butts of roll-ups out of the tin where he stores them after he's finished smoking; with the tobacco from eight or ten of these he can make a fresh roll-up. Robert was flower and bulb picking, and somebody snooped to the Department of Social Security; they have ordered him to pay back £3,000.

'At one time, there were a lot of things you could get to eat free. I was brought up on rabbits', says Caroline, 'but the young people won't eat them. They used to eat hedgehogs, make lapwing pie, pigeon pie. That's all gone now.'

There is plan to improve the site here; the area behind the existing site is to be levelled and upgraded, so that people have more space. 'They want to keep the site open', says Robert, 'because they don't want us near them. When they had a plan to enlarge the site, the local people thought they going to make room for more houses, and they got a petition against us. Five thousand people signed. That shows what they think of us. They plan to barricade us in with trees. There's a garage owner up the road, he built a big house five years ago. He never came and asked our permission, whether we minded or not; but they think they can dictate to us where and how we should live. They call us thieves and tramps, what about them and the way they make their money. We didn't pay the poll tax, and in court the judge said, don't pay until the site has been upgraded. They're still stopping £6 a fortnight out of my dole money to pay it.

'We do want a permanent site, but not one where they can hide us away, forget all about us.'

Robert is under curfew. He has to be in by nine. He got into a fight. Somebody said to him 'Fuck your mother', and he laid into him.

The money they get from the social fund is paid direct to the shops, so they can buy only in kind. Caroline now gets attendance allowance, because she is badly disabled by arthritis. You have to learn to survive, bypass the electricity meter. 'We won't have gas, because it's not so easy to do,' Sophie says. 'There's a lot of people would like to do to us what Hitler did to the gipsies.'

Betsy, Caroline's sister, lives in a new house on the other side of the road. The houses cost about £8,000; they have to pay cash – there are no loans or mortgages for gipsies. She says, 'It's like a Vietnam prisoner-of-war camp. We only want to be free to lead the life we want. It's not us that's the problem, it's other people who can't leave us alone. I'm proud of being a gipsy and I'll live the way I like. I don't interfere with they, why should they interfere with we? No gipsy ever abuses children, they should look at their own problems, and not blame us.' Of her sister, Betsy says, 'Caroline would do good to a dog. I've known her give a bed to a homeless stranger.' Betsy's husband has been thirteen years without work. 'As soon as you say Boscarn Park, people don't want to know. You can't get credit if you've an address down here. We've had stones chucked through our window. You go to the police, they won't do anything. If any member of your family does something bad to you, you might ring the police, but when they get down here, we won't shop them or anything. We have our own ways of getting back if somebody does anything. We get our own revenge.

'I love my way of life. We have outside fires in the evening, and my dad tells us stories. He sold his painted waggon for £4,000 some years ago; it was a beautiful thing, all made by himself, it was worth much more.'

Granny Isaacs was the matriarch and tyrant of the family. She died over a hundred years old, and now there is no family boss. They say, 'She was wicked. She went to DSS and told them my brother was selling daffodils in Redruth when he was dying of leukaemia. We spat on her grave.'

In the centre of Redruth, Lee and Adam are eating burgers. Adam has been offered a job packing leisurewear for £2.08 an hour. He was manager of a sports shop in Sevenoaks, Kent, but when his family moved back to Cornwall, he came with them. He was judged to have given up his job voluntarily, and got only £18 a week. That was after being on £10,000 a year. Lee has just left college, doing an HND in Geology and Applied Computing. 'I have a bad ear and couldn't get a safety certificate for mining. I would have gone on to do a degree, but I already owe £2,000; another two years I don't know how deep in debt I'd be. I thought I was bettering myself. I come back and find kids of eighteen driving fast cars, I really wonder why I bothered.' Adam says, 'We come down here in the early afternoon to the Jobcentre, because the vacancies go up at midday. You don't get tired, so you stay up all night, then sleep in the daytime.' He says, self-deprecating, almost apologetic, 'Our days are measured by the time of the Australian soaps on TV.'

There is a severe shortage of housing in the Camborne–Redruth area; an unusually high proportion of people living in caravans, old cars, lodging with families, seeking refuge in hostels. A hostel built by the Devon and Cornwall Housing Association is always full; people waiting to be rehoused by the council, only families, no single people. Tamsin is about to give birth, any time now. Donald was working in a meatpacking factory for £2.75 an hour; but when he lost his job he was thrown out of the house by his brother. They went into bed and breakfast, which costs the council £140 a week; in the hostel the £80 housing benefit is much cheaper.

Elaine is in the wash room of the new hostel. She and her husband had a small business in town, called the Stork's Nest, a shop selling baby clothes. He was an alcoholic, who denied it, and she was left to do all the work and look after three children. In the end, the business failed, and she was not allowed to take over the mortgage. One of the children is asthmatic and has had thirty-five hospital admissions. The children keep saying, 'When are we going home?' Elaine has seen her dreams of owning her own business realized and then lost. It is a very painful experience. People move in and out of poverty arbitrarily; the image of the wheel of fortune is appropriate; so much depends on whether you have a good partner, the state of the economy, your own health. Those who get stigmatized as homeless, unemployed, are for the most part able and competent people. There is no underclass; there are just victims of a system, some of whom are better placed to cope and fight back than others.

Julie has been in the hostel for a year. The landlord sold the house she and her husband were renting, and they had two weeks to find somewhere else. They spent 4½ months with their two children in bed and breakfast. 'We were all in one room all evening; there was nothing to do but watch TV, but that kept the children awake.' Julie's husband is a maintenance mechanic at a theme park; he looks after the machinery, dredges the pools, leaves home at 7.30 in the morning and is frequently not home till 9 in the summer season. 'It's a very responsible job. If there should be an accident, he'd be in terrible trouble. But he gets £80–£90 a week. It's seasonal, and he doesn't know whether he'll be kept on in the winter or not.' Julie's mother's house was attached to a house which fell down a mineshaft, a crater opened up. It took them three or four years to have it declared unsafe. Julie is paying £61.30 a month to keep her furniture in store in an old chapel. Over the year, she has paid out nearly a £1,000. 'If we were on income support, the council would pay for that, but because Adam works, we have to pay it.'

Opposite the hostel, there is a row of cottages. The door of one stands open, with the sound of the group Europe on the stereo. Tony, twenty-five, is looking through the paper for a job. He has been out of work for eighteen months. He applied for a job at £2.18 an hour in a pottery, but heard nothing from them. He has worked on construction, farm work, bulbs, welding. Seven months ago he moved in with his girlfriend, Sharon, who has five children. She is also unemployed. The DSS pays interest on the mortgage. Tony has also been a nightclub bouncer, and he worked on building the Redruth bypass, driving a dumper truck; at that time, he had the ornate tattoos on his arms done – £475 worth. Since he has been out of work, he has learned to cook and look after the children. The baby in the high chair is eating a burger from a plastic container.

Karen's husband works in Ealing as a Vodaphone engineer. Karen has a baby of three months. She went to join him there, in a room for which they paid £100 a week. Karen was afraid to go out on her own into the streets of London. After six weeks, she came back to Cornwall. She had not been out once on her own in all that time. He calls her every day. She thinks she may try again because it can't be much good for her daughter to be without a father, no matter how much money he earns. She is in her sister's house waiting for the phone call.

Susan's husband is working, but she has to supplement his wages by working twelve hours a week in a supermarket for £32. She says, 'What kind of a future have they got? I found my daughter crying, because she is afraid of the future. When you're young, you should feel your life is before you; any kid with any sensitivity feels afraid. What an inheritance for young people. At Camborne's school, they've even got a nursery for the pupil's children. Then they want to teach them sex education.'

In the poor houses, the children learn how to be dispossessed. I want this. I'm having that. What will you give me? Where's mine? How much can I have? What have you got for me? What have you brought me? The mother of Nicola and Carl tries to pacify them by promising what Father Christmas will bring, while the bonfires are being lighted on the hills around Camborne to celebrate midsummer eve. 'They know what they want,' says Gracie admiringly, but the ambiguity of what she says escapes her. They know what they want, but they don't know what is lacking.

The winds from the Atlantic blow over the high ground of Camborne. Every year, with the gales, tiles and roofs will be blown off; to be a roofer here is the safest work. For the rest, it has all gone, the Bassets, mineral lords of the Camborne–Redruth mines, their mansion gutted by fire in 1919, the old man who was chauffeur to Jim Holman, the assayers and miners, the mine-captains in their villas, now given over to bedsits and rundown flats, or converted into nursing homes where the smudge of pale faces behind lace curtains suggests novel forms of dereliction, new poverties that luxuriate in the spaces once occupied by mining and the making of material necessities.

Britain's Third World:

The Land of Broken Toys

'When I was nine, I lived in the hills of Jamaica with my grandmother. She called me one day: "Dee, come quick. A telegram from England. Your mother and father send for you." I was really excited. I thought I'm going to the land of broken toys, because my parents always sent me toys the other children finished with.'

Layers of 'urban renewal' have still not effaced the Victorian fabric of the Granby Triangle, the black area of Toxteth. The dark-red glazed brick of derelict pubs, the Storage Yard of Liverpool Water Works, the closed public baths and shell of a library are ghosts of what were, in their time, also civic improvements. Within a few hundred yards, there are flats from the 1930s, ruinous brick arches and asphalt covered with splintered glass; from the 1950s, with sunlight pouring through the lattice of bare roofs; 1960 cubes now completely untenanted; and new houses, seven years old, in neat closes, tinned up and invaded by rank grass. The life expectancy of houses, it seems, decreases with each decade.

The sites of the 1981 riots have been landscaped. On Lodge Lane, the spaces of burned-out shops are grassy mounds with saplings; as though this cemetery landscape could lay to rest the injustice and oppression that led to the uprising. The shops that were burned, people tell you, never employed black people.

'Liverpool is a very racist city. You feel secure in Granby, but you think twice before you go to the all-white areas of the North End. Racism? It means shopkeepers don't even place the change in your hand, but throw it down on the counter.

'I was seven months pregnant, walking down Beaumont Street. My husband happened to be a few yards behind me. An unmarked police car drew up, and the driver said, "Want a lift?" They wanted to do me for soliciting and him for pimping. Seven months pregnant, I couldn't believe it.'

'After the riots in 1981, they told us: "Violence will get you

184

nowhere." But it did! All the politicians came, the leaders, the charity workers, the church leaders, pop stars, the poverty tourists. Everybody came!'

'Whenever their is a funeral here, everybody turns out. Traffic comes to a standstill. It's an act of defiance. You make us wait for you all our lives. We'll make you wait, just once, when we're dead.'

'Black boys grow up knowing how to use white racism: we use the fear white boys have of us for our own safety. That's what gets us through life.'

On the end wall in Granby Street, in white paint: 'Pigs Enter Here At Your Own Risk.' The bricked-up windows of some derelict houses have been covered up by paintings of black heroines and heroes: Sojourner Truth, 'Proclaim liberty throughout the land and to all the inhabitants thereof'; Steve Biko, Harriet Tubman, Female Moses of Her Race. Nearby, there is an announcement that a police video camera was found hidden behind a high wall in January 1991, trained onto the entrance of a nearby cafe. A high-tech community spy.

The young men stand on the corner of Granby Street, kicking a football against a blank wall. Denied function and purpose, they are resources taken out of production, like fallow fields, their youth and energy rejected by the society. This waste of human resources is the counterpart of industrial society's waste of material resources – a double prodigality in a poor, suffering world. 'Bread and hope are what the people need; take away either, and they perish.'

Ken Drysdale has a barber's shop on Granby Street. Newly painted, immaculate white interior, gleaming new equipment. But the shop is more than it seems. For Ken also runs the Granby Drug Awareness project. Born in Granby, one of seven children, when he talks of the youth, his voice is vibrant with feeling. 'I see the lads out there, and my heart aches, because I was like them. I see possibilities in them that nobody else sees. If treated right, they will open up like flowers, kids society has written off. I know what I'm saying. I started to get my education only after I left school. I read my first book at nineteen. Look at it – the only institution of the state represented here is the police. When I started the project, the official agencies thought: "Who is this black upstart?" We've had laminated cards printed, telling kids the effects of each drug – smack, crack, ecstasy – and what to do if anyone overdoses. We've just received £5,000 from the Home Office, after working five years at it. I understand the psyche of the lads. I know what disadvantage and low self-esteem do to them. I know why a young man won't even get up in the morning to go for an interview for a job that will have gone the minute they set eyes on him. The youth are full of a righteous anger. The question never asked is "What makes a section of society feel so cornered that they'll pillage and loot and burn?" They haven't asked it in Los Angeles, and they haven't asked it in Liverpool.'

In 1919, there was a demonstration in Liverpool by demobbed soldiers; organized by the Seaman's Union, it called for all non-whites to be dismissed from the jobs they'd held during the war – on the ships, in the engineering factories. They were replaced by whites. Some blacks could not go back to sea and were stranded in Liverpool. The demonstration ended in the first race riot in Britain. Charles Wootton was chased by a white mob, and drowned in the Mersey.

Joe looks at his wife tenderly, and says, 'I admire the white women who don't walk away from the racist pressure. For black women, there is nowhere to go. But white women have a choice. They can leave it. But they don't.' Audrey left school before she was fifteen, and at sixteen was married. 'I hated school. I hated it because they didn't recognize that I was intelligent. I met Joe in the "Cavern", and that was it. None of my family came to the wedding. My brothers disowned me.'

Ann, now in her forties, says she was given away at birth. She was taken by a white woman, who was cast off by her family for doing it. 'She had a terrible life, but she was a beautiful woman, she never let go of me for a minute.' When her husband came back from sea, he assumed that she had had an affair with a black man, and he beat her up. 'People used to say to me, "How come you're brown when your parents are white?" I used to say, "They give me a lot of cocoa." I was sheltered from prejudice till I had my own children.

'I thought my own father was dead. Then one day, talking with a neighbour, it turned out he was a countryman of his. He said "What was his name?" I told him, and said, "but he's long dead." "No he's not, he's living round the corner. I'll fetch him." And he did.

'When I had my first child, the hospital gave me a hard time because I was black and not married. All the married white women were at one end of the ward with their husbands and flowers, and there was I all on my own at the other. Segregated.

'I remember carrying my mother up three flights of stairs when she was drunk. The women used to say, "That poor child, her mother's drunk again."' Ann says, 'I am glad I wasn't rich, because if I had been, I wouldn't be the person I am today.' She would not have the compassion and feeling for others which inform her life. She still lays out the dead and comforts the bereaved. 'I tell the youth, "Now watch what I'm doing, because you'll have to do it one day." I don't know if they will. But there is a strong solidarity here. When joyriders killed the two children in Granby Street, everybody was wonderful. It's hard to explain to outsiders the generosity of the poor. Those who have nothing give the most, because they are giving of themselves.'

On the radio there is a local news item about a man lying drunk outside the pub in Bootle. Police are looking for two men who partly succeeded in gouging his eyes out. People in Toxteth are shocked. 'That would never happen here.'

The redevelopment of Albert Dock and the Festival Park are linked by a new road that avoids Toxteth, so that commuters from the new estates no longer even have to see it. A notice near the Park says: 'You are Now Entering the Pleasure Zone.' Joe Farrag says 'The pain zone has been bypassed. None of the money that came into Liverpool after the uprising has done anything to alleviate poverty or unemployment in Toxteth.' The biggest section of work on offer in the Jobcentre is Jobs in Other Areas.

The most recent newcomers to Granby are refugees from Somalia, people displaced by civil war. The local authority sent them here, assuming that they will be safe in a black community. Adam Hussein, whose father came from Somalia in the 1940s, says, 'There has been friction between the newcomers and the indigenous black community, if I can call it that. It's not the first time. The same thing happened when the Caribbeans came in the sixties. Caribbean kids spoke the nation-language which we couldn't understand, and English-speaking Scouse blacks felt threatened. We assumed they were thick, and picked fights with them.'

In an incident at the end of May, a Somali man lost the fingers of one hand from a machete blow. 'The Somalis were resented, because they got houses. They were houses nobody wanted until they were done up; then everybody wants them. The police know who did the machete work on the Somali, but they took no action. Why? They went to the mosque and told the Somalis that they are entitled to defend themselves. What is that if not an invitation to further violence? Do they want another excuse to move in in force and wreck the place again? There have been a number of attacks on Somali women – people burst into the houses and snatch their handbags, because Somalis are seen as weak and vulnerable. What they don't realize is that they have come from a war zone, are extremely traumatized; many have bullet scars. If the police don't take action, the Somalis will. They have lost family and friends, they're not going to take whatever shit is handed out to them. It isn't as if all indigenous blacks are against them, it is just a certain group. They know what they're doing is wrong – they all take part in the same covert economic activity, they depend on the same people. But some local young blacks say, "They think they're better than us because they're Muslims." Trouble is, some of the blacks have had white values knocked into them.'

Joe's father was deported as an illegal alien when Joe was two. Joe left school at fourteen. He was charged three times with trespass with intent to burgle because he used to go to the university library to read. By the time he as fifteen, he had been before the court five times, and was sent to an approved school.

His son Ben, sixteen, has been excluded from school, the victim of bullying by a racist teacher. After some trivial incident, this teacher said to him, 'You've wasted five minutes of my time.' Ben replied, 'You've wasted two years of mine.' Far from being embittered, Ben went to the Education Department and suggested that each school set up an ombudsperson to prevent problems from escalating into exclusions of black kids. As a result, a pilot scheme is to be set up.

Delroy is a musician, who has just recorded a song with some eleven year olds called 'Stop the Joyriding', a response to the Granby Street deaths. Delroy has a powerful sense of mission with his band, Jah Deeankho. A Rastafarian, he was captured by his Creator who directed him to Liverpool to help save the youth from self-destruction. He says, 'The youth have no sense of the future. They say, "What does it matter, with pollution and the hole in the ozone layer, we shall all die, so who cares if you take drugs, damage yourself." Those who have no perspective are condemned to live in the present.

'I say to my brethren, "We are born in debt." Our ancestors who were slaves ran away from the plantations. They knew if they were caught, they would be hanged, some boiled alive. But they knew some would escape. They said, "We must do it, because then our children will be born free." I say to my brethren, "If you do nothing, you have wasted their sacrifice and their love. We are the posterity they died for."

'I am a prisoner now of what I know: consciousness cannot be reversed. I love words, but words have failed the youth. We have to tell them through music, and they recognize themselves in what we say. We have to show them the map, because they do not know how to describe what is in their hearts.

'I could have hated white people for all they have done to us. But I don't. We have choice. Even the angels envy us, because we have choice and they don't. I have the strength of my grandmother. My achievement is to show a role model to the youth; we have been called Liverpool's finest reggae band. When I came here, I gave away all my earthly possessions, except my guitar and a change of underwear – that was my grandma's influence again.

'The problem is the rich. They have a disease called the desire for money; but when it spreads to the poor, they blame them and call them criminals and cheats.'

Steve Skeete is a footballer, who also offers a positive role model to the young. For the past five years he has run the successful Almithak Football Club, winner of the Liverpool Premier Cup, and voted best amateur team in the Commonwealth by the *Caribbean Times*. Almithak was formed by the merger of two clubs, one of them from the local Yemeni community. Yemen Airways promised sponsorship, and sent for the team to play in Yemen. 'We won against the Yemen national team. As we were leaving for the airport, the coach was boarded by soldiers, who ordered us to hand over the trophy at gunpoint. We never got the promised sponsorship either. But the success of Almithak has rekindled the interest of the youth in football, and there are teams of youngsters, under fourteens, under twelves, who call themselves the Almithak Colts.'

It isn't only sport and music that offer alternatives to young people. Michelle, a single parent, also a school drop-out, is starting a degree course in Media and Cultural Studies. She was a disc jockey on local pirate radio, where she was known as Sister M, and played reggae and soul. The radio station was raided and closed by the DTI. 'We are breaking out of the ghetto occupations open to black people. We fought for black access courses, for law, the civil service, business, social work, the media. I talk to my son about racism: he's only five, but here you know all about it by that age. Toxteth used to be an Orange area; people used to say, "I'd rather you marry a black man than a Catholic."

'The biggest employment here is the administration of poverty. If we were not criminalized, just think how many people would lose their jobs – police, social workers, the courts, probation officers, judges, social security officers. They should praise God we're here, because we guarantee their salary. Weed [cannabis] is the biggest "criminal" activity in Liverpool 8. It is part of daily life. We are criminalized for something that is accepted now virtually world-wide. If you take away cannabis-related crime, Toxteth would be the least criminal area of Liverpool; yet we have the highest intensity of policing.'

Austin Smith came to Granby twenty-five years ago, a priest of the Community of the Passion. 'When we came here, there was a lot of community action in Toxteth. We failed, because we were forced into being mediators, and therefore left the people as powerless as we had found them. Instead of drawing out their richness and experience, we spent our time getting round the bureaucracies and trusts, and getting money. We were selfish and satisfied and felt good. It took time before we woke up and realized you have to take on the institutions, the police, the local authority, employers. By the time of Thatcher, we were in despair, and overtaken by uprisings, when neighbourhoods were burned down. With the rebuilding, we have seen deeper dispossession – more poverty, more unemployment, reduced benefits, more wealth filtered away from the already impoverished.

'Racism is the next historical dialectic. What we are seeing now is the shattering of inherited symbols – power, economic growth, possession. Eternal questions have to be asked in time; and the symbols that reflect those eternal questions inevitably fall into decay. We are living through such a moment now.'

Joe Farrag has taken over the lease of a dilapidated, eighteenth-century building on the edge of Toxteth, formerly the lodge of the Knights of St Columba. In the basement, black groups are practising and rehearsing. He wants to turn the building into a gallery and meeting place, where poets and musicians will perform their own work, artists and craftspeople will sell what they make; 'a place where black and white, young and old, women and men will come and celebrate our community, so that we don't have any more people in from outside to tell the world how bad it is.'

Adam Hussein says, 'More and more people are saying, "Why fight for a slice of the cake, if the cake itself is poisoned? Why fight for equal opportunity, if that only means equal opportunity to exploit and cause pain to others?" '

Scenes from a Developing World

Tarlac is the home state of the former president of the Philippines, Corazon Aquino, and the site of the family's plantation, Hacienda Luisita. The hacienda is a well-guarded area of 6,000 hectares; expansive fields of sugar-cane, green spiky cockades and purple stems. There are twelve *barangays*, or villages, where most of the houses are of metal or wood. The plantation is criss-crossed by sluggish drainage canals, shaded by plantains and ipil-ipil. Waste from the refinery coats the vegetation along their banks with white sugary dust. The conditions in which the *sacadas* (itinerant cutters) live, are the worst. Sweltering tin barracks two storeys high house these workers from Negros, emaciated hungry wanderers, who move from one hacienda to another, almost permanently separated from their families.

Because sugar has lost value on the world market in recent years – partly because of the growth of beet in the rich world and partly by the substitution of artificial sweeteners – the hacienda must diversify, or see its profitability eroded. This is why, on the edge of the plantation, the first phase of an industrial estate has been completed. Luisita wants to expand further; and for those now living outside the compound, this will mean eviction.

The people of Capehan have been given orders to evacuate their properties. Capehan is a long-established settlement, to which no one has ever previously contested the right of ownership by its residents. It was settled mainly by those who had served in the Philippines army: it was given to veterans in the 1920s. None of the residents has ever paid realty tax, which means that they are not recognized as owners of the site where they have built their houses. In February 1991, they received letters informing them that the Tarlac Development Corporation is the owner of the land. The fact that TDC was set up by José Cojuangco, brother of Corazon Aquino, means that the hacienda itself is seizing this land from its rightful owners. The barangay covers 2.8 hectares, which are contiguous with a piece of land sold to the Luisita Realty Corporation in 1987. This company has erected the first phase of the industrial estate, which is occupied by mainly Japanese companies. The owner of the LRC is Miguel Araneta, son-in-law of José Cojuangco. A subsequent letter to the residents said: 'Please realize that by your adamant refusal to be relocated, you have derailed and set back the timetable and schedule of the industrialization programme of TDC, to its irreparable damage and prejudice, and have at the same time, denied the greater number of our people in the area the economic opportunities to be derived from such a programme.'

It seems inconceivable that the former president can be unaware of what is being done in her name, on the edge of her property, to evict people whose right to be here has been unchallenged for sixty years, in order to sell their land to the Japanese.

At the Gateway of India, outside the Taj Hotel in Bombay, a family of street entertainers is preparing to perform. A man, a woman, two young children and a girl of about twelve, with a dog that jumps through an old cycle tyre and lands on a pyramid of rusty cans. The man carries a long pole, like a single stilt, on top of which is a padded cushion. His daughter, the twelve year old, lies on this pad, so that it supports the small of her back. She leans back, arms and legs completely relaxed, so they swing loosely, like a sawdust doll. The father hoists the pole aloft with his two hands. The girl's body bends double, supported by the pad; head and feet almost meet. The father raises the pole now in the palm of one hand. The he places it on his forehead and tilts his head backwards, so that the child is balanced perfectly. He spreads his arms. The girl's body seems to float, perhaps four metres above the father's head. A crowd gathers. The mother collects money. The man lowers the pole. The little girl leaps to the ground. She looks at her father; a look of utmost faith and trust.

An oil-seed plantation in Kepala Batas, Malaysia. The long rows of squat palms create Gothic cloisters as far as the eye can see. Gloomy green light. The workers go from tree to tree, cutting down the bunches of orange-gold fruit. Here, a young man went missing eleven years ago. He had been working alone in the processing room, where the seeds are boiled in great vats. He didn't return to the family's home on the plantation that night. Next day, the boiler was stopped and cleaned. Some bones were found. These were taken to the police. The management said the bones belonged to animals that had strayed into the boiler-room. The police said nothing. The father was told that these were not the bones of his son. They should look for him elsewhere. For five years the father searched for his missing boy. A report was sent to the union. Nothing happened. Only when the Consumers' Association of Penang heard about the case, seven years later, they wrote to the management asking what had happened to the young man, who was in their employment. The father still had his payslip. The management replied that the man had been missing for seven years and they were still waiting for the police report. It was confirmed by the police that the bones were indeed the remains of a human being, but the identity could not be confirmed. CAP pointed out that no one else had gone missing. Denial appeared to be an attempt to avoid paying compensation. The case went to court. It was decided that the bones were indeed those of the boy who had fallen into the oil-vat. Management was ordered to pay. The father has just received $M4,000 in compensation.

The rich enclaves of Manila are secluded compounds, protected by armed guards. Checkpoints at their leafy entrances, with black and yellow barriers and bullet-proof glass booths, are like the frontiers of a foreign country.

Ayala Heights is one of these, overlooking the hills north-east of Manila, a rocky place, with mansions shored up by cliffs of concrete, terraces overhung with bougainvillea and hibiscus. They are built in a wild variety of styles which have plundered time and space for their inspiration: some long and low like airport terminals, others with Corinthian pillars and wrought-iron gates, some like Hansel and Gretel gingerbread houses, others Black Forest Nazi retreats, Spanish colonial, Tudor and Jacobean. The gardens are exotic bowers of orchids, yuccas and champagne palms. Everywhere, construction is filling in the spaces between the villas; 60 hectares of extreme luxury, mostly built within the six years of the Aquino era. This is where those who have done conspicuously well live – launderers of black money, those enjoying the fruits of graft and corruption, as well as judges and army generals, with their leisured wives, their retinue of bodyguards and snarling dogs. In this development live two senators, the Speaker of the Assembly, a former chief of staff, a movie star, the president of Pure Foods Corporation, as well as many of the professionals who supported People Power in 1986. Most of these have since become disillusioned, and have retreated into a very private life.

In the crowded railway compartmenton a Bombay surburban train, a beggar girl is singing, accompanying herself by clicking two stones together, improvised castanets. When she has finished, she goes to the passengers and holds out a tiny hand in supplication. A man is sitting with his daughter, a girl of about six, the same age as the beggar. The man does not look at the beggar girl, but brushes her off with a wave of his hand. His daughter imitates the gesture of dismissal. The father sees his own ugly action mimicked by his child. He places his hand gently on hers to restrain her. He calls back the begging child, and places a coin in her hand.

In Baguio in Luzon, Philippines, the small miners are struggling against the Benguet Corporation, and its extensive open-pit mining for gold and copper. This devastates the communities that live around the pits. To reach the ore, the corporation bulldozes whole mountains. It alters the entire topography of the countryside. In the process, small-scale miners are displaced. These use crude tunnelling methods, but which do not disrupt the hills. When asked why they were against open-cast mining, they said, 'First, the company removes the topsoil, so where can we plant our crops?' The company said, 'We own the place, we can do as we like.' Then they asked, 'Is your ownership so absolute that you can destroy the whole area?' They said, 'We need the property, and that is the most economical way of getting to the ore.' Second, the indigenous people asked, 'That is your property?' The company replied, 'Yes, we have titles.' 'When did it become your property?' 'In 1903.' 'But we own it from time immemorial. Who gave the titles to you?' 'The US government.' 'We don't recognize such titles. The land belongs to our ancestors.' Then they said, 'Even if it is your property, do you have to destroy our source of fresh underground water? When you bulldoze the mountain, our aquifers are ruined.' The company said, 'We will replace them with piped water, which the company will provide.' 'We don't need it, we have our own water.' The open-pit mining destroys the livelihood of the small miners, the pocket-miners as they are called. They say the company always chooses to chop off the mountain at the point where they do their small-scale mining. The company allows local people access to its property, because the local people are the best searchers of the ore. Then the corporation goes to the spot which they have discovered and drives them away. Only then is the sophisticated equipment deployed, which, however, is not sophisticated enough to trace the ore as efficiently as the pocket-miners.

On a length of hessian on the pavement of Marine Drive, the horseshoe shaped seafront of Bombay, sit three microcephalic men, shockingly deformed and disabled. Dressed in grubby grey blouses and shorts, they sit in the shadow of the sea wall. They stare blankly at passers-by. A notice in English beside them on a piece of cardboard reads: 'We are three brothers. We cannot talk or work. We have been handicapped from birth. Our older brother is looking after us. Please help.' People shower them with small-value coins. They do not pick up the money, but let it lie, patches of silver on the dirty sacking. The crowd lingers around them, watching with a mixture of horror and fascination; perhaps the ultimate spectacle in a social and economic order, where the greatest wretchedness that can be visited on human beings become their sole source of income – and of survival.

It is evening rush-hour in the suburban railway station. The trains pull in, and the young men clinging by toes and fingertips to the open doors, leap onto the platform. More people emerge than it seems the carriages could ever contain, and still they remain full, before, somehow, absorbing another wave of passengers.

Some of the people on the platform make no attempt to get on, but remain in place under their whirring fans and the dense orange sunshine of late evening. This station is one of the city's best-known meeting places for gay men. They are unnoticed by the commuters, who make straight for the exit, and the buses and scooter-taxis. The other groups of people who use the station are invisible to both – the workers who service the station, shoeshine boys banging their brushes against the side of the footrest, the servers in the kiosks handing out bottles of sulphur-coloured drink, acid-green iced cakes and sienna-coloured tea, the sweepers and news vendors. And no one sees the beggars, the man with concave chest and arms so thin that his skinny joints look swollen; a man with face half-obliterated by leprosy, a blind man with empty white eyes guided by a child of about eight. A little girl with withered legs sits drawing in the dust, a metal container at her side.

Even the crowd of gay men is sharply differentiated. The boys from the nearby railway slum have learned that there is money to be made here; in baggy blue-jeans, long hair stirred by the dusty wind, they stand in a cluster at the ticket-hall, looking distant and detached, but in fact sharply vigilant for anyone who will make them an offer. The older men move around, wait under the stone canopy in front of the station, as though expecting a friend. The pick-ups are very discreet: the movement of an eyebrow, an imperceptible oscillation of the head, and they walk off, not speaking until they are clear of the station area. Some of the younger men actually meet their friends here: indeed, will remain here from sunset till 10.30 or 11. This is the centre of the city's gay social life. For it is, like so many

Third World cities, a place without privacy. The first thing people ask when they meet is whether they have somewhere to go; and if not, they immediately lose interest. A gay man with a flat can, it seems, take his pick.

India, with Turkey, has for centuries been one of the world's principal producers of opium. While cultivation was encouraged by the Moghul Empire, the systematic growth of opium was imposed on thousands of subsistence farmers only by the British in the nineteenth century, especially in Bihar. The opium was required to be forced onto the Chinese as a commodity they would pay for, in order to finance the British addiction to tea. The enforced crop substitution of opium had profound consequences for the growers. It transformed their culture, disrupted their traditions, created widespread famine.

Since the 1970s, Australia has been producing morphine, using cheaper and more efficient technology for harvesting and processing the poppies. Britain, which formerly depended on India for its supply of morphine, now obtains its requirements from Australia. As a result of the drop in demand, the area officially under cultivation in India has been drastically reduced. For the most part, these cuts remain on paper. In consequence, considerable quantities of the drug have leaked onto the unofficial domestic market. Heroin is widely available, especially in its crude and adulterated form, brown sugar. Following the change of policy of Britain and other countries, there are now hundreds of thousands of addicts on the streets of the cities of India.

Cora left her small town in Rizal, Philippines, to come to London in 1972. EMI was then recruiting waitresses and chambermaids for its hotels. When she arrived, she was given work as a waitress, but there was no accommodation. When she finished her shift each night, she had to call Filipino acquaintances and ask if she could spend the night there. After a few weeks, she was sent as a chambermaid to a hotel in Jersey; and after that, had live-in jobs in a number of hotels. Cora had to abandon her studies in order to send money home: thanks to her, her nine brothers and sisters managed to graduate. Her brother recently gave up a teaching job in Manila to go to Macao as a chef: far more remunerative work. 'They think that anyone who goes abroad gets rich. They don't know what sacrifices you have to make, they don't realize how expensive it is. They don't understand the humiliations of being treated as though you were part of the furniture, the racism and the indifference. Although my life is here now, after eighteen years I still dream of the Philippines every night.'

There is always a cluster of people outside the five-star hotels, simply watching those who come and go. The luxury hotels are the object of a kind of cult; and with good reason. They are the supreme examples of an alien implant in the culture, a microcosm of that technosphere which has been brought to such perfection in the West, and which insulates the people there from the effects of their way of life upon the earth. In the enclosed hothouse of the hotel, fantasy luxuriates. You can see it in the dreamlike way in which people in the hotel behave: they glide across the soft carpets or cool marble floors, sunglasses in hand, flicking their hair, offering ceremonial greetings to acquaintances, chinking the ice in long-stemmed glasses. Beyond the tinted windows, the beggars exhibit their mutilations in vain; the ragpickers pass by with their bulky sacks, the dust swirls in the afternoon breeze from the Arabian Sea. In these air-conditioned refuges, nothing disturbs the purchased distance, the immensity of internal spaces, from a world the people scarcely acknowledge. A man in evening dress is playing 'On the Street Where You Live', on a grand piano; a young couple, coolly immaculate, are reading *The Survival Guide to India*; a man dressed as an imperial sepoy wheels a trolley of luggage held in place by a fish-net. There is an expansive bowl of yellow chrysanthemums; lamps stand on fluted plinths, the curtains hang in shimmering swags at the dusky windows. On sofas in the foyer people sprawl, a novel on the seat beside them. A woman surreptitiously adjusts her metallized hair; a man in Bermuda shorts admires himself in a smoked mirror. Inside the hotel, there is a row of shops, where people stroll, looking at Kashmir carpets, fabrics, jewels, ebony carvings, sandalwood effigies, parasols, silver filigree earrings, glass bangles, copies of Mughal miniatures, Adivasi carvings, ivory–nourishment for dilating fantasies of the rich, calculated to promote the feeling within them that they live in a world without limits.

Maya Krishnan works on a rubber plantation at Kepala Batas. He started work here when he was twelve, and is now in his sixties. His father was brought here from Tamil Nadu to work on the railways. Maya Krishnan wears old grey trousers and wellington boots covered with latex, dried like barnacles. His responsibility is to tap six hundred trees in a lugubrious monoculture which stretches away into the far distance, a stand of trees now nearing the end of their life. His basic salary is M$12 a day, with 37 cents for every kilo of rubber he collects over the 11 kilos he must find to make the basic income. With a deft movement, he cuts the strips of bark and attaches the clay pot to catch the milky latex. He starts work at 6 a.m. His children are leaving the plantation; one works in a factory in Singapore, another is an engineer. It is hard for Tamils to study: their schools are inferior, the facilities in the company house are poor – the electric current goes off at 11 p.m. to encourage people to be ready for work in the morning, the water comes only for a short time in the early hours. The plantation is still British-owned, although the management is now Chinese, and provides even fewer facilities for the workers. This plantation will soon be bulldozed and replaced with oil-palms. Some of the wood will be used for charcoal, the rest for plywood packing cases. The first spots of rain splash onto the leaves. Rain ruins the latex and earnings go down. Maya Krishnan is a lonely figure; a man lost among his six hundred identical trees.

Development and Human Needs

How can the wealth we have seen produce such sad mutations of poverty? How can models of development to which the whole world aspires continue to exercise their power in the presence of a humanity diminished and disgraced by them?

In recent years, there has been much discussion about basic needs, which has, perhaps understandably, focused on the needs of the poor. Need has been generally understood to be the absence of something vital for the maintenance of life and well-being.

There is something incomplete in this formulation. Basic needs are simple, but they are also dual. There is need for food, shelter, clothing and warmth; but that is not necessarily the same thing as being fed, housed, clothed and warmed. For needs are also a potential: a need to do, to create, to have a function. These active needs are met most satisfactorily when they are linked to the others: when we can provision ourselves, furnish one another with those things that lie within our competence to make and to give. These active needs have also passed into the category of passive absences in the rich world. Second, the question remains why, in the richest societies the world has ever seen, so many basic needs none the less remain unmet, or only partially met; or indeed, sometimes smothered by the very wealth that is usually promoted as the pathway to the realization of all of them.

To understand why so many needs remain imperfectly answered in the West requires a more critical examination than this interesting question has hitherto received. The dominant explanation of this is that the only thing wrong with the rich West is that not enough wealth has yet been created to cater to the basic needs of all the people. No doubt this is why theorists of basic needs have turned to the have-nots: it is more comforting to ascertain how little the poor can make do with, when the rich find it impossible to be satisfied with so much.

There is another common explanation for why so much unmet

199

need remains in the rich world; and that is that in the West, more and more dissatisfactions are uncovered precisely as wealth accumulates. Deeper, more abstract needs are laid bare by the abundance of the West; needs far more difficult to fulfil than the need for shelter, warmth or food; we should, therefore, is the implication, feel sorry for those tormented by obscure desires from which the merely hungry and shelterless are mercifully free. In other words, wealth doesn't answer need at all, but merely reveals unsuspected gulfs of want: perpetual economic growth meets a bottomless avidity for more. There is, it seems, thus a perfect congruence between human wants and the economic arrangements that can best manage them. In this way, capitalism and human nature are said to converge.

This impermeable mesh of reason serves, among other things, to conceal the obvious; not merely that in the rich West there are considerable sections of the people who remain badly nourished, homeless and functionless, the human scarecrows who live under the bridges and in shop doorways, the living dead locked into their menacing ghettoes in the inner city and outer periphery. Their very existence serves as proof that the West must create even more wealth than it has yet produced, so that this minority of unfortunates may be brought within the ample embrace of contentment in which the majority now rest.

But a more significant question is whether, in fact, that majority have seen their basic needs answered at all. Manfred Max-Neef, Chilean economist and philosopher, has asked whether the very satisfiers of those needs are not themselves partial, imperfect or even downright subversive of the fulfilment of needs they claim to answer. Perhaps the means whereby some basic needs are attained actually block or impair the attainment of others. Perhaps the pursuit of certain goals, or rather, the manner in which those are pursued, renders others unreachable; and those others may be just as basic as those more or less satisfactorily answered.

To be more concrete: how can the basic need for sufficiently diverse and life-giving nourishment be answered by industrialized food conglomerates, whereby the value-added commodities they supply us with involve no participation whatever by those whose famous 'freedom to choose' is reduced to the selection of items on supermarket shelves? The obliteration of creative participation in the production of food, its growing, harvesting and preparation, is presented to us as though it were a liberation; but another way of seeing it would be as the progressive elimination of our capacity to control and influence our environment. To surrender this is to be dependent on others; and not on the butcher and the baker, as the homely apologists for the division of labour would have us believe, but on vast impersonal companies which determine the food we eat, from the germplasm of the crop that is grown to the pre-cooked preparation of the recipe in its wrapper in the supermarket freezer. This is not some idle hankering after archaic and vanished forms of activity, superseded by the complex and efficient division of work in advanced industrial society. Loss of control over our environment is always an unfreedom; and liberty is supposed to be one of the fundamental attributes of Western society; and a basic need, if ever there was one.

In the cumbrous mechanisms whereby basic needs are answered in the West, it may be that other needs are mangled and extinguished. How far is the health-care industry – that even more industrialized successor of a health service – actually a generator of sickness, a machine for the creation of ill-being, as well as a sophisticated processor of all the diseases manufactured as by-products of other claimed satisfiers of human need: a means of treating a humanity wrecked by carcinogens and poisons released by the 'need' for energy, weaponry or convenience foods? How far are the unwieldy remedial institutions of advanced society merely attempts to find palliatives for basic needs that have been undermined, denied or distorted by delusive answers and bogus satisfiers?

To give another example: the need for creative and imaginative play, as basic as any, has been turned into a craving for ceaseless entertainment and functionless mobility. Escaspe from an escapist society is the most doomed specific for a need which has been disfigured at source. Some of our most urgent and positive needs, those that involve creating and giving of ourselves, have passed mysteriously into the realm of need that is absence, have been rendered passive and inert. The need to tell stories, to invent and amuse, to celebrate and sing our lives, has been superseded by an economic system whose superior need is to make money out of keeping us amused. This generates a real human poverty. The only solution to this poverty appears to be even more wealth, although that wealth generated the poverty in the first place.

This is why the answer to world poverty lies with the rich. What we have to do is retrieve from the elaborate apparatus that claims to provide us with all the necessities of life and a great deal more besides, the living needs that have been stifled, crushed or simply allowed to disappear, for want of being convertible into marketed commodity or service. If the basic needs of the poor remain un-answered, this is because the basic needs of the rich remain unan-swered also, in spite of the accumulation of goods and services with which their lives are ornamented. The goal of universal sufficiency remains a mirage, precisely because neither rich nor poor live in a society which seriously addresses their needs at all. In other words, we persist in the strange paradox, whereby the rich monopolize the necessities of the poor without, for all that, achieving the satisfaction of their most fundamental requirements.

Needs, in all societies, remain few, simply and relatively easy to define, although there may be some dispute over the precise words of those that are less tangible than the obvious needs for food, shelter and health. But these others are located in the area around the need for livelihood, security and affection, a need for play and a need for meaning. The only things that change through time, and from society to society, are the means whereby these needs are met. And it is here that we should look, if we want to discover how some of the most easily answered needs, our most simple desires, are broken, fragmented and dispersed in an ugly machinery of supposed satisfiers. What we see in that mutilating machinery is not a people rich in material contentment and spiritual fulfilment, but on the contrary, individuals tormented by private and unnameable yearning and pain, to which all the wealth in the world cannot minister. Those who would have us believe that economic necessity can ever be even approximately congruent with human need have overlaid an unanswerable truth – that with inadequate material provision we perish – with an even greater falsehood – that well-being is enhanced in proportion to the growth of wealth.

There remains another layer of complexity in dealing with basic needs in the rich world. For entangled almost inextricably in the mechanistic paraphernalia of answering need, some needs are indeed answered, however clumsily, partially and fitfully. It is, perhaps, this partial and imperfect means of answering need that chains us to a system which none the less fails to generate the more ample satisfactions that we require. For we see that system as the provider of our needs; and because we have only minimal control over the ways in which those satisfactions may be attained, it is relatively easy to persuade the people of the West that all we are suffering from is *insufficiency*, that we have not yet reached that elevated stage of development, where the multiple shortfalls, inadequacies and disappointments will be magically resolved. The very imperfection of the mechanisms for answering need ties us to them, indeed, sets up a profound dependency on, and attachment to, them. The addiction to the existing satisfiers suggests that any other mode of answering need would not liberate, but would leave us exposed, resourceless, bereft even of the consolations we now enjoy as substitutes for our thwarted well-being.

For it has been on the erosion of the human resource-base that this dependency on the excessive abuse of the material resources of the earth has been constructed. It is a double wastage: no wonder it fails to deliver the satisfactions it promises! If our needs remain curiously elusive, constantly undefinable, never stilled, this is not because of some theory about the unassuagability of human desire, but rather a consequence of an aberrant form of development, which exting- uishes our capacities to answer our own needs and those of others, and looks instead to a system whose purpose is the accumulation of wealth and not the answering of need.

The ghost of Marx haunts these discussions, or rather, the empty halls and street corners, the blank pages where these discussions ought to occur; Marx, a poor wraith, his magnificent and poetic insights excluded, stifled by his admirers and detractors alike! For when he said that it was the destiny of the working class under capitalism to become more and more impoverished, he was not, as he has triumphantly been declared to be, wholly wrong. It is simply that it has been possible to heap up material wealth, even on the working class itself, while at the same time, those very people live through strange forms of dispossession and impoverishment unforeseen by Marx. The destruction of self-reliance, the colonizing of the inner spaces by extremes of individualistic ideology, the expropriation of the internal substance of humanity and its replacement by depend- ency on whatever the industrial machine can produce, has caused patterns of immiseration beyond the reach of the measuring instru- ments of economics. When the bonds of sisterhood and fraternity, of kinship, friendship and neighbourhood decay, and people stand alone, naked and solitary, and must make the best deal they can with the dependency-generating capitalist machine, they have undergone forms of deprivation, loss and indigence which words scarcely exist to describe. While we continue to chase the source of dispossession to give us back what it has taken, we must not expect to create a politics of hope or of emancipation.

Another way of expressing this might be to say that even our *alienation* has been privatized. The vast pall of unhappiness that hangs over these rich societies, the fear, stress and anxieties, are seen, not as socially determined, but as the fault of flawed individuals. This means that when we are confronted by people corroded by drugs, alcohol, violence, loneliness, psychic disintegration, broken relation- ships, these are never dealt with as though they were part of a social and economic system: we are able to choose, as it were, our own poison, in the hypermarket of privatized suffering, which is a kind of shadow of the hypermarket of good things, installed at the heart of contemporary Western society. Because we seek remedies to the socially inflicted isolation and despair according to our own choice, the pain we seek to numb no longer appears to emerge from society, but becomes of opaque, impenetrable origin.

The squandering of our human resources is not incompatible with Marx's prophetic warnings, although their mirror-image, the squanderings of the material resources of the world, perhaps is. The ways in which Marx was wrong and in which he was right have been radically distorted and falsified. But when we look at the people squatting in the slums of Manila or Bombay – so evocative of Victorian England – we can see that his sulphurous denunciations have not been bypassed by a capitalism globalized; and with a little imagination, we might see a reflection of their suffering in the ruinous inner landscapes, the desolation of millions of people in the West, who are expected to find meaning and purpose in the perishable merchandise destined to be tomorrow's garbage. If our understanding of the meaning of poverty had been less narrow and restrictive, we might have been able to see the common ruin that unites both the beneficiaries and the victims of the capitalist scheme of things.

The Tourist Malignancy

The most privileged people on earth, sustained as they are to a significant degree by the substance of the poor – the produce of their lands, the resources of their oceans and fields, their labour and ingenuity, in short, their wealth – nevertheless remain chronically unsatisfied. The rich are goaded by so many discontents and felt insufficiencies that they are impelled to seek ever more remote and exotic places to flee to, as an escape from their restless privilege. Many of their destinations are in the Third World, where, oblivious of the spoilings set in train by the version of development of which they are such enthusiastic beneficiaries, they none the less look for places which are 'unspoiled', where they may find the peace, fulfilment and satisfactions that elude them at home. In this search, they further modify cultures, degrade habitats and impoverish people in ways they remain unaware of.

PENANG

Penang, off the west coast of peninsular Malaysia in the Malacca Strait, has been intensively developed for tourism; so much so that the object of promoting its clear waters and opal beaches has become self-defeating, because of overcrowding, pollution and industrialization of the island. Not content with this particular form of maldevelopment, the authorities recently signed a memorandum of understanding with the Berjaya Property Corporation, to 'develop' Penang Hill. This is a 365-hectare site, one of the last untouched areas on Penang. The company wanted the hill degazetted for commercial use.

Penang Hill was, at the time of British occupation, a hill resort. Some 800 metres above sea level, it is now a rather ramshackle spread of colonial buildings in a state of melancholy decay. An extraordinary atmospheric place, secluded and beautiful, it has the air of desolation of all such deserted hill stations. The old Crag Hotel, with its tea-room, ornamental garden and cages of exotic birds, evokes languorous afternoons of pampered tedium, the fretful loneliness of functional exile, imperious army wives raising their voices at impassively compliant servants.

Penang Hill has always occupied a special place in the lives of the people who live on the island. There, the temperature is some 8°C cooler than in Georgetown below, the biggest town on Penang. The hill is the spot where many people of the older generation proposed and accepted marriage; and for young people, it is still the destination of a hard day's hike. Cool, secluded and without traffic, it is a place of peace and serenity. The Berjaya plan would have involved an extraordinary transformation: a five-start hotel, a disco, an acropolis, a jungle walk and adventure park, and most anomalous of all, a Banyan Tree-Top restaurant. The banyan is not native to Penang, although hundreds of species of other tropical trees are; the developers proposed to construct a banyan tree in concrete.

There were more serious objections. Penang Hill is an important source of water for the lowlands, as well as for the hill itself. Penang is already buying water from Kedah, and there is no guaranteed future supply from there. Mary Assunta, of the Consumers Association of Penang, which was in the forefront of resistance to the project, says that even if only a small portion of the water-catchment area is disturbed, the ecological balance can be upset by a serious knock-on effect. In any case, the gradient is 25–30 per cent and susceptible to erosion. Any kind of construction will damage the fragile slope. There is already a funicular railway, constructed by the British, which does no further damage to the slopes; a road for the vehicles of residents and officials exists too, and even this causes erosion. The heavy equipment for such a gigantic project would severely damage the hill, and the silt would wash into the Botanical Gardens below, a splendid spread of native and exotic trees and plants. Most existing buildings were constructed around crags and boulders, but modern construction would level the top of the hill by blasting it away, with unforeseeable consequences.

Most of the residents are hill farmers, who grow vegetables and flowers. There are a few bungalows, a post office, a police station, and the people who sell to visitors and hikers. Some of the flora and fauna of the hill are unique, including the slipper-orchid and monkey-cap, nepenthes, which collects water like a pitcher-plant. There is a unique range of ferns.

The environmental impact assessment was conducted hastily and shabbily, and did not even consider the problems of siltation, the carrying capacity of the rivers, the vulnerability of catchment areas or the destruction of flora and fauna. The Save Penang Hill campaign circulated a petition, which drew 30,000 signatures. The campaign organizers drew up, not only a critique of the existing plan, but an alternative which would have a far less destructive impact than the existing proposal. The funicular railway could be improved to take more people up, and its speed increased: at present, it takes half an hour, and you have to change trains half way. But the hill has a limited carrying capacity; there is no point in providing facilities that are going to ruin the natural beauty of the site.

Ahmed Chik is one of the leading campaigners among the residents of the hill. He lives in an old colonial bungalow, with a garden full of English suburban flowers – salvias, dahlias, daisies – and a panoramic view over Georgetown. 'This area was reserved solely for the British in colonial times. In fact, as late as 1953, in this house, a British official had invited a Chinese industrialist to dinner. It got late, so he was invited to stay the night. But a neighbour noticed, and he telephoned the Resident to complain, and the Resident called the house with an order to get rid of him. They had to wake up the drivers of the funicular specially to bring this man down in the middle of the night!

'They are planing a Moon Walk on Penang Hill. I cannot imagine anything more grotesque. This could happen only in Malaysia. They use the word "development", and people think it sounds like progress, it must be good. The structure plan for Penang Hill says that the hill should be preserved; and this was confirmed as recently as 1989.'

Vincent Tan is the power behind Berjaya Corporation. Originally, Berjaya dealt in steel wire products, but is now much diversified, with interests in property, gambling, textiles and leisure. 'There has been such a frenzied rush to "development",' says Ahmed Chik. 'Everybody is frantic to get a share of the action. Ethics have become secondary to the get-rich-quick mentality. It is true that the ruling party has increased the income of people. It has transformed Malaysia, but the country has been sold to foreign developers. Not in the way that the Philippines has; a more sophisticated form of colonialism is in operation here. Malaysia is not a Third World country, it is small and rich, more like Taiwan. But those outside the mainstream have borne the brunt of its development – the forest people in Sarawak, the people on the plantations.

'When we objected to the scheme, Berjaya said, "Why should you worry, your property will go up in value." We objected that the water would be polluted. "You should be thankful, you'll be a rich man."

Those are the trade-offs that are supposed to silence us – untold costs to others and to the future, for the sake of money in our hands today.'

The school building, in ruins, is on a promontory overhanging the valley. Constructed on stone pillars so that the wood should not be destroyed by termites, it was built for the children of planters. The staff quarters are lower lying and inferior to those of the children's accommodation, which itself is spartan. The stone steps are covered with lichen, and wild flowers burst through cracks in the red-tiled verandahs. Saffron-coloured butterflies weave in and out of cavernous and desolate classrooms; broken glass is crushed underfoot. From the crumbling balustrade there is a view of virgin jungle. 'A hundred and fifty million years of growth is to be turned into Disneyland,' says Ahmed Chik. Below the building, yellow-crested bulbuls wheel and settle on the crags. A white-bellied sea-eagle soars overhead; black-headed bulbuls dart to and fro, and from somewhere comes the song of the straw-headed bulbul. There are over forty species of mammals in the forest, among them, monkeys, squirrels, bats, civet, porcupine, mouse-deer, chevrotine. The jungle, at this distance is a multi-coloured foam of foliage, dark greens, yellows, lime-green, olive, with dashes of vermilion flame of the forest.

The adjacent slope is Pearl Hill. It was 'developed' and cut up into building plots; as a result, it suffers badly from erosion. Below, some fig trees grow as parasites on palms; long rattan palms and ferns create a delicate filigree on the skyline. Turquoise and dusty orange butterflies flash in the hazy sunlight. On Halliburton Hill, the Crag Hotel is visible, built in 1890 by the Armenian Sarkis brothers, who also owned the Raffles Hotel and the Strand at Rangoon. There is a plan for the nearby Lomond House to become a 300-bed condominium, and a village of forty apartments for Japanese tourists and golfers.

Lim Teong Huat, who grew up on the hill, is twenty-two. He runs a stall selling drinks, and would benefit from an increase in tourists. He is against change. He has, he says, a decent life, and is attached to the quiet beauty of the scene. His grandfather came from Canton, worked as a dhobi-man, later as a security guard, and was also a coffin-maker. 'When the Japanese came, they took timber from the hill and paid him in useless Japanese money. When the British returned, he was dispossessed of everything. He became a labourer, and later, a guard at the Uplands school.' Lim's father died of cancer when he was two. His mother had to cook rice, which she sold from a stall in Georgetown. Lim and his nineteen-year-old wife earn about M$200 a month. They live in one of the old government houses;

when his grandfather dies, they will have to leave it. The price of property would make the purchase of another house on the hill impossible. Lim doesn't want change. 'Why should we a want to live down there? This is our life. Here we can breathe. We can grow things for our own consumption. Life is cheaper and quieter. We have control over our lives.'

Many of the bungalows are still known by the name of their old colonial owners; the family at the 'Brown house' had extensive plantations of pepper and cloves. The soaring jungle trees create a cool, green gloom: rengas trees with poisonous sap which was used in blowpipes to paralyse animals; the different kinds of shorea, horse-mangoes, macaranga, which is the first tree to grow again wherever the jungle is cleared, damar minyak, used in the construction of traditional Malay houses. Monkey cups hang on the banks at the side of the paths: pale, mottled crimson containers hang from the stalk; the aromatic nectar attracts insects, which drown in it and are ingested by the plant. There are stinging centipedes, reddish-gold maples with hollow stems which are home to thousands of ants.

'This must be replaced, because it doesn't provide enough entertainment to the foreign visitors who will come here,' says Ahmed Chik. Yet if the Penang Hill Resort Plan sounds fanciful, it is far from the most extravagant of Malaysia's current plans to turn itself into an international playground, and to efface its unique natural beauty. At Johor, in the south, they are planning the Desaru Resort – a giant see-through dome, a ski-run and winter sport resort.

The plan for Penang Hill was later scaled down. A more modest version of the project will be undertaken; but still enough of the original intention remains to ruin irreversibly the character of this unique site.

LANGKAWI

Langkawi is an island 100 kilometres to the north of Penang, close to the Thai border. Partly because of the overdevelopment of Penang, it is being promoted as a 'paradise'; and like all paradises, it has to be lost. Those currently opening up the island – and the surgical image is appropriate – are doing their best to ensure that this happens in the shortest possible time.

Most of the 40,000 population until recently lived by fishing and farming, producing rice and copra. But the construction of hotels, holiday villages, the designation of Langkawi as a duty-free zone, mean that more and more of its people are being absorbed by an industry servicing Japanese, Americans and Germans, who have 'discovered' Langkawi.

The highest hill, Gunung Raya, is covered with virgin forest, where the people have traditionally hunted deer, gathered rattan, found honey and medicinal plants. The red wound of a major road cuts into the side of the hill. This infringed the law that such roads should not be constructed on gradients steeper than 20 per cent. As a consequence, the fields of the rice farmers in the plain below have been silted up and have become unproductive.

Langkawi Golf Club occupies hectares of what was formerly farmland. It is cheaper for Japanese golfers to come to Malaysia for a weekend than to play in Japan, where membership fees are prohibitively expensive. The Pelangi beach resort sends its sewage to pollute the Chenang river, and has destroyed its aquatic life. Workers are being brought to the island, because the sons and daughters of padi farmers have been slow to adapt to the requirements of the tourist industry. Along the road beside the beach resort, the palms have been embellished by the addition of artificial trees in red, green and gold.

There is a plan to extend the small airport so that it will take Jumbo jets. This will mean reclaiming part of the sea, and flattening the neighbouring island of Rebak. Not only would the island's ecosystem be destroyed, but the removal of the wooded peak of the island may alter the wind direction in the Malacca Strait. A number of villages will also be razed.

Pak Long Kassim lives at Ulu Melaka kampong, in the rich farmland below Gunung Raya. The irrigation canal has become turbid and sluggish with silt. His two acres of rice farm have seen yields reduced by two-thirds because of mud washed down from the scarred mountain. His fields are whitish-yellow in the hot sun of the dry season. Last year, the young rice plants were buried, and for the first time ever his family had to buy rice. He says, 'There is no benefit to local people from tourism. We could build for visitors, chalets of nipa and bamboo, but the government invites big companies to construct concrete hotels, and small business people cannot compete.' Pak Long Kassim says that land has become so valuable that farmers are selling. The time may come when farming ceases. He believes that those who grow their own food have the most precious of all freedoms – control over their lives. 'If you work for others, you are not free. How is a boy dressed in a uniform behind a hotel counter more free than a man who cultivates his own land? Hotels are slavery.' He is sad to see so much land sold. 'The last harvest the land produces is a pocketful of dollars. After that, nothing. Money makes land barren.' About one sixth of the farmers whose land has been damaged by silt have lodged compensation claims with the government. But many are afraid. Anyone who attempts serious resistance to 'development' of this kind is in danger of being labelled subversive, and will be at risk from the Internal Security Act.

On a Sunday afternoon, some of the padi farmers of Ulu Melaka gather under the corrugated metal roof of a foodstall. Ibrahim Mat, sixty, and Abdul Hamid, forty-three, confirm what Pak Long says. 'The previous generation lived entirely without money. They used to crop every piece of land. They had no need of cash. There was free fish in the sea, deer from the mountain. But now, the best fish goes to the hotels, you have to buy now what you once took freely.' They are afraid of the future: tourism has shown their children the ways of rich foreigners. 'They see our lives devalued, and it makes them impatient; they want to leave.'

A second golf course is planned at Seven Wells on the west of the island. Ninety-two farmers sold out, and only one refused to leave his land. The ruined houses and abandoned farmsteads are overgrown; the fruit trees, mango and jackfruit, as well as coconut and tamarind, are laden with unharvested fruit. The farmer who will not move says that those who went were dazzled by the money – M$40,000 per hectare. It seems a lot, but it won't guarantee a livelihood for the next generation.

Some grandiose tourist projects have been abandoned, like the Promet Company undertakings at Tanjung Rhu. The deserted foundations of a huge hotel litter the ruined padi fields from which the villagers were displaced. Stumps of mangroves and casuarina trees and unfinished concrete pillars stand like gravestones in a desert-like landscape, with rusty barbed wire protecting it from anyone who might seek to use the land for more productive purposes.

Much of the construction material for the building boom is taken from the hills of the island itself: limestone, marble and granite. A marble quarry shows its silver-grey face to the afternoon sun. Close by is a cement factory, which covers the countryside with a fine white dust.

On the northern tip of Langkawi, Teluk Datai Resorts are building. Yet another golf-course is being carved out of the forest, the space cleared by illegal logging. An elephant from Thailand was used to draw the logs to the sea, which simply tore down all the surrounding trees.

Paknan lives near the shore. Now forty-eight, he started work as a fisherman. He says that when he was young, everything was free. The house was built of local materials, fruit and food were available to everyone; traditional oil-lamps were used for lighting. 'Now you cannot even build yourself a house without a plan. People are forbidden to do things for themselves, and that is called development. Previously, we caught fish for ourselves and for the local market. Now the local market has to import it. I started fishing at fifteen, with my four brothers. We caught 15–20 kilos a day. I wouldn't want my son to go into it, because there will be no livelihood for him within five years from now.'

Rahim was also a fisherman. Now he works in the marble factory, cutting blocks for hotel lobbies. He earns M$600 a month. He has spent his whole life in the same *kampong* (village). His wife is from the same village, and they have three children. He says, 'What have tourists brought us? The gifts of drugs, alcohol and cigarettes. These are now part of daily life.'

Evening in Langkawi. You can see why developers regard it as a desirable piece of real estate. The neighbouring islands rise like giant green frogs from a silver-blue sea. The cockle-gatherers on the beach can wade out half a kilometre into the shallow water. The dying sun hits the water like a luminous toxic spillage. Soft pearly shells are crushed underfoot on the sand. Palm-trees clatter and casuarinas whisper; in the shade of the palms, some patches of creeper have burst into flower after last night's rain, a mass of lilac bells.

Tourism brings people whose lives are not in any way articulated towards the life of the place they visit. They are unaware of the effect they have, altering patterns of livelihood, disturbing social practices and customs. Romli, who works with the community to resist the worst excesses of mass tourism, says: 'They are aiming for a million visitors a year. It is too many. There must be better ways of travelling. We want others to share the beauty of our island. But not industrialized travel. It snuffs out the way of life of the island, and in the end it will ruin the natural beauty they come to see. When that happens, what will the fate of the people who live here? The tourists can go elsewhere, the people cannot.'

Thailand

The phenomenon of sex tourism in Thailand and the Philippines is well known; but there is also a growing number of foreigners who have gone to live in those countries primarily for sexual purposes; people we might call sexpatriates. These are overwhelmingly male, both straight and gay, well-off, for the most part no longer young, from the United States, Europe and Australia. Their reasons for living in Bangkok, Chieng Mai or Manila are loneliness, the break-up of marriage, the availability of numerous partners and the absence of constraints which they feel at home.

Although this appears to be yet another form of exploitation by the rich of the poor, the reality is perhaps more complex than moralists might imagine. It is, rather, a doomed encounter between victims, between the wounded of the West and the most impoverished of the South. It is, on the whole, an unsatisfactory symbiosis, based on a mutual desire to escape, from loneliness on the one hand, and poverty on the other; and it thrives on fantasy and illusion.

For there is a terrible sadness in the lives of many of the sexiles, just as there is in the stories of the young people who service them. Indeed, important questions are raised about the failings of Western society, which send people on such distant voyages for the sake of a little human warmth and comfort. For in spite of the advantages of wealth, such people are devoured by dissatisfactions and emptinesses which can be remedied only by people who are seen as more 'spontaneous', 'open', 'gentle', 'affectionate'; qualities which, it seems, have been smothered by the urgencies of life in the West.

Some of the Westerners, many in their forties and fifties, dress like elderly hippies, in denims and string vests, with paunches that overhang the wolf-head buckles on their leather belts, long hair, often dyed, chunky gold rings and chains, cowboy boots, broad-brimmed JR hats, trainers and tattoos. They wear Thai or Filipina women on their arms, fragile as ornaments. These are the picaresque working-class characters who haunt the karaoke bars of Malate, spend their evenings in the Cruisin' Manila disco in the air-conditioned sterility of the Ambassador Hotel, picking up the *Sun* at over £1 a copy, touchingly 'to keep up with what is going on at home'.

Mike was an oil-worker, who had lengthy spells on contracts in Saudi Arabia and Kuwait. When he returned to Newcastle, he found that his kids were grown up and his wife had found another man. Without realizing it, he says, he had become a kind of nomad, an international industrial gipsy. He is indignant about what he sees as his wife's 'infidelity', although the truth is that he was rarely at home during the twenty-three years of their married life. He speaks as though he had made great sacrifices for her sake. Now, he says, he is determined to buy himself a bit of affection, some excitement, some glamour, to make up for all the years he lived like a 'fucking monk' in the Middle East. He has great contempt for Britain, where, he says, everyone has gone soft: men are no longer men and women have become 'fucking man-eaters'. This is a recurring sub-text: Filipinas are anxious to please, they don't question what a man says, they are docile and submissive. 'What you expect in a woman,' says Mike defiantly.

The 'fahrangs' of Bangkok are also objects of fantasy to many of the young people who work in the sex industry there. Most are the daughters and sons of peasants from the impoverished north-east of Thailand, young people whose sensibility has been swiftly reshaped for the very particular specializations required by the sex bars of Pattaya and Patpong. Many dream of someone who will rescue them from the competitive brevity of their employment in the clubs.

Prasert lingers each evening in Lumpini Park, in search of a 'fahrang' who will restore him to the life he had become used to. For twelve months, he was provided with a room and 3,000 baht a month by a Frenchman. This man reserved the right to buy other boys as he saw fit, and Prasert became increasingly jealous. After a year, he was turned out. Now he has to earn through sex, but at twenty-four, he is past his best, and has acquired no skills for the future. From rice farming to the sex industry: perplexed young people, transplanted like the rice seedlings they no longer cultivate; and they cannot go home. Prasert is the fifth of seven children. He tells his parents he is working as a waiter. The family owns land at Nontaburi, but for six months of the year there is no work, and for the rest of the time it is back-breaking.

If many sex workers feel cheated and exploited by the lurid promises inscribed in the garish city landscapes, the same is true of many of the sexiles. Indeed, social and racial prejudice are often not far from the surface. The intimacies of sex, it seems, do not always go very far in mitigating racism.

Guy was involved with a sixteen-year-old girl, whom he 'rescued', as he says, from a bar in Patpong. He complains that it took him months to initiate her into 'giving him satisfactory sex'. He is generous to her, but complains that she is always asking him for money. He says, 'I won't marry her, because it would mean marrying the whole bloody lot of them.' She is the only 'earner', and the whole family depend on her. All Guy sees is ingratitude and rapacity. 'They're children,' he says of Thais in general. 'They have no education. The trouble is, this is a lawless country. There's no incentive for them to improve themselves. They won't even learn English or German for the foreigners.' Sometimes, the exiles sound as though it were their onerous duty to civilize the objects of their desire; an eerie echo of the more archaic complaints of an earlier generation of colonial pioneers.

Many others who rent girls or boys from the bars demand 'relationships'. 'She knows she gets a better deal from me than she can ever expect from anyone else. Why can't she give me what I want? You never know what they're thinking.' They speculate with other sexiles on whether she 'is beginning to care', whether he 'really is gay', whether 'real affection is growing now'.

Terry comes from a family of farm labourers in the West of England. He went into service at fifteen, and was later footman to a duke. Later, he went into business as a market gardener, and with the money he made, retired and came to Bangkok. He is anxious to distance himself from the pederasts of Bangkok, for whom he professes the greatest revulsion. He talks of the ped who opened a children's home, whose enterprise finally erupted in scandal. The man, a German, was deported from Thailand. 'That gets foreigners a bad name.' A few months earlier, there had been one of those accidents that occur so frequently in cities of the South: a train carrying chemicals had been in collision with a crowded bus on a level crossing. Virtually all the passengers had been killed. A child of five had lost all his family and sustained third-degree burns. Every day for five months Terry visited him in hospital, bought him toys and presents, coaxed in him the will to live. The child recovered and went to live with his grandmother in the village. Terry is generous to the families in the slum where he works voluntarily. The older slum boys come to his flat to get a meal or have a bath. Terry likes 16–18 year olds, but will have nothing to do with anyone who sets a finger on a child.

The sexpats have their own folklore, much of it spun around the celebrated tolerance of Thais towards sex; although the government has expressed its intention of cracking down on the sex trade. 'Thais are tolerant because for Buddhists, the head is sacred and the feet unclean, but the genitals are neutral.' There is a story that the police stop a tuk-tuk, in which a tourist is riding with a suspiciously juvenile-looking youth. They order the boy to open the zip of his trousers, and having ascertained that he has pubic hair, wave the tuk-tuk on freely to its destination. 'They like it' is a common justification for exploitative relationships. 'They are always smiling.' 'It gives them work.' 'It's better than breaking their back ankle-deep in ricefield mud.' At times, they sound like nineteenth-century mill-owners justifying industrial patterns of employment.

Rachel has been in Thailand since the early 1960s. Formerly a man, she fled England in the days before homosexuality was decriminalized: she was always very obviously gay. Now she teaches in a kindergarten and also runs one of the more up-market gay clubs in Patpong. She says she was forced into exile and would never go back to England. 'You were never safe in those days from queer-bashers, police provocateurs and blackmailers. There's nothing I miss about England. Yes there is – I miss the varieties of cheese you can get. But I shan't be going back for that.'

Here, says Rachel, people accept you. 'They're not obsessed with the indecency of the human body. The trouble is with most of the boys in this business, they're uneducated. They come from the poorest parts of the country. When they can no longer attract the men, they look for a bar-girl who will keep them. The girls have a longer working life. Some of the boys will be reintegrated into the mainstream, but others will find it hard: coming from rural backgrounds, this life spoils them. They may make up to 1,000 baht a night, then next day, they'll come to and complain they're hungry. They have no sense of the future. Some might get a job in a hotel, drive a cab or a tuk-tuk. The most attractive can earn up to 30,000 baht a month, but that doesn't last many years. Some do go home, get married, work on the family's land.'

Most boys in the gay clubs are straight. Before they go on stage for the show, they use straight hard porn to turn themselves on; and they increase the size of their penis with a plastic vacuum distender. The boys wear nothing but paper collars and ties, and a number above their genitals. If a punter fancies one of them, he pays the bar and takes the boy to an upstairs room. The price paid to the boy is negotiated. Some won't pay him anything, because they think they have already paid the bar enough; but most are generous to them. 'You mustn't expect gratitude,' says Greg, a retired teacher from

Canada. 'You just have to live for the day. There are always more boys than there are punters. It's a buyer's market.'

At two in the morning, the Magic Bar is still in full swing. A catwalk over the bar, the walls lined with leather benches, where the clients sit. Over the stage, in green and silver tinsel, it says Merry Christmas: the date is 24 March. A woman poses, body arched across the catwalk, with hand and feet on the ground, stomach upwards. She lights two cigarettes, places them in her vagina and proceeds to smoke them down to the butt. Then she stands and expels some eggs from her vagina into a beer mug, where they shatter. She lights a candle, and lets the hot wax drip onto her breasts, stomach and thighs, where it congeals. She opens her mouth and catches it on her tongue.

The man sitting next to me turns out to be a real refugee from Myanmar. He asks me what I think. I grimace. He says that he fled from the tyranny of Myanmar to the freedom of Thailand. It was, he says, an escape from repression into corruption.

Ek works in a bar called My Way, a small club with bar stools and hard sofas with red leather cushions. There is no sex show here, only the dancers, who are athletic and inventive. The stage is a round podium, with three steel pillars and a mirror behind them. The boys swing around the poles, turn somersaults, dance on the ceiling, spin and dive, and climb the pillars at right angles, using only their hands. Ek is a compelling performer. He has a wide face, high cheekbones and a broad smile. His father was a US serviceman during the Vietnam War. His mother later married and had two daughters. With the money she had received from her American boyfriend, she set up her husband with a taxi in Isaan where they lived. The father fell ill, and Ek brought the taxi to Bangkok to earn a living and support the family. After a year, Ek was involved in an accident. The taxi was a write-off, and he spent three months in hospital, with leg and face injuries. 'While I was driving, a katuei [a 'lady-boy'] once asked me why with my looks I didn't work in a club. So I taught myself to dance with a cassette recorder and a book, and taught myself English from tapes.' Now, he is the best dancer in the club. He is saving up to buy a new taxi, and so far, has 100,000 baht – about one eighth of the amount he needs. He hates wearing the number that tells clients he is available, but he enjoys dancing. Is he gay? He says 'fifty-fifty'. He wants to earn enough to start driving again, then go home and get married. He tells his parents that he is a bar-captain. He takes the 200 baht we offer him and makes a *wai*, relieved to have done nothing more for his money than talk.

At five in the morning, the boys and girls who have found no clients still walk the streets, where a few sex tourists are still looking for contacts. 'The nice thing about Bangkok', says Greg, 'is that you need never feel lonely. You only have to go out, any time of the day or night, and you'll find someone. Of course', he says wistfully, 'it isn't a relationship, but beggars can't be choosers. And we are all beggars, aren't we? Economic beggars or emotional and sexual beggars. That's the way of the world, my dear.'

Thailand is one of the countries of South Asia hailed as the site of yet another economic miracle. Growth in the past five years has been over 10 per cent, and per capita income has reached 41,000 baht in 1991 (£942). This success conceals the fact, not only that there is now a debt of $26 billion, and a current account deficit of 8.5 per cent of GDP, but more significantly, in the period 1975–88, the share of income earned by the richest 20 per cent increased from 49.3 per cent to almost 55 per cent; while the share going to the poorest 20 per cent has dropped from 6.1 per cent to 4.5 per cent. Agriculture still employs two-thirds of the people, and farm production is expected to grow more slowly than the rest of the economy in the next five years. This can only mean that more and more young people will migrate to the cities; whether the sex industry will continue to be a major employer will depend on fear of AIDS, the availability of alternative work and the effectiveness of campaigns to resist the sex industry.

RESISTING THE SEX TRADE

The idea of a 'sex industry' suggests that industrialization by no means limits itself to manufacture, but is a far more comprehensive process, which leaves few areas of human experience untouched. Of course, prostitution long pre-dates industrial society; but its organization for mass consumption is more recent; and its concentration in certain countries, as a result of a changing international division of labour, is very new indeed.

Sex tourism was a natural development of the use of Thailand as a 'rest and recreation' centre for US troops during the Vietnam war. There are now several thousand women working in the Patpong area of Bangkok. Patpong had originally been designated as the Wall Street of Bangkok, but it never took off as a financial centre. The sex industry came to fill the vacuum; and sex, too, means fast money. No great investment is needed. And although under Thai law businesses must be 51 per cent Thai-owned, this is easily evaded by using Thai names but not Thai money.

After the bloody coup of 1976, the military government wanted to present a good image to the outside world. This was when tourism was first promoted: it would gain foreign exchange and project Thailand as an agreeable international playground.

There is, however, increasing resistance to this demeaning role for Thailand. Chantawipa Apisuk works with *Empower*, and has been with the women in the bars, clubs and parlours of Patpong since 1985. 'More and more women are entering the entertainment industry. It requires no training, no skills. Many of the women left school at twelve or thirteen. Skilled labour goes into the foreign-owned factories. The unskilled come to Pattaya or Patpong.

'Women and men are equally poor in the rural areas, but men have more opportunity in the cities – construction, driving, industry. Their earning power is higher. Surveys show that 60 per cent of factories pay women less than the minimum wage. It is easy for them to move into the sex industry.'

It is also easy to be exploited. Many of the women cannot read contracts, they know nothing of their rights or such legal protection as there may be. They cannot speak out against the violence and abuse they are exposed to. *Empower* helps them to take some control over their lives – literacy, dealing with the bank, negotiating with bar owners and customers. 'Later, we discovered it was not only formal education that was needed, but sexual education about AIDS and sexually transmitted diseases. Since 1986, we have created an AIDS education programme. We produced a leaflet for women, specially telling them how to minimize risks to themselves. To protect *themselves*; it is *not* a question of not giving AIDS to men!'

Empower has also tried to find alternative employment and to safeguard the human rights of workers in the sex industry. 'Prostitution is a big institution. It is not a personal or a community problem, but international. The outside world sees only the women, and blames them. Prostitution in Thailand is related to political and economic issues. Who decided it was the role of the Thais to service Americans during the Vietnam war? Even during the Gulf war, American soldiers were allowed to come here with no visa or passport, each of them with $2,000 to spend for one week; enough to buy a woman, ten women.'

Of the sex industry, Chantawipa Apisuk says: 'The poor accept it because it is what the rich want. The poor accept what the rich do as a basic standard: that softens them up to follow the same path. They see the people from Malaysia come to Phuket on a day trip for sex; the Japanese for a weekend; Europeans sometimes for months.

'When business is bad, as at the time of the Gulf war, the women go home as failures. Some of them return, HIV positive, and with no money. Can you imagine a more horrible fate? Used up like any other market commodity, and thrown away. Some of the families reject them.'

The Thai government has been trying to pass an AIDS law to detain infected women, and to order compulsory testing in high-risk groups. There is no policy to help HIV people, only control. At a national conference in March 1991, the Health Ministry said there was no hope of medical treatment, so the law must be used to protect the nation. The law would permit the statutory authority to enter any house where there is believed to be a risk. There has been much official discussion about compulsory testing of at-risk groups, and registration of prostitutes.

'The rules of bars, brothels and parlours are very stringent. The usual hours are from 6 p.m. to 2.a.m. If they come late, one baht per minute is deducted from their salary. If they fail to take their turn on the floor, exactly as the music starts, they will lose 50 baht, even if they are in the bathroom. They go to the doctor twice a month, and must pay for their own check-up or lose their salary. They are obliged to go with customers at least four times a month. If they fail to, more deductions. When the customer takes a girl out, he pays 300 baht to the bar, and the girl negotiates her share. If she doesn't make 1,200 baht a month for the bar, she's fired.

'To work in the sex industry, a woman must be at least eighteen; by law it is twenty, but this is easily evaded. In theory, no one under twenty is allowed in the bars. No woman may enter unescorted. There are, of course, no bars for lesbians. No one tells a woman she is too old; she knows it herself. Then they go back home, marry, open a business. Many cannot add up, don't know how to use a bank. It is quite common for a woman to put money into a friend's account; and then, when she wants to draw it, she has no legal right to it. This is an exploiting community; people cheat each other. It is difficult to tell friends from enemies. Older ones exploit the younger, older relatives sell their nieces and nephews as a business.'

In the tourist hotels, late at night, many older women are accompanied by young girls; the older shrewd and vigilant, the younger nervous. 'Flesh auctions take place in the open. Some of the older women become agents who do the trafficking. There are also traffickers attached to the bars, and to certain airlines flying to Japan or Germany, who sell girls to the brothels.

'Controlling the women is no substitute for the prevention of exploitation. If women are able to control customers and the owners of the bars, then there is no problem. We respect them, if that is what they choose.'

For the women, the rules of the bars are stronger than state laws. If they do not do as they are told, they may be beaten up or even killed. There are an estimated 700,000–1,000,000 prostitutes in Thailand. If true, that is about one in six of the 18–25 age group. Ms Apisuk says that the numbers matter less than whether they are free or not. 'We have a different culture, different beliefs as well as different skin colour from those who come here as tourists. Men who come from abroad should behave to Thai women as they do to their wives. Women's issues are as important as the issues of militarization and politics; and the sex industry is a women's issue, not a prostitutes' issue.

'I can take control of my life, but many women cannot, and as long as they cannot, I am not free either. I've learned much from my daughter. When she was six, I took her to swim. She cried and begged me to come into the water with her. I couldn't swim myself, yet I was forcing her to do it. I realized I had to do it *with* her, to learn *with* her. And this is what we did with the women of Patpong. We went to the bars, sat and talked with them. Our first project was to teach them English, so they could deal more equally with their customers; and to read and write Thai. We became friends, shared their food and their lives. I have learned much from them, and I am grateful.'

Natee is a dancer, whose group has been touring the gay clubs in Thailand to reinforce the message about safe sex and the danger of AIDS. He says that, unlike women, only a minority of male sex workers sends money home to their families. Most find the life of the clubs easy-going, and spend all they earn on drink, gambling and clothes. By the age of 23 or 24, they must either go back home and marry, or find other work in the city economy.

'The work we are doing has two purposes: to encourage the emergence of a gay identity, to open ourselves up and be comfortable with being gay. On the whole the rich are too cautious to come out as gay, the poor have too many problems to care. Our other aim is to stop AIDS, and not only in the gay community. This has given gays a crusading purpose in Thailand, which is far more positive than merely begging for acceptance. The Western gay sensibility is not right for Thais. Thai society is more conservative; we cannot demonstrate on the streets. Gays are attacked by straight society, because they are seen as extreme – transvestites, promiscuous, seducers of the young. We are trying to do something to correct this misperception; but we have to be restrained, because being showy is not successful in Thailand. We want to establish gay and straight society in an integrated way.

'There are good cultural reasons why the sex industry should have developed in Thailand. There are two groups in Thai society – the moral group, upright, the good; and the others, who are there to be used. The culture accepts this. People here do feel ashamed of being in the sex industry. Young people in the bars do *not* tell their parents what they are doing. It is a fiction that we like the sex industry. I want the world to understand that we do it because we are poor. Tourists imagine that all Thais are available. Young men come from a poor peasant society, and suddenly they're among big spenders. They find it hard to control their lives. The children of peasant communities are not used to the cash economy.

'We gay activists are concerned with integrating the boys into society. They have problems when they go back to the rice fields. When you ride the tiger, you can't just step down. It is easier for straights and bisexuals to go back, and they are consoled by the religious idea of being content with what they have. It is hard, but they can adjust to reduced circumstances. Gays have had a change of consciousness, they can't adapt. Consciousness is irreversible. They may look for a 'fahrang' to take care of them. We tell them that being gay is worthwhile in itself; they don't have to depend on fahrangs.

'There are about two thousand male workers in the industry in Bangkok, although many more pass in and out, working for six months or a year at a time. The number of women in the sex trade in the city is somewhere between 60,000 and 70,000, so you can tell the scale of it.

'The gay community were the first to talk about AIDS, and this has done us good with the wider public. The Fraternity for Aids Cessation – FACT – has been seen to take a positive role. We've educated gay people, distributed condoms, talked about safe sex through plays and dramas. If a customer refuses a condom now, he will be thrown out of the gay clubs. Formerly, the customer was king, but we have changed that. In fact, in the gay community, the rate of increase in the number of people with AIDS, ARC [AIDS-related complex] and HIV is lower than in any other group.

'The government wants to reduce the sex industry. They have said they want to discourage Thai men from the tradition of using prostitutes to gain experience. The most effective way to reduce it would be to ensure alternative livelihoods to the poor people up-country, who feed the sex industry by migrating to Bangkok and other urban centres.

'Our message is to judge people according to whether they are good people, now whether they are different. "Be anything, but be good" is what we say. I started this work, because I felt comfortable being gay. I had to struggle to achieve that, to find a gay identity, because I'm the youngest son of a Chinese family, and the Chinese in

Thai society are even more strict than the Thais. I have done good things to show my family what I can achieve. I've shown that you can do good work and be gay; and they have accepted it, after a long battle. If you are straight, 7 out of 10 is good enough, but being gay, you have to get 11 or 12 out of 10 to be good enough. In the beginning, when I started to go round the clubs, explaining the need for condoms, there was a lot of hostility. They thought I would scare the boys away, it was bad for business. That is all changed now. The seriousness of the situation is too obvious. The health of the people must not be subordinated to the need to earn foreign exchange.'

What is Development?

Voices from the South

D. L. SHETH, DIRECTOR OF THE CENTRE FOR
THE STUDY OF DEVELOPING SOCIETIES, NEW DELHI

'It seems that you can no longer survive as a nation-state without IMF
loans and the tutelage of the Western economic institutions. I have
little doubt that in time, the IMF conditions and loans will achieve
what they promise to do, statistically at least. Exports will go up. The
balance of payments may become tolerable. We may even get out of
the debt-trap. The stimulus to the economy will come. You will see
modern offices coming up in Delhi. The telephones will work better.

'On the other hand, there is no promise that employment will be
augmented. There is no safety net for the poor. There will be 12–15
per cent inflation, maybe higher. Wages will not increase nor keep
pace with inflation. Two-thirds of the rural economy consists of
landless labour, wage-earners, for whom there are only 220 days
work a year. Even if they are assured the minimum wage, which is far
from likely, and there are two wage-earners in a family of six, that is
only Rs40 for 220 days a year; Rs8,000 a year for the daily needs of
survival; that means fuel, edible oil, lentils, rice, salt, clothes. It is
certain that the bottom 20–30 per cent will sink further. They cannot
fill their bellies as it is, let alone find the necessary nutrients to sustain
health. These people will be pushed further, from indigence to
destitution. Social turmoil will follow, because it is a fight for survival.
There will be more crime, more prostitution, with more people dying
on the road. Not perhaps in a way that will make big news, because it
won't be a collective famine. Two or three bodies more a day on the
streets of every town and city is not big news. The news will be more
full of the success stories of the economy. Turmoil can lead to more

militarization, more terrorism, more separatism. With more monet-
ization and less money for the poor, those who survive will have no
other resource to lean on in the village: as the commons are privatized, the poor will no longer be able to take two bunches of leaves
from someone else's tree without being criminalized.

'Economists rarely link their nostrums to the social consequences.
They behave as though their prescriptions operate in a quite separate
sphere from that in which the people must live.'

ASHIS NANDY, AUTHOR OF *THE INTIMATE ENEMY:*
LOSS AND RECOVERY OF SELF UNDER COLONIALISM

'When I hear the word "development", I think of more industries,
more cities, pollution, uprootedness, organized violence. What it
ought to be is more limited small-scale urban development, less
bombardment of the senses, more time for reflection on ourselves
and the world, more time for people to enjoy themselves, less
pressure from the state. The proponents of existing development are
losing the battle of words; but they have the technology of coercion to
force it upon the people. We see the triumph of economics at the very
time when its power is declining, faith in it is waning. It's quite
obvious that they have lost. Their arguments are barren. What rate of
growth, on their terms, would be required in India, to reach the
poorest? With the growth rate of 30 per cent, it would take 100 years.
And what would be the cost to the country, to its people, its environment, to social cohesion in the meantime? It would lead to intolerable
levels of exclusion and breakdown. It cannot be maintained, this
system, whereby the Westernized quarter of India has hegemony,
while the other three-quarters just have voting rights.'

ELA BHATT, SEVA, SELF-EMPLOYED WOMEN'S ASSOCIATION,
AHMEDABAD

'Over almost two decades, SEWA has organized and strengthened
groups of workers previously believed to be beyond the scope of
organization. SEWA has shown that the belief that the "informal"
sector cannot be reached is false. We have demonstrated that many
women can be brought together to work for radical change, against
the current of existing development.

'The women are mostly self-employed; they have created work for
themselves at the lowest level of reward. Great profits have been

made out of the invisibility of their labour. They are *chindi* (quilt) makers, vegetable vendors, bidi-makers, block-printers, headloaders, sellers of secondhand clothes, makers of *papad* or *agarbatti*, cane and handicraft workers, recyclers of paper, metal, plastic, rags. If they remained invisible to economists and planners, their presence was all too clear to middlemen and wholesalers, who took advantage of their isolation to pay miserable wages. One of the greatest inhibitions on their ability to upgrade their work and skills was the unavailability of credit, which led to dependency on moneylenders. The formation of the SEWA bank in the 1970s has transformed the lives of many such women.

'SEWA found that many traditional skills had been lost or degraded through "development". Many women in the city are well aware that they have been driven there by technological change, have been ousted from settled ways of living by development. For instance, a vendor who borrows Rs50 a day to buy vegetables, and pays back Rs55 every evening, may have been forced to leave land degraded by river effluents: memories of her former agricultural role live on in vegetable-dealing; a farm labourer who used to weave cloth has been displaced by cheaper mill-cloth; and she has become a rag-picker in a gesture to her former purpose. Bamboo workers can no longer buy bamboo because it has been sold to paper-mills. The forest dweller who harvested grass, seeds and honey is now banned from the forests.

'SEWA believes that its members will progressively work out from a perception of the local exploitations and constraints on their lives, and come to understand from those the nature of the wider oppressive forces, both nationally and internationally. What we can say is that the ninety per cent of workers in India who have been unorganized no longer need now be counted outside the agents working for change: they show the possibility of transformation by people who have never before figured in programmes for radical change.'

URVASHI BUTALIA, EDITOR OF *KALI*

'The effects of "modernization" and "development" on women have been ambiguous and contradictory. There has been the influence of a Western-inspired liberation ideology, which affects principally urban-educated women, and which is of varying utility in India, being yet another imported ideology. Equally, however, in terms of grass roots activism, many movements have been inspired and led by women, especially those around resource-base conservation.

'When the issue of *sati* (suicide of widows) arose recently in Rajasthan, many women's groups saw it as a response of ethnicity. The indicators of development in that village were not of poverty and backwardness. There was a higher level of education than average, there were schools for girls. There was wealth, in terms of business, upwardly mobile trading families. There were links with urban areas, notably Calcutta, from where trading families were remitting money. Where is development located, in external factors, or within? Until change happens within the mind, there will be no social transformation. You may have many comfortable things in life, but until that impulse to change comes from within, anything that alters is only superficial. In a way, the rise of fundamentalism is itself a reaction to outer, imposed forms of change, a way of reasserting identity in the presence of what seems like an onslaught against it.

'Women have been present and transformed many campaigns and movements within India: Chipko, Bhopal, Baliapal. The courage to resist is a strength of women. Where men's instinct is to fight or to escape, women's is to resist and endure. It is an altogether more effective and courageous stand; and this has nourished much activism in India in the last ten years.

'With dowry deaths, it is difficult to say whether the incidence has increased, or whether they are being more widely reported now. As a thing is named, so it becomes visible. What is sure is that there have been very few convictions of men who have killed for the dowry. We thought it was a lower-middle-class phenomenon, used by an upwardly mobile group to get itself easy money to set up in business. But it cuts across classes and even communities. There are ways in which "development" might be expected to worsen the situation. With the more intensive monetizing of the Indian economy, the penetration of an older domestic economy by money might make the lure to kill for it irresistible.

'Of course, there is police cover-up of dowry deaths, because the police can be paid off. The government set up dowry cells in police stations, with officers to help women, and informal courts for advice. The officers were given no training, and therefore they force women to go back into the home, they persuade them to reconciliation, which is against the intention of the initiative.

'The same thing is true of rape. The rape campaign by women's groups led to a change in the law that was 150 years old. In law, there are good provisions; only the implementation fails. Women still won't report for fear of reprisals. If you're from a lower caste, the police are violent and aggressive. One change in the law has been in custodial rape. If the crime is committed by a public official, policeman or government servant, and the crime proved through medical evidence, the onus of guilt is on the man till he is proved innocent. The minimum punishment is ten years. The first major case came in Haryana: a young woman was raped by two policemen. In the lower court, High Court and Supreme Court, the men were convicted through medical evidence and their own admission. In the Supreme Court, however, the punishment was reduced to five years on several grounds – the woman was of loose character, the men were poor and the only earning members of their family, putting them away for the ten years wouldn't help anybody, etc. We asked for a review of the case. The judge refused, saying that medical jurisprudence all over the world concurs that women are given to lying! When the dispensers of justice talk like that, it makes you despair.

'Amniocentesis is an example of modern technology that has fed into malign tradition. This allows people to know the sex of their child, and was found to lead to abortions of females. In Maharashtra, a law has been passed to ban it. Anything that worsens the deficit of females can only make things harder. In India in 1901, there were 972 women per 1,000 men; in 1961, 941, in 1971, 931, and in 1981, 933. It is reflected in child mortality, where in many places in India, girls make up two-thirds of the deaths between the age of 0 and 4. There are currently 417.6 deaths per 100,000 births; and the majority of these are girls.'

RANDY DAVID, DEPARTMENT OF THIRD WORLD STUDIES, UNIVERSITY OF THE PHILIPPINES

'The market system is undergoing prolonged and undeserved celebration. We in the Philippines have been involved in discussions of socialist renewal long before the fall of Communism, and we began this in response to the failure of capitalism. For capitalism has failed in the Third World. The collapse of Eastern Europe cannot be compared with the breakdown, violence and poverty of the Philippines. When they cite the triumph of capitalism in Taiwan, Korea, Singapore and Hong Kong, these are not examples of capitalism at all. There, the state played the most decisive role against the logic of the market. They could not be more wrong, when they point to the triumph of market forces in those places.

'We have been looking for an alternative model which does not sacrifice democratic or human rights or nature to development, social order or socialism. We think it possible to evolve models of political intervention as well as recreating society along the lines suggested by the social movements, NGOs – old and new – and popular local struggles. Movement politics distinguishes itself from traditional Third World politics, both from the colonial and feudal legacy, as well as from the familiar revolutionary politics.

'In many ways, the Marcos years were fortunate, in that they showed alternative modes of intervention. When Marcos came to power in 1965 and declared martial law against his own government in 1972, he had in mind the authoritarianism of South Korea. That was his inspiration for revolution from above. That project was attractive to the intelligentsia. Although fascistic in temper, the ultimate attraction of the Marcos project to intellectuals was that it offered them access to the corridors of power. All intellectuals nourish illusions of actualizing the models which they can normally only lecture and dream about. The main idea was that all who cared to join him were given full freedom to explore the limits of their dreams. If you could sell an idea to Marcos, absolute power existed. It was Camelot in its way, Third World style. Most people assume dictatorships and authoritarian figures keep power because they control the military. That is only part of the story. The other part is that in all instances, members of the intellectual community lend it legitimacy and their brains; and this model of authoritarian techno-cratic government was deeply attractive to many intellectuals. You can see it in the West now, the numbers of intellectuals only too eager to underwrite the triumphalist project of capitalism, even though it enslaves and destroys the South.

'We are now confronted by Western fundamentalism. Do we need an alternative faith to deal with it? This question we brought to our Indonesian friends, after the 1966 massacre of the Communist movement. Then, all activists went underground. They were com-pelled to use more sophisticated methods. This is why, both in Indonesia and the Philippines, innovative and creative interventions have occurred at the community level. If you are an activist, con-fronted by a powerful state, supported in turn by a world system that appears almost invincible, you have no choice but to operate in the sphere over which you have some control. Think globally, act locally has a powerful resonance in the Third World. While you operate at the micro-level, you also have to think of macro-forms, local, regional, national, global. The alternative paradigm exists already, waiting to be properly expressed and articulated. That will happen when the majority of people also see the injustice and unworkability of the model they are trying to operate in.

'General MacArthur in 1902 described the Philippines as a "tui-tionary annexe" of the USA; and that is what we remain. For us, nationhood has remained an incomplete project. Look at the farce of the Aquino government, lobbying for foreign troops to remain; the idea being that we cannot stand on our own feet, at least not yet. The time is not right. It never will be.

'We are still a major exporter of people. I have asked officials, does it not send a shiver down your spine that our country's economy depends to such a degree on the export of our people? Their response is "Our people are in such demand abroad because of their knowledge of English."

'I come from Betis in Pampanga. This is the centre of woodcraft in Pampanga, skilled traditional carving and wood artisanship. Ninety per cent of these men are now in the Gulf, as construction workers. As a result, we have seen the death of those artisan skills, their mutation into brick and carpentry work for the rich Gulf states. Those men were artists. What we see is the degradation of a culture. Who assesses the cost of those things? They inherited exquisite skills from their ancestors by observation and practice; and every day they spend in the Gulf, they are losing these skills; every day they work on construction, their hands become more blunted. They cannot pass it on to their own children, because they do not see them growing up. In our consciousness, this legacy of our forebears means nothing compared to their earnings as bricklayers. These costs never enter the calculus of economics. All that registers in this violence is the remittances in the formal banking system. We do not have an adequate calculus of pain to measure these processes. These are the costs we should be counting, integral to any assessment of development.

'One thing we have been concerned about is the effect of overseas contract worker migration on the Filipino family. Does anybody care? One wife said to me: "The dinars keep coming, although they are sometimes not enough to pay the instalments on the initial loan taken out in order to pay the recruiter." It is accepted that the first year's income will be used to pay the moneylender. The recruiters are not supposed to charge the workers, but people are so anxious to go, the rate is between 20,000 and 30,000 pesos just to get the job. The same woman said her husband is a carpenter, and he built their house. They have nine children. She said what he loved most was to potter about in their small garden. He liked to grow orchids and roses, and at the same time, raise hogs. Most of the workers don't write letters; many can't, anyway. But they send voice-tapes. And this man requested that his wife record the grunts of his pigs and the whistling of the wind in the bamboo-trees, as well as the voices of the family.

'They have appropriated all the riches of our consciousness. The economy has colonized society. This means that the non-economic realm of human life is shrinking. And that dwindling area has to absorb the higher and higher costs of the pain, loss, injustice and exploitation inflicted by economics. This might once have been called the contradictions of capitalism; but now that capitalism has been rehabilitated, the contradictions are not only not counted, they are not even observed. Recuperating and naming the violence that occurs in the processes is a prerequisite for any alternative that may replace the dogmas of communism. The economy is no longer a sub-system, but has become the dominant system.

'I was in Japan for a year until March 1991, at the University of Kyoto. There was a story in the local newspaper, "Filipina Needs Help". This woman had had a stroke. She couldn't speak, but she looked sufficiently Japanese for them not to question her nationality when she was taken to hospital. If it had been known that she was Filipina, it is doubtful whether they would have treated her, because Filipinos rarely have medical insurance. Anyway, she survived; but when they discovered she couldn't speak Japanese, they were worried she would not be able to pay the bill. Half the Filipinos in Japan are undocumented, illegals. Every year the Japanese Embassy in Manila issues 32,000 non-immigrant entertainment visas to Filipinas; and this makes us the largest exporter of entertainers in the world.

'I visited this woman in hospital. I said to her in Tagalog, "Are you Filipina?" She looked and said "Hai" in Japanese. I said, "It's OK, I'm Filipino." She wept; she held on to my hand and broke down. She had been a schoolteacher in Cubao, Manila, a graduate of the Far Eastern University. She had seven children, and had left her family two years earlier to become an entertainer in Japan at the age of forty-three! Well, at that age, you have little chance of lasting, because of the competition from younger women; and she became a daily worker in a plastics factory. She was the common-law wife of a Japanese truck-driver. In spite of her family here, she closed her eyes and took a Japanese husband, because that would offer her some protection. When she was found to be Filipina, she knew she would be deported as an overstaying alien.

'But first the bill had to be paid. My Japanese friend started a collection from the public. He said the people come from the Philippines to serve us; it is our responsibility to look after them. The donations poured in. There was enough to pay the bills and to send her home. She came back to the Philippines in September 1991. She thought she would go back to teaching here. But she hadn't realized how much prices had gone up in the two years she was away. She said,

"I can't imagine how I and my husband can support our children on our wages. He is a jeepney driver. I shan't go back to teaching." "What then?" "I'll go back to Japan."

'Ninety per cent of Filipinos in Japan carry fictitious names, because they all mean to outstay their visitor's visa. Then they will be deported. In fact, when you feel homesick, you surrender yourself to the authorities, they take your picture and your name. Therefore, you use a fictitious name. Then you can always return under another one. So this woman said she would get another passport and go back. Meanwhile, one of her daughters has applied for work as an entertainer in Japan.'

VANDANA SHIVA, PHYSICIST AND ECOLOGIST

'We have to make visible those connections which have been concealed. Any critique of "development" must look at the total costs, in so far as these can be measured, and not simply allow the dominant ideology to count the few selective aspects which they present in their balance sheets.

'Making visible means above all including the work of women. Women have had to stay underground in terms of sustaining production: they couldn't enter the market, because the market has depended for its operations on their staying outside and on their efforts to keep things going. Women have had to lead their life where their contributions are not bought and sold. Their invisible work has helped the system to perpetuate itself. Women know that no market can be all-embracing. Women's role is to operate in the areas of exclusion created by the market. They must bear ever greater burdens of the degradation inflicted on the earth and the people. As the economic wounds become deeper, so women's healing role increases; but it has to operate in spaces diminished by the spread of market forces. It is for us to make visible the parallels between the world of nature, of women and the Third World in this scheme of things; the degradation of all three is a symptom of the uncounted costs which the world must bear as the price of success of the market economy. Until the South articulates itself upon what parallels and mimics the feminist critique, we will be trapped into new subjugations.

'The roots of violence in Punjab, for instance, can be traced to the way in which the human material itself had to be transformed in parallel with the way in which land use and inputs were being transformed. The Green revolution was seen as a struggle between the entrepreneurial farmer and the backward farmer. Society had to be remodelled into competitive entities; a new energy was unleashed of go-getting entrepreneur, people who were farmers in name only, and solely in wheat and rice. What happens to those who become redundant, the boys who leave the farms, either because their fathers have generated a lot of wealth, or because they have become super-fluous labourers? Both rich and poor of a new generation are affected. It is an explosive process. Young people feel injustice, and they articulate this feeling as available – communalism, liberation through militaristic struggles – they have learned from the main-stream state, which must then control its own offspring, its own creation.

'Punjab is the product of good planning. It worked wonderfully. Even now they are still saying the Green revolution worked, because they separate and externalize its consequences. The problems are now seen as external – caused by blood-thirsty Sikhs; they don't see it as socially determined, as a response to the destruction of diversity, which was India's special quality. In fact, that diversity is now defined as the problem itself. That then creates a reason for the separation and for the snuffing out of more diversity. Separatism is a response to the state, which wants communities to be controlled militaristically, or through economics, but not by themselves, organically.'

RAJMOHAN GANDHI, MEMBER OF THE RAJYA SABHA, GRANDSON OF MAHATMA GANDHI

'The IMF and World Bank speak of integrating us into the world economy; the truth is that the vast majority of Indians are not even integrated into the Indian economy. No one can deny that the state sector is not a success, but then the private sector in India is no paragon of virtue, whether in terms of paying its taxes, observing pollution laws, minimum wages, labour laws, research and develop-ment, long-term planning. More deregulation can only be a blue-print for disaster.

'There are 72 million tribals in India, 120 million Untouchables. In the tribal areas, facilities are absent, schools inadequate. Teachers hate the places where they serve, they feel punished and devalued going there; some draw their salaries without even teaching. They visit the school twice a month to draw their salaries, and that's it. The number of Indians who wish to emigrate is a hundred times the number of those who want to go to the deserts of poverty within the land.

'The loss of the Soviet Union has been a grievous one. We were entranced with the Soviet dream. Into that vacuum marches the West with flying colours. I feel sad now; my illusions have been broken. I try to will myself into confidence and vigour, but that is not easy. The non-appearance of our dreams following freedom is saddening. India has not meant for us what we thought it could mean. So much sadness, so many tears, so many drops of blood, so much hunger! My anger and disappointment are above all directed at myself and Indian society. The Indian contribution to our present state is substantial; I think my grandfather's attribution to the British of the woes of India was greater than was justified. The British presence in India was by no means the biggest single obstacle to our progress.'

ANIL AGARWAL, CENTRE FOR SCIENCE AND ENVIRONMENT,
NEW DELHI

'There is, it seems to me, nothing wrong with the creation of wealth through human enterprise in doing things. But beyond a certain point, it becomes destructive.

'There have to be checks and balances which are built in, through value systems. And this is what we are losing. Values are being overtaken and submerged by market values: the very things that need to be checked are seen as a source of value themselves. The West is always blaming the South for corruption, but the profiteering of the multinationals is the same thing in another guise. The system of corruption has been legitimized in the West.

'Much nonsense has been written about sustainable development. Nature cannot remain the same for all future generations. Who is to decide what is sustainable? Who can know? All societies, in order to survive, use and change the environment. Agriculture profoundly altered the environment. Sustainability lies in the speed with which any society can correct its mistakes. Any society will make errors in the use of resources. And those best placed to correct these are those who suffer the consequences of them. Therefore, if you want sustain-ability, or rather, a higher order of sustainability, you must empower those elements in the society who have a vested interest in self-correction.

'Liberate enterprise, but not so that it usurps people's control of their resources. In their decision to allow enterprise to use those resources, they will have to live with the consequences. If they suffer, and they find long-term disadvantages, they will says, "Stop, that is enough, the costs are too high." The social and ecological costs will then be built into the model of enterprise and wealth-creation. It is not for the entrepreneurs, the economists and experts to build these costs into models, but the people who must grow the crops, harvest and cherish the earth.

'Why are people now destroying the forests they depend on? The question should be, what has anyone, government or business, ever given them for their knowledge, their biodiversity, for their careful tending of the forests? They have never been rewarded by the people who come and take away their knowledge, their resources. When was the price ever paid to the people of the Amazon for that incomparable storehouse of riches, medicines and crops and genetic diversity, its rubber, its quinine, its curare, its corn, its avocados? The Amazon has nourished the transnational food and pharmaceutical industries. It should have received, or rather, its people should have received, royalties on every potato and tomato grown in the world. If they had received their due, the Amazon Indians would be the richest society in the world. What we have done is stolen their knowledge and patented it in laboratories, and then sold it back to them. We have been to the forests with guns to wrest it from them.

'We who come from the Chipko tradition were saying that we should conserve the forests, because it is in our long-term interest to do so. We will do it in a way that will ensure their survival. We are agents of sustainability. The tribals have become industrial fodder in the furnaces, steel-mills and mines, because their forests were destroyed. If they had received the true prices and costs that were their due, their life would not have been so degraded that to work in appalling conditions in a city slum would seem an acceptable alternative.

'The present system *is* sustainable. The only question is, who will pay the price for the privileged to sustain their riches and their lifestyle? It has to be a question of social justice, distributive justice. But there is nothing to say that the present system could not continue for some long time yet. It will involve more dispossession of the poor, there will be more casualties of environmental destruction, more urbanization, more degradation in every sense.'

ARUN KUMAR, ECONOMIST, JAWAHARLAL NEHRU UNIVERSITY, NEW DELHI

'The finance minister, negotiating with the IMF, said that in the next round of negotiations, we will change the policies if we see fit. By then, it may be too late. Unemployment, inflation, social tensions, the reaction of labour, the farmers – it all may be so much worse when the next meetings take place, that there are no options left. At the same time, referring to liberalization, the minister says there can be no going back. It may be that irreversible processes have been set in motion by economic decisions whose results will be felt in the social and political arena.

'The correctives required should deal with the crisis in all its dimensions – social and political, as well as economic. We should take account of unemployment, increased social problems and tensions, and that includes terrorism, migration, social violence. While we measure only the economic indicators, we shall have no clear picture of what the *economy* is doing to *society*. In all these dimensions, the problem confronting India is very deep. To imagine that economic correctives can deal with profound social consequences of those very correctives themselves is both deluded and eccentric; absurd, if it were not potentially so tragic.

'According to figures from the Planning Commission, the 1980s saw a population increase of 2.1 per cent per annum, while employment generation was at a rate of 1.55 per cent. That means 0.5 per cent per annum increase in unemployment. And those figures take no account of those forced into doing any kind of work, services that are not real employment, the educated underemployed. Unemployment is officially 35 million; underemployment is more difficult to measure, people doing socially unsuitable work, especially the educated. This is an important feedback mechanism for the future: the expectations of educated people cannot be fulfilled through the employment system. The young, now so eager to learn, are doomed to disappointment. What happens when these social pressures build up? Expectations have been raised through TV and the mass media. In rural areas, people become conscious of their poverty, areas formerly untouched by awareness of the world outside. And the more the prosperity in one area, the worse the unrest, especially if it is unequally distributed. Look at Punjab.

'The political base of the ruling class is narrowing, and that means more social problems. Formerly, a coalition of large, medium and small business, rich farmers, middle-income farmers, the urban lobby, government servants and organized labour, provided a powerful base for Congress support. The base has now narrowed, and the IMF package will narrow it further. This can lead only to more fundamentalism on the one hand, and increasing state authoritarianism on the other. The Latin American scenario is there.

'Those who come from the IMF to tell us what to do are devoid of human values and of human sentiment. For instance, a subsidy is a concession to a group: take fertilizer subsidy, benefiting the poor indirectly, because it increases food production and keeps prices down. There is some benefit to the poor, however much one might disagree with chemical fertilizers. But why should the rich have all these concessions on property (Rs40,000 crores or more), while the fertilizer cut is a mere 4,000 crores? Ten times more could be obtained from a wealth tax, and from the black economy, which reaches as much as 30 per cent of the official economy. To cut the subsidy to the poor shows that the political economy is changing; it shows the government are agents of the rich.

'The Indian elite are increasingly linked to the Western rich. It is clear that India does not lack resources. We are not a poor country, yet we are seen as beggars. The resources are being maldeployed by the rich. The IMF approach is an ideological attack on the Indian system. The property owners of India are traitors, economic traitors. During the Freedom Movement, at least the wealth was kept here. Now it is leaking away. The character of the business class is no longer national in outlook. Why has Indian business not opposed the opening up of the economy? They should be losing out in this process. The truth is, they have their capital outside; therefore, they have changed. This is what integration into the global economy means. They live in five-star enclaves, guarded and protected. Indigenous capital has now secured its base outside India, and has therefore ceased to be nationalist. It has integrated itself into the global network of wealth and power, and is prepared to leave the poor to their own devices. This can lead only to disintegration, unrest and violence. And they don't care.

'We need unity between workers, employed and unemployed, organized and informal. Political action must include many of those traditionally seen as outside the political arena – women, rural people. The majority should be mobilized against what the powerful are doing to this country, and against their blindness, which will lead us to ruin if they are allowed to continue this criminal folly.'

LEONOR BRIONES, PRESIDENT,
FREEDOM FROM DEBT COALITION, THE PHILIPPINES

'Human rights are being suppressed in the name of the market, a market which is far from free anyway. We are sacrificing the poor on the altar of market economics.

'In the case of the Philippines or Peru, riddled with crisis and poverty, the first thing is always to put the country back into the market economy. The same draconian measures are advocated.

They kill for the sake of the market. They will not listen to reason. Even after Pinatubo, the most horrific natural disaster, the secretary of finance refused to adjust a single digit of the objective of the IMF stabilization programme; no matter what social instability comes from it.

'Even the bankers were never expecting total acceptance of the Marcos debt by the Aquino government; no doubt, they couldn't believe their good fortune. The Aquino administration was supposed to be a rejection of Marcos plunder and greed. She could at the very least have renounced the fraudulent loans. But she chose to take an heroic stance. The debt went up, in spite of the debt-reduction programmes, because they were financed in the same way as the debt itself – by further loans. The character of the debt crisis has changed now. In the 1970s, we were borrowing to finance "development". Now we are borrowing to pay back debt. It can't be done.

'The payment of the debt leads directly to human rights abuses. Development is a human right, guaranteed by the UN: it is not only the physical right to life – adequate shelter, food, education, participation, although these rights are also ignored. In fact, what we see are human rights violations in the name of "development". Nothing more perverse could be imagined. Areas that are going to be developed are militarized: development at gunpoint is the most flagrant denial of development.

'The IMF adjustment programmes almost invariably suppress human rights. In Poland, Venezuela, we have seen IMF-inspired riots. Economic rectitude above human well-being. What kind of system are we serving? The IMF comes into our countries, there are no public hearings, legislatures are ignored. It is all deeply anti-democratic; it violates all norms of humanity.'

DHIRENDRA SHARMA, DIRECTOR, CENTRE FOR ASIAN SCIENCE
AND INDUSTRIAL POLICY RESEARCH, NEW DELHI

'The Third World countries spend collectively a larger percentage of GNP on arms than the rich ones. But they import weapons of mass destruction from the rich countries, in the range of $50 billion a year, in order to fight one another. India, for example, spends more than 65 per cent of its science and technology budget on research and development efforts related to defence-oriented activities. China and Pakistan divert 6–8 per cent of GNP to war-based activities, based on mistrust and hostility to their own neighbours. Hostility and competitiveness have kept us divided for so many centuries and this folly has benefited no one but the arms dealers.'

The arms trade supports national entities and pseudo-entities which are largely the creation of Western colonialism, and which prevent Third World unity and effective resistance to later forms of colonialism. The prolonging of national rivalries, many of them artificially engendered, shaped in the image of Western nationalisms, is the most powerful means whereby the West inhibits serious attempts at South–South co-operation. The recreation of the nation-state, the growth of which convulsed Europe only recently, has been a source of discord, bloodshed and carnage all over the South. 'Development' is supposed to have eliminated these antagonisms in Europe; although for the moment, the shared privilege of Europeans is their sole unifying impulse. The rich have always upheld collective and solidaristic action among themselves, although they have denounced, outlawed and brutally crushed the same tendency wherever it has appeared among the poor, both locally and internationally. Arms sales are essential to the West's universalizing mission as is its economistic ideology.

DHIRENDRA SHARMA

'If the Indian economy is to open up, this should take place within certain parameters. If foreign companies want to come here, they should be the ones to provide us with the infrastructure required to support their products. If a motor manufacturer wants to come and produce, say, 200,000 motor cars a year, then that company should also provide resources to cope with the predictable number of accidents and diseases due to pollution. They should furnish blood banks, hospitals, as well as telephones so that accidents can be reported. They should supply petrol pumps, roads and flyovers. They should tell us the levels of lead likely to be added to the air. If they can give all that, we should say, "Go ahead." If Union Carbide had indicated the dangers beforehand, do you think it would ever have entered India?

'Another example. The new *Hindustan Times* building here in Delhi, a high-rise building, was erected without anyone realizing that there was no fire tender in Delhi capable of reaching a skyscraper, nothing higher than the 4th or 5th floor. There was no pressure in the hydrants, no hosepipes to reach that height. The building was 10 or 12 storeys. A fire broke out on the higher levels of the building. The fire lift did not work, people could not be rescued. The army was called in. They brought a helicopter, which only fanned the flames, because of the wind it created by its blades. They tried unsuccessfully to carry water drums in the helicopters. On the next site, there was a building under construction, and the citizens from the streets res-cued the people spontaneously, using builders' ladders and ropes. But the fire services and the administration collapsed and could not cope. We should be saying that the builders of hotels and office blocks should also provide all the safety and firefighting infrastructure if they are going to establish themselves here.

'The same thing is true of the nuclear industry, the supreme generator of unseen costs, invisible damage. You cannot detect who is exposed, and therefore you cannot monitor the effects. The dangers of the technology are ignored, because we don't have the infrastruc-ture to measure the effects. Therefore there is no accountability. The nuclear power stations have a high level of radiation leaks. The technology is not advanced, often obsolete; the joints of the pipes leak. High-ranking officers and engineers are high caste, 80–90 per cent of the scientific personnel are upper elite, the top 10 per cent Brahmins. If there is a leak, the Brahmins don't go near. Nor do the engineers. They say, "If you expose me to more than the permitted dose over two years, you won't be able to use me. I have to be protected." In this way, the top echelons ensure they are not exposed. Therefore, low-caste people, backward castes, tribals, criminals, sol-diers are used. Anybody hired by the establishment has to have a geiger-counter and protective clothing. These persons on the regular payroll have medical cover too. Contract labour does the dirty work. The work is given to a contractor, and how he does it is nobody's concern. He hires people on daily wages, at a high rate of Rs200, when the ordinary rate may be Rs40 or 50. He brings dozens of them. They do the job, they may be exposed to radiation, and then they are dismissed. Those who have been exposed to more than the limit are given Rs500 and sent back to Bihar, Orissa; they disappear. More than 10,000 such people have been exposed over twenty-five years. They are not traceable. They are illiterate. If they have deformed children, they will say it is fate, karma; no proof of exposure exists. In that way, you can bury the malign consequences of radioactivity in the folk-beliefs of the people, perhaps one of the most inventive ways of burying the costs of industrial development. It also shows how 'modernization' and 'development' simply build on older patterns of exploitation and disadvantage. This is seen as progress – electricity is generated, and to make energy is the essence of progress. No word about the social costs, the ecological costs. The negative value never enters into it. They don't see or count the consequences.

'Scientists themselves may have lacked consciousness of the social concerns of what they did; but after Hiroshima and Nagasaki that is no longer possible. Till then, science might have seen itself as exploring objective truth. After the A-bomb, many scientists came to see the degree to which they had prostituted themselves; an unholy alliance with politics, destructive energies linking them to the state and the military. Einstein himself said he would have preferred to be a vegetable seller. They had been unaware of the context in which their power would be used. Once the genie was out of the bottle, they could not stop the industrial, military and political powers. They could do nothing against US conservative thinkers who said: "Now we'll show the world the meaning of manifest destiny."

'The Critical Science Movement began to question the scientific paradigm. CND, END, Concerned Scientists in the USA, all this has nourished the environmental movement of the 1970s and 1980s. There will be no more free hand, no more non-questioning, no more claims of dispassionate objectivity. Now people ask: "What are you doing, what are the advantages, the implications, the disadvantages, what are the social and environmental costs?"

'I am not anti-science and technology. I'm not opposed to development per se. Development and change are necessary for human civilization to continue. Not all new ideas are good and old ones evil, nor vice versa. In the overreaction of people against the misuse of science, there is a risk that they will fall into another form of fundamentalism; a worship of the traditional, which can be just as damaging as the uncritical chase after the new.'

ANISUR RAHMAN, BANGLADESH

'Many people have been forced to surrender their own accumulated knowledge and wisdom by the sheer power of the "development" effort, which has concentrated power, privilege and wealth in a few hands with the ability to exploit and subjugate the broader masses; and which has uprooted vast numbers of people from traditional life and life-styles to become *inferior citizens in an alien environment.*

'There is no problem in agreeing with this critique of development. That does not mean that we should jettison the word, simply because it has been abused. It is a valuable concept. What might development mean to people who have not lost their sense of identity and are expressing themselves through authentic collective endeavours? Can we understand how such a sense of identity and collective self-expression could be restored to others who have lost them?

'The existing paradigm gives precedence to economics. Economic growth is tempered by concern for "distributional equity". In developed societies, social disease formation is going beyond human control, and this presents another constraint.

'Development is endogenous. Yet today, development is regarded as overcoming the problems of poverty, thus reducing human aspirations to the attainment of a bundle of economic goods. Poverty cannot be overcome by identifying it as the problem to be solved, as this creates negative motivation.

'Many people have *internalized the gaze of the rich upon the poor*; so that human dignity, self-worth, esteem, are the root of the "problem". The human quality of people is independent of their economic condition.

'The elements of an alternative must include endogeneity; non-hierarchical relationships; the generation of knowledge, that is the relevant reality is the people's own, constituted by them only; the recovery of history, with the people as principal actors, and giving precedence to the values and culture of the people themselves. Knowledge is non-transferable. It can be memorized for mechanical application, but learning is always an act of self-search and discovery.

'The failure of the first real alternatives to world capitalism (in the form either of socialism in the USSR, or decolonization in the Third World) does not in any way exonerate capitalism from its globally negative record, past and present, including colonization, ethnocide, exploitation and alienation, misuse of resources, destruction of nature and war. All the deviations and distortions of alternatives have, in some manner, been determined by the dominant paradigm.'

MANEKA GANDHI, FORMER MINISTER FOR THE ENVIRONMENT, NEW DELHI

'The cities of Delhi and Bombay are now receiving something like 30,000 environmental refugees a month. When I was minister, all over my own constituency, brick-kilns were coming up. People were selling their land to brick-makers for a flat sum of Rs50,000. The land would then be scooped out to a depth of 8 or 9 feet. After two years, the brick-makers go away; the topsoil has gone. Most of the small landholders who sold make a capital investment with their money, they buy a scooter or build a house. The money is used up, and two years later, they realize the land has gone for keeps, and they are poorer than they were before. It is the lottery-winner syndrome – people feel rich and buy a one-off luxury life, and nothing is replenished. And just as that occurs at the individual level, this is the model we are following both nationally and internationally.

'The whole of western Uttar Pradesh is an object-lesson in how not to develop. Growing apples and sugar-cane is an efficient way of exporting water. And then a million bottles of Himalayan spring water go to the USA each year. It is madness. I would rather export blood, because that is what it amounts to. Our best produce goes for export. Indians use the dregs of tea, the powder that is left when the best leaves have gone. Our fragile mountain-slopes have been turned into tea-gardens. The producers say they are greening the hills. What nonsense. It is a monoculture; the pesticides they use run into rivers and streams. The costs of the economic success stories are horrendous, before you even look at the failures.

'We have taken Rs165 crores from Japan for greening the Aravali mountains, which were completely denuded. No trees came up, because they failed to fence off the greened spaces in what is a goat-breeding area. They were dropping seeds aerially. Billions of rupees were spent, and nothing happened. Goat-breeding should have been stopped on those mountains. Why are we breeding goats to export meat to the Middle East anyway? To earn Rs20 crores for India, we have to borrow Rs165 crores from Japan.

'We get a loan, in the form of aid, from Sweden, to plant trees in Tamil Nadu. What happens to that so-called aid? First, the donor country spends 30 per cent of it for the travel of executives. They have to be able to assess the situation on the spot. They insist on employing their own people – people want to come to see India; the money does not come to us. There was a 9 per cent success rate in planting. They wanted to do a mid-term review of the project. This meant flying the executives to Sweden, I said: "Do it here. How can you expect people to assess such projects from Sweden?" We refused to pay back the loan.

'The people in the Environment Ministry expect to go abroad three times a month. They are on a heroin-drip of going abroad. The minister has to keep the officials happy or they'll tell the truth about the way work is conducted, and that would never do. Two-thirds of all the files I looked at in the ministry were about trips abroad.

'The system we have is absurd. A hazardous polluting company can set up anywhere, as long as it is not within 20 kilometres of an urban area. Well, as soon as a big company sets up, say 25 kilometres outside of Muzzaffarnagar or Meerut, the ancillary companies and services come closer to it. The employees live near the works. Shops, schools and houses are built, and within no time it becomes an urban area itself, often linking with the bigger conurbation.

'Then the government offered a 50 per cent reduction in company tax to those companies that would go to tribal areas, because the tribals don't complain. They don't get jobs either. What happens is that islands of affluence come up where the company workers live. The company dispossesses the tribals of their clean air and water and land, displaces them with no compensation; and all they get is work as chowkidars [watchmen] and roadbuilders. It enslaves the tribal people.

'I framed a law that said any company using any chemical that was dangerous must take out insurance, so that any incident or accident that occurred to anyone living around the factory or downstream from where the pollution happened, can demand compensation. There would be a fine of Rs12,000 for injury, Rs25,000 for death. That may not sound much, but if it goes on day after day, the company will soon be out of business. After the fiftieth person has claimed, the company will be closed down. This will be done by the insurance company, because they will not want to go on paying out. This law was passed in January 1991, and implemented on 1 April. Then the new government came in. The new minister is a business-man, he stayed the Act, because he said it harasses business. As everyone knows, it is now the economy that has got to be protected, the economic and investment environment, not the real one, the business climate, the atmosphere of confidence, the sentiment of the market – not the global climate, not the air we breathe, not the feelings of the people.'

SWAMI AGNIVESH, PRESIDENT OF THE BONDED LABOUR
LIBERATION FRONT

'Our experience with the liberation of bonded labourers shows that most are not born into bondage. The system first impoverishes them in every way. The terms of trade between the urban and rural sectors, between industry and agriculture, North and South, mean that more and more farmers become marginalized. Landlessness is increasing, as is assetlessness; more women are thrown out of work by mechani-zation. This creates a congenial atmosphere for the bonded labour system to perpetuate itself.

'Here enters the moneylender: loans must be taken to meet con-sumption needs; and the moneylender exploits to the maximum the illiteracy, the social and economic backwardness of the poor farmer, in order to get him into the trap of debt and maybe of bondage. The rates of interest are so manipulated that the borrower can never get out of the trap. The loan is on the creditor's terms, and the wages the bonded labourer receives are dictated by the creditor. This is a colonial type of trade practice; and is replicated in the relationship between North and South at the global level.

'The North in our South is trying to catch up with the West; and the notion of development which they promote plays havoc with our people and our natural resources. The "new economic policy" as it is called is not very new. It is the logical corollory of the suicidal path which the West has adopted for itself and on our behalf.

'Bonded labour is of pre-colonial origin, but it was given a boost by Lord Cornwallis with the creation of the land tenure system, which created a division between owner and landless. The merging of the feudalist, colonial and capitalist culture that followed has been defined as development.

'The real crisis is in the West; they have appointed us to resolve it for them. It is the West that needs aid from us. We have the tradition of Gandhiji and Buddha to call upon, a tradition of living simply, and elevating, not an excess of consumption, but the minimum we may take for our needs. The West needs help, because it has created a closed system and sees no way through the impasse it has reached, except to intensify and extend the very processes of dispossession that makes the West, and us, so unhappy.

'We can see the outlines of a new global feudalism, in which the industrial overlords will plunder the world at will. When the collapse comes, it will be the West that will suffer. Three-quarters of the people in India have lived without electricity and other so-called modern amenities. For the average US citizen to be without electricity is unthinkable. They are more at risk than we are, because we have used our ingenuity in order to survive; they have used theirs to find more ways of becoming dependent.

'I would like to see the Third World rise to the occasion and say no to debt repayment. When the bonded labourer contracts his debt, he puts far more labour than the equivalent of the sum borrowed; in the same way, we have paid many more times than we borrowed. The West has taken far more than it has ever given. We are already in bondage as a country. Just as there is a cut-off date, where a bonded labourer says the debt is fictitious and is a fraud played on us, and I will not repay, so the South should do likewise. We need to re-orient our society towards *svadeshi*, self-reliance. Full employment must be our guiding principle, and this must underlie all economic activity. To use other criteria – profit, competitiveness, modernization – will condemn masses of people in India to inactivity, and then to protest and violence.

'In Chattisgarh, there are two cement factories near Bhilai. The older one, owned by Tata, is the Asian Cement Company, which employs 1,800 people. It produces 3 lakh [i.e. 300,000] tons of cement annually. A new works came up, Modi Cement. It produces 10 lakh [i.e. one million] tons annually, and employs only 300 people. Our friends there met some of the experts installing the machinery, and said to them: "What are you doing? You are employing only 300 people. You are employing less and producing more." He was told: "We have the technology whereby we can produce 10 lakh tons with only three workers. We are employing 300." That so-called efficiency should override livelihood is a vicious imposition.

'The Bonded Labour Liberation Front is associated with the Anti-Slavery Society in Britain. Perhaps we should extend our actions to the West. Slavery emerges in some strange guises. There, the people are bonded consumers; tethered by debt to the melancholy enjoyment of things for which they pay over and over again.'

Conclusion

In the name of 'development', 'progress' or 'wealth-creation', 'economic adjustment', people all over the world are being subjected to constant upheaval and involuntary change. In the service of these noble abstractions, the landscapes of whole countries have been devastated, whole populations forcibly uprooted. The sensibility of human beings has been drastically and violently reshaped in accordance with the relentless changes these require; the psyche of peasants and tribals have been reworked to transform them into urban dwellers and factory workers; the world-view of workers has been dismantled and reconstructed in the image of 'service industries' or of 'consumers'. It is a driven and irresistible experience, and there is, it seems, no place on earth to hide from it, neither in those societies called 'developing', nor in those declared to be 'advanced'.

The refugees and migrants who make a mockery of national boundaries, camping in deserts and no man's land, living in city slums, held in camps and detention centres, represent only the most visible fraction of a humanity that is incessantly being evicted and moved on, disturbed and uprooted. All over the world, people are denied the security and space in which they can rest and bring up their children, free from harm, sheltered from economic necessities that drive them on in search of improvements that often turn out to be illusory.

This experience of relentless change has fateful implications for those who have always advocated change as the basis for radical politics. For they risk being misunderstood and repudiated by those whose lives have been tormented precisely by incessant and dispossessing change. The devastation of ways of life, environments, cultures, traditions and sustainable ways of answering human need has been in the interests of conserving only one thing – the maintenance of wealth and power where wealth and power are already concentrated.

247

Change, then, in the lives of the people, is a visitation whose purpose is, ultimately, the preservation only of privilege. And in this act of conservation, it does not matter what valuable experiences, practices and customs are swept away. Resistance to this is scarcely to be sought in appeals of yet more change. Opposition now means, rather, the construction of places of refuge, spaces of stability, tranquillity and peace, where people can live out their lives with an assured and decent sufficiency. For this is what people try to do; holding on to traditional associations, to the ties of self-reliance, of kinship and village or neighbourhood. When they are exhorted to follow ideological prescriptions for 'change', is it any wonder that they are seldom moved? For they are trying only to safeguard, preserve and strengthen control over their own lives, to value traditional ways of living in the world that are under threat from an industrialization that can leave nothing alone. Industrialization can acknowledge no adequacy, no sufficiency, no stability, but must goad us on in search of forms of wealth which, whatever amenities they may bring, are always accompanied by impotence, loss of self-reliance and increasing violence.

In such a context, a truly radical struggle would involve a disengagement from the eager embrace of a remorseless colonizing and monetizing of human experience, which is then sold back to us. It would mean opposition to this malign process, wherever resistance is possible and appropriate. Opposition would mean enhancing and retrieving ways of answering need outside the market economy; the rediscovery of all that we can do and make and create for ourselves and each other, freely. It would be to reclaim the greatest gift of our humanity. The failure of socialism in the world derives, not from its too radical departure from capitalist-determined development, but from too close and imitative an adherence to its ruinous prescriptions.

This is why, in the late twentieth century, more and more people have been looking at the values of indigenous peoples, tribal communities, forest dwellers, subsistence farmers who, they feel, have something vital to say to the world, especially if the world is serious about conserving and harvesting and husbanding the resource-base of the earth prudently. This does not mean trying to live like those peoples; such an ambition would be clearly impossible; but it involves trying to see how the values they bear may be applied in our own, very different, context.

It is only to be expected that the eager messengers of ever-extending industrialism, the apostles of endless change, will see the search for more enduring values as a version of nostalgia. Nothing must be permitted to inhibit the convulsive transformations, which, within the next two decades, will turn more than half the world's population into urban dwellers. These changes are expected to provide humanity with its best hopes: the melancholy realities of people wounded by the multiple dispossessions and the new poverties conjured out of the very wealth that was to have rescued them, does nothing to abate the fervours of the missionaries of global economic expansionism. Anything that stands in the way of these voracious and devastating transformations of the world will be presented by them as backward-looking and archaic, an obstacle to a 'progress', no longer defined, but written into the rigours of the economic machine. 'The economy' has become an autonomous entity, no longer biddable by mere human beings to the answering of whose needs it bears a dwindling relationship.

The desire to conserve what is good is not a question of going back to the past, least of all to a mythical one of harmony and stability. It is a question of taking from cultures that have endured precious lessons in self-reliance and sufficiency, and bringing these back to the wasting, threatened world whose resource-base must sustain us all. The advocates of industrialism without end are the ones leading us into a mythic world, for theirs is a figment, maintained by faith that science and technology will deliver human beings from the consequences of their own actions. This is clearly a project based on faith; one that has strayed from the realm of religion. The branding of conservation as nostalgia is an attempt to clear all obstructions on the path to a development to which human purposes and values have become the real 'externalities'.

Sustainability in the lexicon of the West now means sustaining Western privilege. This means preserving a form of wealth-creation that diminishes us and tears humanity apart by the monstrous inequalities it imposes, at the same time as it culls the forest and mines the oceans, guts the earth and extinguishes civilizations, destroying all value and values but those that can be measured in money.

We need to think of a different relationship between conservatism and radicalism from that which has governed a stale and empty political discourse for so long. We need to think of ways of conserving what is of value and of uprooting only that which enslaves. And what enslaves more than anything is the violent advance of an industrialism that knows no limits, does not stop at the frontier of the material world, but invades, colonizes, industrializes our deepest needs, our profoundest longings; which rearranges the internal landscapes, just as it spreads its desolation over the face of the earth.

The struggle of the Left against the Right was always undermined by its faith in the possibility of applying existing forms of wealth-creation to more benign ends. What is in crisis now are those very forms of wealth-creation themselves; indeed, the definition of wealth, the instruments whereby it is measured and judged, as well as its ownership and distribution. Systems which reduce all the living richness, abundance and diversity of the world to the sterile mono-culture of money are the real subverters of human purpose. To stand against these is to be, at the same time, both radical and conservative; but more radical than seeking mere changes of ownership of the means of production, and less conservative than those who see nothing wrong with existing patterns of privilege. It is to be more truly conservative than those who affix conservative flags of convenience to their violent disruptions and discontinuities; and to be less radical than those who seek to reduce the treasures of the earth to the measure of money.

It can be seen that the victims of 'development', and those who resist it are not merely residuals, being swept aside by the forces of progress or history or any other serviceable abstraction. They are articulating a powerful and growing, if subterranean, feeling that economics, and the 'development' that serves it, are blunt instruments with which to beat humanity into submission and silence, and to compel us into forms of 'improvement' that impoverish and disempower. The economistic ideology of the West is designed to perpetuate privilege and to prolong social injustice; and it is applied with a merciless rigour in the world.

A new, dynamic mix of energies is emerging – an imaginative use of more human resources in the rich countries and a lesser dependency on material ones; and for the poor, an enhanced access to material resources, and a little less abuse of their human energies. The aim of this reconstructed form of development is sufficiency for all, a space for human ingenuity and creativity to find answers and to fulfil our own and each others' needs.

It is an extraordinary moment. Our allies in the adventure of reclaiming human development from wealth-creation are every-where, if we know how to recognize them and join with them in their struggles, which, in the end, are ours also.

JEREMY SEABROOK
Manila – Bombay – Delhi – London
February 1991 – May 1993

250